HOSTAGE IN HAVANA

ALSO BY NOEL HYND

The Russian Trilogy

Conspiracy in Kiev
Countdown in Cairo
Midnight in Madrid

The Cuban Trilogy

Hostage in Havana
Payback in Panama (forthcoming)
Murder in Miami (forthcoming)

Available on Kindle

Flowers from Berlin
Revenge
The Sandler Inquiry

THE CUBAN ★ TRILOGY

NOEL HYND

HOSTAGE IN HAVANA

BOOK ONE

ZONDERVAN

Hostage in Havana

This title is also available as a Zondervan ebook.
Visit www.zondervan.com/ebooks.

This title is also available in a Zondervan audio edition.
Visit www.zondervan.fm.

Requests for information should be addressed to:

Zondervan, *Grand Rapids, Michigan 49530*

Library of Congress Cataloging-in-Publication Data

Hynd, Noel.
Hostage in Havana / Noel Hynd.
p. cm.—(The Cuban trilogy ; 1)
ISBN 978-0-310-32454-6 (pbk.)
1. Americans—Cuba—Fiction. 2. Havana (Cuba)—Fiction. I. Title.
PS3558.Y54H67 2011
813'.54—dc22 2010050414

Cover design: James Hall / JWH Graphic Arts
Cover photography or illustration: 123RF.com
Interior illustration: istockphoto®
Interior design: Michelle Espinoza

Printed in the United States of America

11 12 13 14 15 16 /DCI/ 22 21 20 19 18 17 16 15 14 13 12 11 10 9 8 7 6 5 4 3 2 1

Havana traps you. A Cuban woman seems to walk on air, not on the pavement. A Cuban man the same. We are gifted with fleeting happiness. We don't expect a death or an accident either. That's why people are so emotional and cry and shout and stamp their feet if something happens that isn't part of the daily routine.

Cuban novelist Miguel Barnet, *Rachel's Song*

PART ★ ONE

ONE

Alexandra LaDuca stood in the elevator with Andrew De Salvo. She used the time to collect her thoughts, prepare her words, and set her shoulders squarely. This wasn't her first press conference, but it would be her most important.

The trip was thirteen floors down from the fifty-seventh floor to the forty-fourth floor of a Manhattan skyscraper at Duane and Wall Street and its expansive chamber used for press conferences.

She checked her reflection in the mirror above the brass buttons of the elevator's controls. What she saw was a woman who was fit, strong, and thirty years old. Her makeup was fine, her hair was loose to her shoulders, and she looked good. She wore a navy Chanel suit, a white silk blouse, and sensible pumps.

The elevator continued its descent: fifty ... forty-nine ... forty-eight.

Thirteen flights. The unlucky number, if one paid any attention to such things. Forty-seven. Forty-six. Almost there. She drew a breath and was ready to go.

"When you face the press, kiddo," De Salvo said, "don't smile too much. We don't want them to think we're having too much fun."

De Salvo was Alex's boss at the Financial Crimes Enforcement Network — "Fin Cen," for short — a division of the United States Department of Treasury. He was an expert on many things, prominent among them, lawlessness in Central America and the Caribbean. De Salvo often used his sly, dry sense of humor to keep Alex calm.

She appreciated it. "I'll try to keep my priorities in order."

De Salvo, silver-haired and silver-tongued, gave her a wink. "About time someone around here does ... Go get 'em," he said. "Kick some butt, girl."

She grinned, then suppressed it. The elevator stopped at the forty-fourth floor. The brass door slid open. They stepped off. The hallway was crowded and crackled with excitement. As Alex and her boss moved quickly down the hall, people recognized them and gave way to let them pass.

Moments later, conversation stopped as Alex entered the conference room. Camera lights went on. All heads turned her way.

Operation Párajo was about to enter a new phase. Glancing around, she made a quick estimate. About fifty people, including coworkers, reporters, and camera people, were there. Good. Everyone she expected. Some of them she knew personally; the rest she had worked with via secure phone and internet.

A few approached her and greeted her. Rick Edwards, her CIA contact from Washington, gave her a congratulatory hug, as did Leslie Erin, a New York–based FBI agent who worked in international bank-and-security fraud for the same agency.

Alex's boss moved to one side of the conference table, pleased with how well Alex, the "new kid" at Fin Cen in Manhattan, related to the press. She glanced at her watch. Almost 9:15. She nodded to those in the room whom she knew from previous contacts.

"Good morning, everyone," she said as silence fell and cameras started to record the event. "First, a special word to my peers who have worked with me on Operation Párajo. Thank you for being here. I was hoping to see you all here. I wanted to thank you in person and let the media know where we are on Operation Párajo. To the media, I'll be putting hard-copy documents in front of everyone, and you'll also find flash drives accompanying them."

Two young assistants, a woman named Stacey and a man named Alan, had followed Alex into the room. They distributed the documents and software. The sound of large white envelopes being torn open could be heard everywhere. Then Alex called the conference to order as everyone settled into their chairs.

"Over the last forty-eight hours, and continuing this morning," she began, "a joint strike of American and Panamanian military and law enforcement agencies have dealt a significant blow to the operations of a major international criminal enterprise. At this hour, I can announce the arrests of two hundred and fifty-two individuals and the seizure of an ever-increasing amount of illegal drugs, weapons, and cash. Raids have been coordinated in six countries and five American states. The law enforcement activity has been aimed at the Central and North American operations of the Dosi money-laundering enterprise as well as four of the newest and most violent of this hemisphere's major drug cartels."

So far, so good. She paused for a breath and continued.

"While this enterprise may have operated from Panama, its reach extended well within the U.S.," she said. "On Wednesday, fifty-two people were arrested in Miami. In New York City, forty-four. Beyond these arrests, authorities seized 81 million dollars in U.S. currency, 4,700 pounds of methamphetamine, 5,000 kilograms of cocaine, 26,000 pounds of marijuana, and 56 pounds of heroin. More arrests are expected. The Dosis and their various undertakings finance the bulk of the drugs and weapons that arrive on our streets. That's why we're hitting them where it optimally hurts them — their revenue stream. If we upend their supply chains and financial underpinnings, then we disrupt 'business-as-usual.' "

After a pause, Alex continued. "As you all know, Panama remains particularly vulnerable to money laundering because of its proximity to such major drug-producing countries as Colombia and Mexico. It also maintains a highly sophisticated international banking sector. Its economy is based on the American dollar. Panama City is where globalization meets the black market, and the Panama Canal is the key bottleneck of global trade in the Western Hemisphere. Panama City is also a choke point for black-market trade between Colombia and the rest of the world."

She surveyed the room and felt calmer. No major gaffes so far, so she felt more confident and continued. "Panama is also home to the 'Colón Free Zone,' which is located by the city of Colón at the Atlantic gateway to the Panama Canal. The CFZ is the 'trading showcase' for Central and South America as well as for the Caribbean region. Think of it as the world's largest duty-free mall."

A hand rose in the audience. Alex pointed to a man with a question. "How big is the CFZ, financially?" asked Rick Edwards, a friend of hers at the CIA.

"Massive," Alex said. "In 2009 the CFZ generated exports and re-exports valued at more than 12 billion U.S. dollars. That figure includes all the services and facilities offered by the Colón Free Zone. In other words, all importing, storing, assembling, repacking, and re-exporting products from all over the world. We're talking about everything from electric appliances to pharmaceuticals, liquor, cigarettes, furniture, clothing, shoes, jewelry, toys, even packaged food. Name it, they sell it. But naturally those are only the legal products."

There was a restlessness in the room. Half of those present were reading her documents as they listened. The other half had eyes locked on her.

"So, here in the CFZ," Alex said, "is where many problems begin for the U.S. Treasury and its enforcement arms. Many goods transshipped through the CFZ are bought with narcotics proceeds, often through a black-market peso exchange in Colombia. That's an overview. Now look at the surrounding financial establishment."

More rustling as those assembled examined Alex's paperwork.

"There are three thousand international companies established in the CFZ. After Hong Kong and the British Virgin Islands, Panama has the highest number of offshore-registered companies in the world, approximately half a million. Panama also has a large international financial sector, which includes fifty offshore banks. The volume of trade in the CFZ presents a 'perfect storm' for narco-money-laundering operations."

She paused and looked again around the room.

"You all know that much," she continued. "That's what each of us who combats international financial fraud and the monetary underpinnings of various terrorist movements lives with day-to-day. What I'm here to announce, however, is a new phase of Operation Párajo — the takedown phase. If our conviction rates are good, few of the owners will be enjoying their real estate any time soon."

Alex adjusted her prepared notes and made a note in a margin with a silver Tiffany pen with her name on it, a gift from Andrew De Salvo when she had started work there.

She moved to her final remarks, after which there were several questions.

"Incredible progress," Rick Edwards of the CIA said. "How did it fall into place?"

"The dominos started to fall when we received a major break in mid-March," Alex answered. "A Caracas-based narcotics trafficker named Hector Darío solicited a Panama City customs inspector to ease the smuggling of twenty bales of U.S. currency into Panama. Darío gave us our link to two individuals named Misha and Yardena Dosi, a husband-and-wife team, who are our principle targets. The Dosis hold Israeli passports as well as Panamanian. We believe they also have emergency 'escape' passports, forgeries, possibly South African or Canadian. Here at Fin Cen, we became interested in Señor and Señora Dosi after the U.S. Drug Enforcement Administration established that Misha Dosi maintained several islands on both of Panama's coasts, islands that have been used for running narcotics and currency via a fleet of state-of-the-art speedboats. The ships are designed with long V-shaped hulls and driven by a combination of high-speed motors. They can travel at one hundred miles an hour in smooth or choppy water, and even maintain thirty miles an hour in two-meter seas — "

"Outrunning any coastal patrols, in other words," Andrew De Salvo chipped in.

"Outrunning our navy, coast guard, and anyone else on the

water," Alex said. "These boats can also haul multi-ton loads of cocaine."

Without notes, she continued, focused on a distant but bitter enemy.

"On the Caribbean coast of Panama, Señora Dosi owns two islands in the Islas Marias archipelago, near the Panamanian town of Veraguas. On the Pacific side, Señor Dosi owns Isla Escondida, near the Panamanian coastal town of San Carlos. The Dosis' central company, Nauticabonita, is the top marine supplies business in the country. Nauticabonita launders money. Here's how. Merchandise sold by Nauticabonita to normal customers is discounted off the books by twenty-five percent. The difference between the true retail price of the item and the price paid by the customer is then filled with dirty money. Money from cocaine enters Nauticabonita's financial statement as part of a legitimate sale, thereby washing the money of its origins. This stage, the "placement," is often the most difficult to accomplish. Once the illicit money is circulated into Nauticabonita's normal business accounts, it is then transferred to a number of banks — or 'layered,' or 'integrated' — and used to purchase items in Panama's free-trade zone. These items are then shipped to Colombia, where Dosi's clients receive them and sell various products such as refrigerators or washing machines in Colombia in exchange for Colombian pesos. Seems simple, but it went on successfully for more than a decade. But in the last months our sources began to get blowback in Miami and Panama City. There was a pervasive rumor that arrests were imminent and a Federal case in the United States was building. This, of course, turned out to be true. We were afraid we'd lose our two big fish, our 'barracuda,' Señor and Señora Dosi. Given the proper warning, he and his wife might have used their Israeli passports to flee to Israel and fight extradition for years."

She answered several more questions, then glanced around. "Anything else?" Alex asked. There was nothing.

She flipped her folder closed and managed a smile. She gathered up her papers and put her pen away. De Salvo passed by her as the press conference broke up.

"Excellent work, Alex," he said. "I'm proud of you."

TWO

Manuel Perez, freelance contractor, sat in a short-term rented apartment in Bogotá, Colombia, shortly past nine on a hot morning in the middle of May. He anticipated the moment that, after weeks of preparation, was almost before him.

He set down the Spanish-language gossip magazine he had been reading as a television droned in the background. Enough of the love life of Paulina Rubio, a Latin singer he adored. Enough of the fabulous Shakira in her magical short skirts and explosive concerts. It was time to go to work.

His hair was gray, long, and shaggy, somewhat like a sixty-ish latter-day hippie. Gray stubble crossed his face. By the door of his poorly furnished apartment were the two canes that he used when he went out for groceries or ventured into the public park on the other side of the expressway. He was kind and polite, had a good word for almost everyone, and most people simply addressed him as "Juan."

Since he spoke with a pronounced Argentine accent, some people referred to him as *El Viejo Porteño*, "the old man from Buenos Aires." A rumor had circulated that he had been a political prisoner in Argentina in the 1980s, but he never talked about that himself. He mentioned Juan Perón and Evita a few times, never favorably, but did speak well of Che. Yet with El Viejo Porteño one always knew to leave the past alone.

Perez wore latex gloves on both hands and a digital watch on his right wrist. In his line of work precision was an absolute necessity, a split second was the difference between life and death, much like a professional athlete or a neurosurgeon. That's how he thought of himself. He was as skilled as any of those people, smarter in most cases, and every bit as deserving of the money people paid him. Nanoseconds separated success from failure, as did millimeters. As for the latex, fingerprints were a bad idea.

It was not a coincidence that he had been educated in his craft in America two decades earlier. He liked Americans, most of them, the people, their lifestyle, their cities, their music. Yet he was wary of them as well. Part of his survival depended on knowing which ones to coddle and which ones to steer clear of.

Well, no matter. He turned off the television. It had been tuned at low volume to one of those goofy Mexican *telenovelas* that all the women drooled over. An old set of rabbit ears flopped to one side.

He needed quiet now and concentration to focus on his assignment.

Perez used the arm of the sofa to brace himself as he hoisted himself to his feet. His first step had a small wobble to it. On hot days like this, his right knee bothered him. He still suffered from a childhood injury that had plagued him for three decades. In the small town he had grown up in, he had been hit by a car when playing soccer on the streets. Medical intervention was primitive. The bones recovered but never set properly. He recovered from the accident with his right leg a quarter inch shorter than the left.

But that was long ago. This was now. He gained his stride, went to the door that led to the public hallway beyond, and glanced out. No one was there. Nonetheless he used one of his canes since neighbors were used to seeing him chugging along in his unbalanced way.

He limped down the hall to a spot near the emergency stairs. There he ran his fingers over an area in the wall till he found the one cinder block that he had rigged to come loose. He pulled it out. It opened a space between the inside wall of the hallway and the outer surface of the apartment building. There was a gap of about a foot between the two. He slid the block back into place. Only he knew it was loose.

He went back into his apartment and locked the door. Setting his cane aside, he withdrew a heavy steel case from under the sofa in the living room. He unlocked it by combination. Then he opened the case and gazed upon a thing of beauty.

The case contained the parts of a sniper's rifle, high tech, high caliber, high price tag, and high stakes. He checked for any tears in his latex gloves and found none. Then he removed the parts from the case, laying them side by side on the floor. He assessed the workmanship of the breech, the stock, the laser-telescopic sight, the three tubes that fit together to form the barrel, and, last but not least, the silencer.

He admired the craftsmanship of the interlocking parts. They meshed together as if God had created them. They were that good.

Perez gazed at the pieces for several seconds, in an almost meditative state. Then he assembled his weapon. When he finished, he buffed the rifle with a chamois cloth to remove any fingerprints. Even though he had been careful not to touch the weapon at any time since he had received it, he also knew that the gunsmith in Cali who had crafted it for him could eventually identify him to police or the military. So he buffed it vigorously, even though he had done this twice before.

Then he froze. Outside the door he heard voices. Two men were arguing in loud, inarticulate Spanish. One could never be too careful in his line of work, so he set down the rifle, drew a small Chinese-made handgun from his waist, and went to the door. Peering through the eyehole, he studied the scene before him and slowly relaxed.

He had been in this location for six weeks, waiting. He knew who should be in the building and who shouldn't. The players in the hall were Suárez, the fat peasant handyman with the cleft palate, and Gómez, his boss, a smelly runt from the Bogotá barrio. Well, Perez reasoned quickly, these two nonentities were just that, nonentities. Nothing to be afraid of with these guys.

So Perez returned to his work. He had six bullets in a small box. The custom-made magazine of the weapon was designed to hold only three, two of which would be emergency rounds in case the first shot missed. At the fringe of his consciousness, he heard the two disputants in the hall walk away. Perez loaded the three rounds into the weapon and put the others in his pocket.

The rifle was a fifty-caliber sniping special: the weapon that Soviet snipers had used in Afghanistan and the Americans still used in Iraq. The target that Perez wished to hit moved about Bogotá in an armored sedan with extra-thick bulletproof glass and a bombproof chassis. Perez needed a weapon that could propel an explosive bullet far enough with enough accuracy to hit a vehicle at just the right angle and still maintain enough velocity and impact to break the existing rules of armor penetration.

It would first need to smash the destruction-proof glass and then become a small fragmentation grenade upon second and final impact. It was no small challenge. But in his hands, he was sure, he had just such an equation.

Perez laid the weapon on the floor and stepped back. As if by magic, he began to move with an increased dexterity. He went to the window. The building was old, just perfect for his purposes. The old air conditioner churned away. Because of the imperfect fit, Perez had been able to poke a hole into the weather stripping that was supposed to close the gap between the conditioner and the window frame. The hole was just big enough for him to poke the nose of his rifle and the sight through.

He stood at the window and admired the view. Ten floors below, winding through the center of Bogotá, a highway ran toward his building, then cut close by on the eastern side. The highway was walled off from the city streets and passed under a bridge two hundred yards in front of him. From his contacts in the government, Perez knew that Ramon Inezia, the chief of the national anti-narcotics squad, would pass this way in the middle of a three-car convoy in about forty minutes. Perez had been waiting for this opportunity for weeks.

He assessed the day. Bright, humid, and hot. Good shooting weather. His bullets would travel two thousand feet per second at a weight of 185 grains. Location, time, distance, temperature, wind direction, mental state of the shooter, everything factored in.

Perez was anxious to take his shot. Maybe even a second shot if time and logistics permitted. He scanned the highway with his binoculars, mentally picturing the short convoy of official cars that he had been tipped off would pass by this afternoon. He unwrapped some baked chicken and tortillas, ate his lunch, and returned to the window.

For several minutes, each of which seemed like an hour, he waited, his pulse quickening. Then, at a few minutes before 10:00 a.m., he saw what he was looking for: traffic giving way to a trio of black Mercedes limousines about a mile away, the front car with a small blue beacon. This was his cue. He knew the distance, 1.2 miles. He had sixty-eight seconds to get ready and hit a target moving at a rate of a hundred feet per second.

He shouldered his weapon and went to one knee. He protruded the long nose of the rifle through the hole in the weather stripping and found his bearings on the expressway. Steadying the rifle on his shoulder and on the window sill, he then locked in the laser sight. He wondered if the cortege had any radar detection. But he reasoned that they moved around the city with a confidence bordering on arrogance. Unless he had been betrayed within a small circle of conspirators, he was fine. No way anyone would suspect that this day was different than any other. And anyway, if they *did* detect sights on them, they would alter their speed and that would tip him off.

He saw no sign that they were doing that. Thirty seconds passed.

Squinting, Perez fixed his sight on the first car, then moved it to the second. He had a full profile of the speeding car and locked into the sharp downward angle he wanted. Seconds flew off the clock. The trio of cars hit an area a quarter mile away that was crisscrossed by overpasses. He knew the cars would hurtle out from under the final overpass at about seventy miles an hour. He would have less than two seconds to make a final fix with his sight and fire.

The vehicles hit the first overpass and disappeared. On instinct, Perez made a final recalculation, spur of the moment, completely reflexive and intuitive.

He moved his rifle sight into the open area beyond the underpass. He would not track the cars but rather let the motorcade run into his sight lines.

He looked at the laser dot on the highway a hundred fifty meters away and then saw the first car speed through it. He counted off half a second. When the front bumper of the second Benz streaked into his view he pulled the trigger.

He saw the rear window of the Benz explode into shards. And within that same breathless moment, he quickly tracked the nose of his rifle along the mid-section of the car. He cheated a hair toward the rear seat and volleyed a second shot, then brilliantly following with the nose of his rifle, a third.

The vehicle spasmed and swerved in reaction to the explosives that had hit the car and the fragmentation that had detonated within it. Perez thought he saw a nanosecond of reddish mist exploding within the car, which was wonderful. He had been successful! The car erupted in flames. The second bullet, as he had hoped, must have nailed the fuel line. The vehicle fishtailed and spun. It suckered the car behind it into hitting it, then left the asphalt, struck a wall, and went into a violent forward tumble and crashed.

Manuel Perez had no need to admire the rest. He withdrew his weapon and laid it on the floor. He knelt and broke it down. Within ninety seconds he had wrapped the pieces in a towel and was in the hallway. He held the rifle pieces under one arm, the two canes in the other hand. He let his door lock behind him. He had paid his rent two months in advance. No one would come looking for him.

The hall was empty. No inconvenient witnesses. He found the cinder block that he had checked earlier. Outside, distantly, he could hear police sirens. He removed the cinder block halfway, then stuffed the pieces of his weapon into the area within the wall. He heard them clatter and fall to an area somewhere below the floor. He dropped the towel in behind the weapon parts. Then he pushed the cinder block back into place. He stepped to the chute of the trash incinerator and threw in his latex gloves. The chances were that no one would ever find this weapon, at least not until many years hence.

Perez could hear sirens approaching from a distance, but he knew he was already one step ahead of the police and the army. Confusion and panic were his allies.

He went down the building's back stairway and stopped on ground level long enough to discard one of his canes. Then he was out on the street within another minute, this time accentuating the limp since it fit so well with the profile of an old man.

He shuffled along at a steady pace through several crowded city blocks as police began to flood into the area. He stooped over a trifle more to give himself an even more *ancieno* look. In his peripheral vision, he watched the foolish, always-too-late authorities begin to cordon off the neighborhood behind him. But this was already many seconds after he had distanced himself from the area.

Knowing the airports would be watched, as well as the bus terminals, he had an old car ready and waiting. A second pistol and several rounds of ammunition were in the glove compartment, in case of unforeseen trouble.

He settled into the car. He kept the cane next to him and drove through city streets until he was outside of Bogotá. Then he accessed the two-lane road that led out of the capital to Villavicencio, an uncontrolled lawless city to the southeast.

A modern road shortened the driving time to one and a half hours. On the way, he threw his other cane out the car window. He did this while passing through a village where some poor old soul would pick it up and use it. Discarding the cane here, he told himself, was an act of charity, one of which, in a small way, he was proud.

THREE

By mid-afternoon Alex had returned to her office and had begun to unwind from the morning briefing, which had been followed by a private teleconference with various national police agencies up and down the hemisphere.

At her desk, she felt at ease. She had risen early that morning, after working late the night before, a pattern she had fallen into in recent weeks. She had been living in New York, at her new job, for fewer than six months now. At the end of the previous year, Alex had been promoted from her old position in Washington, D.C. Her job was now more hands-on. Fluent in Spanish as well as Italian, French, and Russian, she headed her own investigations into various financial schemes that emanated from Central and South America, schemes that targeted American victims, both corporate and individual.

She did a quick scan of her emails to see if anything was blowing up in any of her operations worldwide. The internet seas seemed calm. Maybe too calm, she thought to herself. She flicked through the message slips that Stacey, her assistant, had left on her desk, the personal mingling with the professional. Two names she didn't know. There were messages from a district attorney in Illinois, her friend Ben in D.C., another friend from college, and a final one from a name that looked familiar but took a split second to remember.

Paul Guarneri. No message. Just the name and a phone number on Long Island. She had known Guarneri only fleetingly. He was a suburban real estate entrepreneur who had done business with Yuri Federov, the recently deceased Russian racketeer whom Alex had professionally tracked the year before.

As for Guarneri, he enjoyed better fortune than Federov—at

least he was still alive. Or at least he was when he made the phone call. Who knew what could have happened in the past hour?

Guarneri's father, she recalled, had organized-crime connections in Cuba, where his family had lived. So what, Alex wondered as she stared at the slip, did Paul Guarneri want with her? Not having time to agonize over it right now, she zipped through a half dozen emails and arranged the call slips on her desk.

Then she spotted a sealed envelope delivered by private courier. It was from the office of Joshua Silverman, a New York attorney of either renown or notoriety, depending on one's point of view, who had the reputation as a mob lawyer, as well as the mouthpiece for some white-collar sleaze balls. Humanitarian issues were not his thing.

She tossed his envelope aside. She would get to it later and pass it up the Fin Cen food chain as needed. Chances were that Silverman was using her as a contact, and Alex would end up directing him to the department lawyers anyway. They deserved each other.

She looked at the final message. This one was friendlier. It was from Ben, a close friend of hers who lived in Washington. He was completing his second year of law school at Georgetown and was looking to intern in New York over the summer. He was lining up interviews. He had called a week ago to say that he would be in town this coming week for a short time. Did she know any reasonable place to stay?

She did indeed. She invited Ben to crash at her place for two or three nights. She had a sofa bed in her extra bedroom for just such occasions. Today was Monday and she expected him on the weekend. He was phoning to reconfirm.

Ben was a U.S. Marine veteran who had lost part of his leg in Iraq. After Alex's fiancé's death in Ukraine sixteen months ago, she and Ben, together, had learned how to walk again, she emotionally and he physically. She enjoyed his company. They had played in pickup basketball games together at the YMCA in

D.C., which was where they'd met. Ben was a good man and a good friend.

Right now, however, that was all. Just a good friend. The loss of her fiancé, Robert, still weighed heavily upon her. The desire to move on, as well as the pain of clinging to the past, to what had been a nearly perfect relationship, pulled at her almost every day. She was ready for a new romance—but then again, she wasn't.

She returned Ben's call. They chatted. When she returned to the challenges on her desk, she glanced again at the envelope from Silverman, Ashkenazy & DeLauro. Might as well get this over with, she decided as she tore it open.

The letter was from the founding partner, Joshua Silverman. Alex had been named in a legal proceeding, the letter announced, and she was asked to schedule an appointment so she and Silverman could discuss it further.

Alex phoned Silverman. A receptionist put her through. A few seconds of small talk followed, then, "Just tell me this," Alex asked. "Is this request personal or professional?"

"Personal for you, professional for me," Silverman said. "I can confirm that it's a financial matter. But I'm under instructions from my client to discuss things with you face-to-face or not at all. You're free to bring your own counsel, obviously, if you wish."

"Is there a time element involved?"

"The sooner the better," Silverman said, ". . . for you."

Alex looked at her calendar. "What about tomorrow morning? Can we get it done in half an hour? What if I'm there at 7:45?"

"That'd work."

Alex clicked off. Then, as long as she was dealing with pests, she thought she might as well deal with another. She input the number for Paul Guarneri.

He had been first introduced to her by the late Russian mobster, Yuri Federov, and Guarneri had also protected a young female witness for Alex the previous year. Alex owed him a dinner engagement, a marker that, she supposed, he now wished to call in.

Very well. She would go and listen.

On the phone they arranged to meet for dinner in two days. She set down the phone and marked the new appointments on her calendar: Silverman and Guarneri, with Ben visiting on the weekend.

So much for personal distractions. She clicked into her email again and caught up on what had recently transpired as the Operation Párajo strikes continued. Within the last half hour, she noted with satisfaction, Panamanian authorities had arrested three Mexicans and one Colombian-born Panamanian while driving a truck loaded with 511 kilograms of cocaine. Authorities concluded the cocaine was to be transported overland to Mexico. At the same time, a Panamanian Army helicopter crew identified a Colombian go-fast boat at a pier in Panama's Bocas del Toro island archipelago near the Costa Rican border. The Panamanian navy intercepted the watercraft and seized more than two tons of cocaine, presumed to be on its way to Florida by way of the Dominican Republic.

Alex was pleased. She was scoring major points against the opposition. But one thing worried her. Señor and Señora Dosi — the enemy king and queen on her chessboard. No confirmation of where they were, no hint that they would be in custody anytime soon.

As long as the Dosis were out there, the battle continued.

FOUR

In Villavicencio that evening, Manuel Perez shaved. With the help of heavy soap and cleaning solvents, he washed the gray dye out of his shaggy hair, and a local barber trimmed it. His hair regained its natural dark brown color.

The assassin now looked twenty years younger than the old Argentine whom his neighbors had known in the Colombian capital. Before the mirror that night, a man of forty-one emerged, handsome, muscular, and striking. *El Viejo Porteño* had disappeared.

Perez was happy this evening. Word came from Bogotá that both the justice minister and the driver-bodyguard had been killed in a sniper attack. Rebels connected with the cocaine traders were suspected.

The minister and his bodyguard: two for one. Good news indeed. So Perez relaxed and breathed easier. While political murders were common in Colombia, this one had a particularly high profile. Perez reasoned — correctly — that the airport and even the bus terminals would be saturated with police and army. But he also knew that these things blow over quickly. Among friends and allies, he had good reason to spend the next few evenings in the sleazy bordellos of Villavicencio and celebrate. So he settled in, planning to remain for several days.

FIVE

Early the next morning, Alex arrived in the reception area of the New York law firm Silverman, Ashkenazy & DeLauro. After being summoned by a sleepy receptionist, Joshua Silverman greeted Alex personally.

Silverman's office was a vast space, twenty-five by twenty feet, with two plate-glass windows that looked northward onto Park Avenue toward the Graybar building and Grand Central. Thick pile carpeting covered the floor, and there were several leather chairs and a matching sofa. The walls were done in Asian art, Chinese mostly, which seemed contemporary and for which Silverman had probably paid a good price.

The dark green walls gave the cherry legal cabinets some pizzazz, while antique Tiffany lamps dotted the end tables. Silverman's desk, which dominated the chamber, was the size of a small Buick. It was dark and expansive and featured inlays of cherry and mahogany. Lion heads were carved on the legs.

"May we get you some coffee? Water?" Silverman asked.

"I'm fine, thank you," Alex said.

Actually, she wasn't. She had a middle-range headache brewing and some stiffness in her left shoulder, an affliction that had grown worse recently as some internal flesh healed from a recent bullet wound. This appointment wasn't helping.

Silverman seated himself behind his desk. He took a long look at Alex, then threw her a question that seemed to come out of the blue. "I'm told you're a religious woman," he said. "Should I believe that?"

"I am a Christian if that's what you mean. Who told you?"

"A Russian told me," he said. "About a year ago. And if I told you that a piece of business has come forth from our Geneva office, would that suggest why you're here?"

Alex drew a breath. "It might."

"Last week one of our associates in a Swiss firm read the last will of Yuri Federov," Silverman said. "Mr. Federov named you as a beneficiary."

Silverman stood and leaned forward, handing Alex copies of the papers. She stood, took them, and sat down again. She scanned them quickly. The will was written in French, English, and Russian. Reading such documents, and the legalese therein, was hardly her specialty, since, strangely enough, she had seen very few in her life and none had been happy occasions. It would have taken her several minutes to wade through this one, but it quickly became unnecessary.

"This is for you, Alex," Silverman said. "Congratulations. I hope you will treat it well and use it wisely. That was what Mr. Federov intended."

He handed her a small envelope. Her name was written on it in handwriting that she recognized as Federov's. She glanced at Silverman as she put a finger into the envelope and pulled it open.

Within was a letter from the law firm in Switzerland. It was in French and addressed to her. She scanned it. There was another piece of paper, folded in half. A check. She unfolded it.

Silverman said, "I'm sure you will handle it wisely."

She barely heard him. The check was made out to her, drawn on Credit Suisse's offices in New York. She saw a line of zeroes. Then her eyes froze on the second line, the one that conveyed the amount.

Two million dollars.

"Your life just changed, I know," Silverman said. "It must feel strange."

"What's this about?" she asked. "I don't get it."

Silverman shrugged. "What's it about?" he mused. "Who knows? That's not my department. The funds come with no strings attached and no further message from Mr. Federov. Apparently he had great affection for you and wished to leave you a gift, something that would impact your life in a positive way. That's all I know. Other than that, all federal, state, and city taxes have already been deducted. It was apparently the intent of Mr. Federov to leave you a flat two million dollars. I also need a final signature from you on a letter, confirming that you've met with me and received the check. I have the letter prepared. It will need to be notarized. I have a notary on call." He paused. "I assume you're willing to sign and accept."

She was hearing all this but had trouble believing it.

"Of course," she said.

"Then let's proceed."

Twenty minutes later, back down on Park Avenue, Alex was still stunned. She stopped outside the office building, trying to put things in perspective. Yes, this had really happened. The check was in an envelope in her purse, along with a business card from a banker named Christophe Chatton at Credit Suisse in New York. Chatton would be at Alex's disposal if he could assist in any way with the management of the money.

As she took a few steps away from Silverman's building, her purse had never seemed so heavy. Was this Federov's strange final way of corrupting her, she wondered? Or was he expecting her to use it to buy his redemption?

She had two million dollars about to go into the bank. And now, it seemed, she had two million new things to think about.

SIX

Manuel Perez rested, never leaving the small compound where he lodged. Respectfully, with even a small touch of sympathy, he watched the televised state funerals for the men he had killed. A day and a half later, confident that no one was looking for him, he was ready to travel.

His escorts were part of a network of cocaine traffickers loyal to one of the big cartels from Medellín. They didn't know what Perez had done or for whom, but they treated him with courtesy. They showed him to a van. The driver was a muscular young punk, about twenty, with black hair, a silk shirt, and a cocky attitude. His name was Mauricio. He was Mexican, Perez noted. Perez didn't like the looks of him, his surliness, or his singsong Mexican working-class accent.

The plan was to ferry Perez by highway to Cali, and from there he would fly out of the country. They began their trip by the roads that went through the farm areas south of Bogotá. Half an hour later, Perez began to talk to Mauricio. The two men discovered they shared a common background: fatherless and dirt poor in the state of Guerrero in Mexico. The driver's eyes kept shifting between the road ahead, the road behind, and the ominous single passenger in the backseat. A backup team of bodyguards followed in case there was trouble with police or army roadblocks, but no trouble ensued. Perez started to warm up to his chauffeur and wondered if the kid knew who he was and what had been his business in Colombia. Eventually, Perez asked.

"I know you're important. I'm supposed to get you to the airport," Mauricio said.

"Do you have a gun?" Perez asked.

"Not with me. Not allowed while I drive you." Mauricio tipped his head toward the car behind them. "If there's trouble," he said, "they're the shooters, not me."

"You *like* guns?" Perez asked.

"Love them."

Perez nodded. "A man needs his guns in this world," he said philosophically.

At the airport, before Perez stepped out of the van, the bodyguards went into the airport lobby to trawl for potential trouble. They saw none. Returning, they gave Perez the all-clear signal.

Perez drew a breath. This was the tricky part. Getting home.

He tapped his driver on the shoulder in a friendly gesture of thanks. He gave his pistol to Mauricio as a souvenir and gift. Then Perez walked into the lobby as routinely as any other passenger. He used his escape passport, an American one under the name of Martín Lopez, to check in for a flight to Tegucigalpa, Honduras.

The flight was announced. Perez departed. In Tegucigalpa, he connected to Mexico City. When the aircraft touched down in the Mexican capital, Perez heaved a sigh of relief. He couldn't wait to embrace his family. Sometimes these business jaunts were pure torture, and he agonized about the day he might never return from one.

Here in the capital, Perez had a luxurious and spacious home. He was anxious to return to it. His wife, Nicoleta, worked for an American pharmaceutical company. Their three daughters were twelve, nine, and five. They were dark haired and very pretty, like their mother.

He lived quietly in the wealthy suburbs. All who knew him, even his family, thought of him as a business graduate from the huge university in Mexico City, who now ran a successful and highly visible shipping and import-export business. His company, as everyone knew, dealt in dried fruits and processed foods from Colombia, Venezuela, and Argentina. They knew he traveled a lot, and of course, judging by his wealth, he was successful. But no one knew what else he did for a living.

After breezing through customs and emerging into the terminal where friends and families waited for arriving passengers, he spotted a strikingly pretty Latina sitting beyond the edge of the crowd. She had light brown skin, with a delicate face behind large round sunglasses. She was wearing a short blue summer dress and matching espadrilles.

Immediately Perez noticed that her legs were spectacular, beautifully tanned from toe to mid-thigh. Exactly what he loved. A private security man flanked her. In her lap she held an expensive leather purse, one of those beautiful designer bags from Italy or Spain. She sat with her legs crossed, clutching a pack of Marlboros and nervously fidgeting with it.

Perez smiled, stopped, and studied her. She was the sexiest, most beautiful woman he had ever seen. On the woman's hand, there was a ring with an expensive sparkle. The stone must have been five carats. She was obviously waiting for a lucky someone.

Then she looked at him. She smiled and came quickly to her feet.

"¡Nicoleta!" he proclaimed.

His wife opened her arms and rushed toward him.

He opened his arms in return and embraced her. It always felt so good to return safely from a dangerous mission, like a warrior back from battle. The bodyguard, a Chilean named Antonio, protectively stood by, then guided the couple to a waiting Cadillac Escalade.

It was wonderful to be home.

SEVEN

Two evenings later, Alex and Paul Guarneri met for dinner at Peter Lugar's Steakhouse in midtown Manhattan. Guarneri had offered to send a car and driver, but Alex preferred to travel by subway and then on foot.

Guarneri was already at the restaurant at 7:30 when Alex arrived. The maître d' obviously knew Guarneri and escorted Alex quickly to his table, which was one of the better ones—in the back, spacious but private, and out of the view of most of the other diners.

Guarneri was fifty-something, dark and handsome, with gray at the temples. He had a strong face. He was reading the menu when she saw him and had put on a pair of reading glasses, which gave him an almost scholarly look.

He looked up, smiled broadly, and put the glasses away. Alex always knew when a man had some personal interest in her. There was something about the focus of the eyes, the body language, and the tone of voice. She had sensed it from the start. She felt nothing in return.

"Well, well," he said, on his feet and giving an appreciative nod to the maître d'. "My favorite federal employee. Welcome. Nice to see you."

"Hello, Paul," she said.

He gave her an embrace, which she returned. The maître d' held the chair for her and disappeared. They sat.

"If I'm your favorite Fed, chances are you don't know many," Alex said.

"I've met a few, for better or worse," he said with a dismissive laugh. "You've earned your special status."

A waiter arrived and asked if they desired drinks. Guarneri

ordered a vodka martini. Alex went with a Pellegrino. She needed to stay sharp.

After a few minutes of small talk, Guarneri asked, "So you're in New York now? You've relocated?"

"Yes, that's correct."

"New job?" he asked.

"Same old same old," she said, "but more responsibility and more challenge."

"Like it?"

"It's a living."

"So is riding elephants in the circus."

"It's a bit different than that," she said.

"I'm sure it is," he said. "How's that cute young lady my people were protecting last year? Janet? Was that her name?"

"She's fine. Your people did a great job keeping her out of trouble."

"It was easy," he said. "I knew some off-duty NYPD people, and they took care of things. All I did was set it up."

"Nonetheless, she stayed safe. I'm appreciative."

"Appreciation has its price," he warned with a smile.

"Of course. This dinner," she said. "And some more free advice."

He laughed again. "I'm afraid I'd like to call in a heavier IOU than that," he said. "Cuba. That's what we discussed last time, wasn't it?"

"You might have mentioned something," she answered. "I'd forgotten."

On that occasion Paul had, in fact, elaborated a long family history, both professional and family, and their connections to Cuba.

"I doubt that," he answered. He winked at her. "You're good, Alex. 'The smartest beautiful woman I've ever met.' That's what the dear departed Comrade Yuri Federov used to say. I must say, I miss him. Life was never dull."

"It wasn't, no," she said. "I was at the funeral in Geneva."

"That was good of you. I didn't know he had died till afterward. I might have attended myself. Sad, in its way."

"Sad," she agreed.

More banter. The waiter reappeared and they each ordered steaks, even though Alex knew the portions were enormous. Guarneri ordered a bottle of California burgundy. They enjoyed the meal and conversation drifted. Then toward the conclusion of dinner, Guarneri snaked around to the subject he wanted to discuss.

"Okay. Cuba," he said. "Let's backtrack. First things first. You promised to go there with me, to Cuba, in exchange for my having protected Janet. Surely, you recall."

"Refresh my memory," Alex said. "Let's see if you tell it the same way twice."

She had left half her meal and asked the waiter to pack it to go. They ordered coffee, and the waiter cleared the table.

"I was born there in 1955," Guarneri said. *"Mi madre fue cubana,"* he said. "My father was a part owner of a racetrack and a casino near Havana. He also owned some strip clubs. When Castro took over, my dad had to get out—fast. At the time, he was holding a half million dollars in American currency. There was no way he could take it with him to the airport. The police or Castro's soldiers would have taken it." Guarneri paused. "So he buried it."

"I remember," she said.

Guarneri reached for his wallet and produced a pair of photos. One showed his mother as a casino showgirl in a chorus line in 1957. The other was a grainy picture of himself with his mother, a faded color shot, from Long Island in 1966. "My mother and I got out of the country in 1961, February."

The coffee arrived. The espresso was scalding. Alex sipped carefully.

"My father had another wife and family here, but he smuggled us out, anyway," Guarneri said. "My dad could have left us there, but he didn't. God bless him for that. I grew up in the U.S. instead of Communist Cuba. What a difference, huh?"

"Absolutely," she said.

"I remember when we left. My mother got me in the middle of the night, wrapped me in a blanket, and put me in a car. She told me it was time to leave and we couldn't bring anything. We drove without headlights and went to a boat. The boat went to a seaplane, and we flew to Florida. I'm told we flew eighty miles at three hundred feet. There was a storm, but I slept through it. When I woke up the next morning we were in a nice apartment in Key West. Everything was new and clean. My father had set up everything. Then came the Bay of Pigs, the American invasion at *Playa Girón*, a month later. It was harder to get anyone out of Cuba after that. Years went by. My father always fretted over the thought of those greenbacks rotting in the Cuban earth, but he also always said he was glad that he got us out when he did. But he died first and never got back to Cuba. Remember me telling you all this?"

"I do," Alex said. "The hidden money, do you now know where it is?"

"If I could get back to Cuba, I know I could find it."

"Then what?" she asked. "The rightful owners, if you could call them that, were the pre-revolution gangsters who ran the casinos and strip clubs. Are you planning to get in touch with the original cast of *The Godfather* and reimburse everyone?"

Paul glanced away, then shot back, "Look, I have my reasons. When you came to me and asked me to protect Janet, I just did it for you. Friend of a friend. No questions, no moral agonizing."

"So you expect me to trust you?" she said.

"Let's just say I'm not planning to grab the money just to enrich myself. I'll be frank: I've been successful in business. Half a million is a nice sum, but not enough for me to risk everything to grab it. But the money will go to a good purpose. One you would approve of, something my father always wanted done."

"So you're obeying the commandment, 'honor thy father and mother'?" she asked.

"If you called it that, I'd be flattered."

"Are you planning to tell me what that purpose is?"

"No," he said. "Not yet. You don't need to know until we actually get to Cuba."

"That's not very convincing, Paul," she said.

"Maybe not. But it was *you* who came to me and asked the favor. I bent a few laws, took some risks, and did that favor for you. And you *did* tell me that you'd return the favor someday," he said. "You said you'd get us into Cuba. Or at least make the effort. That's what you promised."

She sighed.

He sighed, mimicking her in good humor, and smiled.

"All right. Let me do this," she said. "I'm slammed at the office right now with an investigation in Central America. I can't see how I'd be able to do anything away from the office for several weeks. But I'll run your request past my boss, explaining the past history and the favor you did for us in protecting Janet. And in a morbid sort of way, I'm intrigued. But my boss makes the final call. We'll see what he says."

"Fair enough," Paul said. "Thank you."

"Keep in mind, if it were up to me, common sense would prevail, and you'd have to think of another favor to ask ... and I think it's time for me to get home."

The waiter reappeared with a handsomely wrapped takeout bag, which he presented to Alex. Guarneri settled the bill, tipped generously, and they were out the door into a balmy New York evening.

"How are you getting home?" Guarneri asked.

"Taxi."

"Nonsense," said Guarneri. "My car and driver are here somewhere. We can give you a lift." He turned to the restaurant doorman, who obviously knew him, and asked, "Have you seen Michael?"

A moment later, Guarneri's black limousine appeared and eased to the curb. The driver popped out and greeted Alex by name. He came around the vehicle to open the back door on the curb side.

"I live on the Upper West Side," Alex said to Guarneri. "That's out of your way if you're going to Long Island."

"What a coincidence. We're going to the Upper West Side as well," Paul said.

Alex hesitated, assessing Paul and the situation. "No, thank you. I'll take a taxi. Good night, Paul," she said. "I'll phone you after I discuss this with my boss. Thank you for dinner." She looked to his driver. "Thanks anyway, Michael. I'll be fine."

She allowed Paul to embrace her and give her a social kiss on the cheek. Then started walking away. There was a taxi at the curb and she grabbed it.

EIGHT

At Andrew De Salvo's office the next afternoon, De Salvo's secretary, Elsa Nussman, greeted Alex. Elsa was mid-fifties, stout and prim, with round glasses that gave her an owlish look. "Go on in," Elsa said. "He's waiting."

Alex opened the door and stepped in. De Salvo sat behind his wide mahogany desk. At Alex's feet lay a wide Persian rug. On the walls hung De Salvo's many awards and diplomas, plus photographs of him with the last four American presidents.

Her boss looked up in his distinguished, if slightly stooped, way. Alex liked him. He was a Midwesterner from Indiana, just past sixty. He smiled. His blue eyes showed indictment-fatigue. He looked up from his desk.

"Got a couple of minutes?" Alex asked. "I need to run a few things past you."

"Sure," he said. A trio of hardcopy classified folders sat on his desk. Alex could tell by the bold red binders. He flipped all three shut as she pushed the door shut and sat down. "What's on your mind?"

"Last night I had dinner with a man named Paul Guarneri," Alex said. "I know him from last year's operation out of Washington. Guarneri was a fringe player in the Federov operation," she said. "Guarneri did Fin Cen a favor by babysitting a witness while we cleaned up some business. So I owe him one."

"We have IOUs all over the place," De Salvo said. "Big deal. But keep talking."

"Guarneri was tight with Federov's business associates," Alex said, "but it was the legit end of Federov's businesses. I've run him through the files. No arrests. His father was an accomplice with the crime families in Cuba pre-Castro: the Trafficantes, Gambinos, Frank Costello, Lucky Luciano."

"Interesting. Where does it go?"

"I know that Guarneri's dad was the victim of a gangland hit in the 1970s," she said. "I don't know what it was about, but the case is still open. So he's from a connected family, seems to be clean himself, and makes his money in real estate."

"So? 'Dinner' as in 'dating,' or just 'dinner'?"

"'Dinner' as in he called me and wants to call in the favor," Alex said. "He wants me to go to Cuba with him on some piece of old business relating to his father."

"Cuba?!" De Salvo laughed. "You sure can pick your spots. It can't be Bermuda or Hawaii or Bonaire; it's got to be to a place where you can't legally travel?"

"Guarneri has ideas about trying to get back some money that was hidden years ago. That's the link."

De Salvo laughed again. "Well, sure. The Castro *hermanos* start to fade away, and all the Mafia families are going to be looking for recovery of lost property. It's going to be a mess. How much?"

"Half a million dollars ... so he says."

"I got to say, times must be tough if a connected guy has to go out and scrounge for half a million. Didn't he get any TARP funds?"

Alex smiled. "Guess not."

"So it's just been sitting somewhere for fifty years? A bank?"

"Stashed. Hidden. Buried. Literally."

De Salvo folded his arms, then ran a hand through his hair. "If it's cash, it's still legal tender," he said. He shook his head. "Obviously, Operation Párajo isn't keeping you busy enough. Has anyone arrested the Dosis yet, by the way?"

"Not that I've heard."

De Salvo cursed quietly. "The longer they're out there, the better the chance that they land somewhere beyond extradition. Can you turn up the pressure?"

"I can try," she said.

"Okay, look. This Guarneri-Cuban thing. What do you want to

do with it? You feel you want to make this trip? Scope things out? Think there's something in it?"

"I'd prefer to avoid it," Alex said. "As long as Párajo is in progress, I don't have time for Cuba."

"Well, then, tell that to your Mafia guy."

"Okay," she said. "I'll try. Maybe he'll lose interest."

"Half a million bucks and fifty years," De Salvo said, thinking it further. "Your guy's not going to lose interest. Play him along as an asset. You never know."

Alex gave him half a grin and half a nod. "Good advice."

She sat tight. De Salvo looked as if he expected her to stand and leave. She didn't.

"There's more?" he asked.

"I need your input on something. Professional and personal. Confidential."

"Okay."

"Federov's will was read in Switzerland two weeks ago. I was named in it."

"The dear boy left you some rubles? Is that it?"

"Yes. Dollars, actually. A significant amount."

"Oh. Lucky you. Throw us all a party. Classy hookers for the guys, Chippendale dancers for the ladies. What's not to like?"

She grinned. "I'm inquiring about the ethics. Will it make any waves here if I keep the money?"

De Salvo's gaze ran out the window, across the concrete canyon of Wall Street, and to the harbor beyond. He glanced back to her. "No strings attached?" he asked again.

"None."

De Salvo shrugged. "The Federov case is closed; the man is dead and likely to remain so. And you're not in a position to help his estate or heirs. Right?"

"Not to my knowledge."

"So bank it," he said.

"Can you give me a memo saying we discussed it and you advised me?"

"Sure. You draw it up; I'll initial it. How's that?"

"Perfect," she said.

She got up and headed toward the door. "Alex, if you're looking for something to blow it on, the Ferrari Testa Rosa comes in at about a quarter of a million dollars now. Would you be in the market?"

"Sure. But I don't think I need eight of them."

"Oh, my," he said. "Eight times two-fifty. Significant, indeed. Congratulations." He paused. "You coming in to work tomorrow?"

"Probably," she said. "What else would I do?"

"Don't even go there," he said.

In Mexico City, phones were ringing and back-channel connections were falling into place. Manuel Perez had no sooner settled into his home than he received yet another request for his services. He would need to travel again.

Well, all right, he thought to himself. At least this was one assignment he could parlay into a family getaway. Yet a mood of caution was growing within him. He thought of himself as a player at a roulette wheel, a player who was riding a long winning streak. He knew there would be a time when it would be wise to take his chips and walk away from the table. The problem was, walking away when one was winning was no easy matter.

NINE

A few minutes before eight, Alex arrived at Hastings', a small Manhattan pub down one flight of stairs, in a basement, from the sidewalk on West 64th Street. It was midway between Central Park to the east and Lincoln Center to the west.

She gave Jack Hastings, the owner, a wave as she entered. She selected her own table after Jack waved back and indicated that she might sit anywhere she liked. The eatery was a neighborhood hangout and popular among visitors to Lincoln Center in the early evening. It was small, dimly lit, and comfortable. Red tablecloths anchored the room with a small candle on each table. There were usually only two waitresses from a roster of nine, all of whom worked part-time, grad students at Columbia, NYU, or Juilliard nearby. The waitresses patrolled in red T-shirts and black skirts. Jack worked the bar six nights a week. Harp and Guinness were on tap. Legend had it that throughout Prohibition, Jack's grandfather Michael hadn't missed a shift or a sip. The plasma TVs high up at each end of the bar were usually tuned to sports. Since taking up residence on West 61st Street, Alex had become a regular.

One of the Columbia girls, Martha, appeared quickly and took Alex's drink order. Martha had no sooner disappeared than Ben appeared in the doorway, holding a shopping bag. Alex waved. Ben smiled broadly and came to her table. She stood for a tight embrace and a kiss on the cheek.

Ben was a strapping guy from North Carolina. He had been a Marine gunnery sergeant in Iraq before a roadside bomb in Anwar Province had taken off his leg below the knee. He now wore a prosthesis. In Washington, Alex and Ben had been gym rats together in a co-ed basketball league.

Ben was the slowest guy on the court, but at six four he was also the tallest. Prosthesis and occasional jerky movements and all, he had played center for Alex's team. From their comradeship on the court, a deep friendship had emerged. They'd been there for each other during some of their darkest personal moments, most notably when Alex had plunged into a nearly fatal depression following the death of her fiancé, and another time, in Paris, when she had been hospitalized after a shooting.

When Martha returned, they ordered drinks and then they ordered food. They exchanged small talk about recent events, Ben mostly talking about his search for an internship in Manhattan, and Alex telling him about her successful start at the new branch at Fin Cen.

Ben reached into his shopping bag and presented Alex with a small bouquet of roses. They caught her off guard. No one had given her flowers since Robert, and she still didn't know whether to associate flowers with love or funerals. But she thanked him. They finished eating, ordered coffee, and he asked what else was new.

"You're not going to believe this," she said.

"Try me."

"Do you remember that Russian? Yuri Federov."

"Of course," he said. "I used to be jealous of him, you chasing him down all over the world, going dancing with him or nightclubbing or whatever."

"It was *all* work related," Alex answered with a smile.

"Still," Ben said. "It happened ..." For a moment, Alex reassessed Ben — flowers, an admission of jealousy. Then, she said, "You know Federov died a few weeks back ... His will was read in Switzerland two weeks ago. I didn't attend the reading — but he left me something." She produced the envelope that she had carried all day. She handed it to Ben. "Open it," she said. "Take a look."

He pulled out the check. The front of it was facing away from him when it first left the envelope. He flipped it over. His eyes widened as they settled upon it.

"Holy cow!" he muttered softly. "This is real? Two million dollars!"

"Two million dollars," Alex said, "and the taxes have already been paid."

He shook his head. "Don't know about you," he said, "but that's the most money I've ever held in my hands. When I got discharged from the Marines, I had nineteen thousand dollars in the bank plus a VA card — and I thought I was rich." He stared at it for several more seconds and handed it back. "Wow," he said. "Incredible."

"Really," she said. "Incredible. Seriously. But I have some hang-ups about it. I know the type of man Federov was. I know that at the end of his life, facing death, he was looking for salvation and forgiveness." She paused. "Think I should keep it?"

"Don't even think twice. Think of the good you could do. Really!"

"That's what you'd do?"

"Listen, Alex," he said. "Maybe Federov *was* looking for salvation. Maybe he thought you would know exactly where his money could do the most good."

"Maybe," Alex said. Then, seeing the look he gave her, she said, "So what?"

"So what does it matter if it can't buy him forgiveness? It could do a lot of good, anyway. Good in your life. Good in the lives of others. You could give it away, or you could use it to sustain you while you give your time and effort away to others. How's that?"

"Good." She nodded.

"Think about Itzhak Perlman," he said, "the violinist."

"What about him?"

"He contracted polio when he was four and lost the use of his legs. Instead of cursing his fate, he saw it as a gift from God. As he tells it, no one would have put a violin in his hands if he hadn't been in a wheelchair. And from the hands in that chair came some of the most beautiful music of the twentieth century. So from a quirk of fate, or divine intervention, or whatever you call it, lives get changed. That's happened to you, so just go with it."

She pondered. Ben sipped his drink and continued, "I'm happy for you. You know the old joke: 'Money isn't everything, but it's way ahead of second place.' "

She smiled. "Funny, but not necessarily true."

"Of course not," he said, "because money can bring misery too." He paused. "When I was growing up in North Carolina, my mother used to tell me about this nasty woman she knew named Darlene. Mom and Darlene had gone to high school together. When Darlene was about thirty, she inherited a pile of dough from her family, and it changed her. She spent her life safeguarding it, being suspicious of other people, never having fun. She became churlish, hostile, lost all her friends. My mother was a Christian, a woman of faith. She used to say, if that's what money does to you, she prayed to God she would never be rich, because that's not the person she wanted to be."

"Point taken," Alex said.

"Now, let's get back to Itzhak Perlman. Did you know he's playing at Carnegie Hall on Friday?"

"I *did* know that," she said. "I tried to get tickets but it's sold out."

"So who's your pal?" he asked. "*I* am, that's who. I have my own magical envelope this evening."

Ben reached into a jacket pocket and flipped a small envelope onto the table. "Two tickets for Perlman. Bought them as a gift for letting me stay with you. Hope you can go."

She picked up the tickets and looked at them. Orchestra, fifteenth row. In terms of grad-student dollars, Ben had taken a plunge for these.

"Wow!" she said. She stood, leaned over the table, and kissed him.

"It's already worth it," he said. "You'll go?"

"I'd love to."

He took them back. "I'll hold them for now."

"Ben?" she asked, a trace of anxiety. "Is this a 'date' date?"

"What if it were?" he asked.

"If it were," she said, "we should talk first. I think you're wonderful. But last year was so traumatizing. I'm not sure that I'm ready for — "

"Look. It's you and me as friends going to a recital where we happen to be close up to one of the great violinists of our lifetime. We have a great evening and hear some great music. Does it have to be any more than that?"

She shook her head, mildly relieved. "No. That's already splendid enough."

TEN

Before work on Friday morning, Alex went to the office of Credit Suisse at 11 Madison Avenue. By appointment, she met Christophe Chatton, whose card Joshua Silverman had given her at his office. Chatton was a thin young man with dark hair, about thirty. He wore a three-piece suit and spoke with a mildly irritating accent that suggested a year or two in British public schools. He met her in the bank's vast lobby and ushered her to his private office.

The banker was up-to-date on why she was there. "I do congratulate you," he said, "on your good fortune. An inheritance from a late gentleman friend." He presented her with another business card and a brochure about the bank.

Late gentleman friend. His phrasing made it sound like she was an ex-mistress who'd struck gold. She let it go.

"I'm hoping that you're here to open an account," he said.

"That's correct," Alex said, "I am. So let's get it done." All in all, she thought, she should be happier about this than she actually felt.

"Excellent," he said.

Alex placed the check on his desk.

"I have some forms for you to fill out," he said silkily. "Applications for an account. Please be assured that we can handle all aspects of private banking for you. We like to build long relationships with our customers and tailor our various investment services to your needs."

"Forgive me," she said, "but I'm going to go slowly on this. I've only been wealthy for less than a week."

Chatton laughed. "I fear that Swiss banks have long been thought of as exclusive and only catering to the very rich," he said. "That is not a fact. Swiss bank accounts and private banking are available to those with less than one million dollars."

"Paupers," she said.

"You're familiar with Credit Suisse, I'm sure," he said. "Foremost, we have protected the wealth of our clients for nearly a hundred and fifty years. During the American Civil War, our headquarters in Geneva stood on the same spot where it stands now. Before the Suez Canal was completed, before man flew the first airplane, we were doing business. Continuity and security, Madame LaDuca. That's what we stand for."

"Yes, I'm familiar with the bank," she said, bemused.

"You know much about us?"

"I know that like most Swiss banks, ninety-nine percent of your private clients are wealthy law-abiding citizens. Another three quarters of one percent are tax evaders, bribe takers, and arms dealers. The rest are drug traffickers."

"You have a delicious sense of humor," he said.

"Thank you," she said. "And don't worry. I'll leave the money here for a while."

"Let me explain the possibilities for investment," he said. "Do gold bars interest you? Certificates of deposit?"

"I just want it in one insured account right now, earning interest. Nothing exotic."

"Very well." His tone conveyed a sigh of exasperation. He looked down and put his own signature on the documents. "Please wait for a moment," he said.

Officiously, he was on his feet and out of his office, leaving the door slightly ajar. For several minutes Alex sat alone, surveying Chatton's lair, the teak of the desk, the signed Miró print on the wall, the standing plant in the corner. Then Monsieur Chatton was back with all her documents fully executed and a book of temporary checks. "All done," he said. "Your deposit is complete. Again, my congratulations on your new wealth."

Alex smiled. If only she knew what to do with it.

ELEVEN

Friday evening arrived. At Carnegie Hall, Alex and Ben sat in the fifteenth row of the orchestra and watched in awe as violinist Itzhak Perlman played seemingly two concerts. The first half was remorselessly formal, as Perlman delivered the music, nodding but otherwise not saying a word to the audience between pieces.

The concert opened with one of Handel's violin sonatas. In this work, Perlman's tight musicianship came across to Alex as a lovely, chaste melancholy. Already fatigued, she felt her spirits dimmed from the sadness of the music.

But after intermission, the formal virtuoso was transformed into the casual, accessible violin player, a man who, in his fifty years of performing, had not only performed in every great concert hall but had also easily joked with the Muppets on *Sesame Street*.

"The good news is that the piece is not very long," Perlman quipped from the stage about Messiaen's modernist *Theme and Variations*. "Just pretend you've heard it ten times before and maybe you'll like it."

Ben and Alex laughed. Ben gave Alex's hand a squeeze and then pulled it away, awkwardly and self-consciously. After that, Perlman played six short pieces. At the end, he was rewarded with a roar of acclamation from the audience.

Alex and Ben emerged from Carnegie Hall into a balmy June night. They walked up Seventh Avenue to 61st Street where Alex lived. They chatted amiably, enjoying the evening. She felt relaxed with him in a way different than any man she knew. His body felt strong, his gait smooth, even with the prosthesis.

"Hungry?" he asked as they maneuvered the crowds. The New York Philharmonic and the theater where a revival of *South*

Pacific was playing had let out from nearby Lincoln Center. The sidewalks were busy.

"Yes. A bit," she said. "What are you in the mood for? Italian? Greek? Pub grub? Coffee and pastry?"

"You choose."

They looked at various store fronts. Then the answer presented itself to her. "Know what would be good?" she said.

"You tell me."

She motioned to her neighborhood pizzeria, Raimondo's, a bright place that sold pies whole or by the slice. "Let's just get some slices and take them home," she said. "I've got drinks in the fridge."

"Works for me," he said, "if it works for you."

"Works perfectly for me," she said. "The place is owned by an Athenian named Chris who grew up in Calabria and is staffed by people who barely speak English," Alex said. "That's always a good sign for pizza in New York."

Ben laughed. "You always break me up with stuff like that," he said. "How do you know all that? You just moved here."

"I've been here five months. This is my neighborhood. Raimondo's is open late. I stop by sometimes when I don't get home till midnight. I talk to the owner in Italian. He grew up in Sicily. He likes me because I speak Italian."

"Does he know you're a Fed?"

"Of course not," she grinned. "If he did, he probably wouldn't like me anymore."

They stepped into the crowded pizzeria. They bought half a pie to take out, four generous slices with various toppings. Ben paid.

They were back at Alex's apartment in ten minutes. They entered. Alex dropped the blinds in the living room. At night she could see hundreds of windows, and they could see her. Ben loved the nighttime view of Manhattan and spent a few minutes peaking around the blinds, looking downward onto Seventh Avenue where traffic moved southbound toward Times Square and the theater district. She loved her view, but one never knew when one was the target of a voyeur with a telescope. It was New York, after all: plenty of weirdoes out there.

Alex went to the kitchen. She put the pizza slices on a cookie sheet and warmed them in the oven. She grabbed two bottles of pop from the refrigerator and set them on her small kitchen table. Ben wandered back to the kitchen a few moments later and sat down.

"Want a glass?" she asked.

"Nope."

"Me neither."

They clicked their bottles and talked about times they had shared in Washington. Ben told her again how much she was missed by the gang at the gym and how no one before or since could sink a three pointer from that particular spot, two feet beyond the three-point line, like Alex could.

She laughed. It was a good memory. She got up, retrieved the pizza, and put it onto plates. "Knife? Fork?" she asked.

"For pizza? You're kidding, right?"

"I'm kidding," she said.

They ate and laughed some more over old times.

As they sat in the cozy kitchen a seditious thought came to Alex's mind. It occurred to her that she and Ben were acting like a couple, a man and a woman who might already be lovers or who might be lovers in the future—or even husband and wife someday. She didn't know whether to embrace the idea or reject it. She felt she was ready to move on romantically—except for the fact that she wasn't. In some ways, she was as confused as she had ever been. Eventually, Alex looked at the wall clock; it was nearly 1:00 a.m.

"Hey," she said, "I have to put in time at the office tomorrow."

"Saturday?" he asked.

"And Sunday too," she said. "More of a pain than anything, if you want to know the truth." She stood. "Anyway, I need some sleep."

"Yeah," he said, looking at her.

"Well, look," she said. "You know where everything is. Towels. Bathroom. Let's just leave the dishes in the sink. I'll deal with them tomorrow."

"Yeah," he said again. There was an awkward moment and he stood.

"Did you enjoy being together tonight?" he asked. "The concert?"

"Of course."

"I really enjoy it when we're together, Alex," he said.

"Ben ..."

He stood before her. Their eyes locked. "What?" he said.

"I thought we decided ... I thought we agreed," she said. "There were some places we just weren't going to go. Not now."

"We decided, we discussed, we agreed," he said. "But I want to know something, Alex. I need to ask." He paused, then asked, "Do you have feelings for me?"

Her heart banged and felt as if it had gotten stuck somewhere between her throat and the pit of her stomach.

"Tell me if you do or if you don't," he said, "because I think it's obvious by now that I have feelings for you."

It was not a conversation she was ready for. Ben was a decent, kind man, a pillar of strength who, with his tough love, had pulled her back from the abyss of suicide less than a year before. Deeply, she did not want to let him go. And yet she didn't even know how to phrase her answer, or, for that matter, what her answer was.

"Yes," she admitted, "I have feelings. And they're strong feelings. But maybe they're not the right ones just yet. Or maybe the time just isn't right yet."

"When *will* the time be right?" he asked.

She looked into his eyes, set as they were in a rugged, strong, kind face. Her instincts told her not to say anything, but to take him by the hand and kiss him.

She did not know what to say, didn't even know what was

right to feel. She could keep her feelings inside her, bury them, suppress them, but sometimes her physical desires had the pull of a runaway horse. Bubbling beneath the surface, she realized, were feelings that she was struggling to keep inside; she was afraid to fall in love because the last time she did, she had fallen hard and then everything had been taken from her.

"I don't know," she said. She felt as if she had muffed her response. "I mean, I *do* know. But I don't know if I'm ready for another relationship yet."

"It's been a year," he said. "More than a year. I understand your loss. I can't replace Robert. We both know no one ever can, but— "

"Sorry," she said. "It's not something that I can put a clock on. I hope you understand, Ben, because the last thing I'd want to do is lead you on or hurt you."

She sensed his disappointment. Meanwhile, her mouth had gone dry, her heart hammered, and her knees felt weak. She was shocked but not surprised. Everything was turned on its end because a friend was suggesting that he might now become more. A couple of uneasy seconds went by and she couldn't figure out how she could be so on top of things at work and so adrift in her personal life.

He released her hand. "Okay," he said quietly. "I asked. It's been driving me crazy, this attraction I have for you, unable to do anything, afraid to even say anything. At least I asked." He paused. "I hope I didn't wreck our friendship."

"Of course not," she said. She drew another breath. "I'm just not ready to pour out my emotions again. It doesn't feel right yet."

He nodded. "It's okay. I understand. But then there's something else I want to tell you about if you and I aren't going anywhere."

"Go ahead."

"One reason I came to New York was not just to do those interviews but to see if, you know, maybe we could start going out. I wanted to know because, honestly, you're the most terrific woman I've ever met. And I wanted to see if something would spark between us."

"Where are you going with this, Ben?" she asked.

"I was at an interview the other day in D.C. One of the big firms. Very politically connected. And I met this woman," he said. "Her name's Carol. She's smart. Like you. I guess that's my type. She went to one of those prestigious colleges up in Boston; you know, one of those places that bankrupt you if you're not rich."

They shared a smile. Hers was nervous. So was his.

"She's blonde, about five-seven. Beautiful figure. Working on her master's degree in public affairs at Georgetown."

"And you're going to ask her out?" Alex said, suppressing a tinge of jealousy.

"I wanted to ask you first," he said, almost shyly. "Before I get to know her any better, I wanted to see if there was anything that could happen between you and me. Because if I start falling for her and then realized I could have fallen for you, well, what a mess, huh?"

"Really," Alex said. "What a mess. What about your plans to get a job in New York?"

"Carol's moving here too," he said. "It's like, you know, you go on for years. You never meet anyone you're interested in. Then suddenly, wham."

"I can relate," she said.

"Sometimes it's hard to know God's will."

"Not sometimes. *All* the time," she said.

"Well," he said with a long exhalation, "that's my spiel. I'm done. It's out. Hope you don't hate me for it."

She shook her head and embraced him. "I never could hate you."

They embraced again and said good night, disappearing to their separate rooms.

TWELVE

Manuel Perez sat on the shaded veranda of the Sorentino, an expensive resort in Belize. He nursed a tall glass of tropical iced tea. He was clad in a light linen suit he had bought in Italy. It was of a weight that breathed easily with both the sun and the breezes that rolled in from the western Caribbean.

He was deep in thought. The woman at his table, a guest, had just presented a business proposal. She waited patiently for his reaction.

Perez looked across the off-white sands of the beach to where his beloved wife, Nicoleta, and their daughters, all equipped with snorkeling gear, romped in the water. With them was Maria, their bilingual mother's helper and housekeeper and the children's tutor. Maria had, as always, accompanied them on this one-week vacation.

At the door leading to the veranda stood the man the children knew as *Tío Antonio*, Uncle Tony. Uncle Tony always watched Perez's back when Perez took his family on vacation. After all, a wealthy Central American entrepreneur needed personal security in these troubled times, even a conventional importer and exporter of fresh and dried fruit. So the Chilean bodyguard seemed to be a wise precaution.

The Sorentino was located on Ambergris Caye, the largest island along the Belize Barrier Reef. Perez had chosen it for this meeting for more than one reason. Before Perez and beyond his family was the most spectacular scuba-diving paradise in the world, including the Blue Hole. Once the meeting was over with this businesswoman, Perez and his wife could dive.

Yet as much as the diving and the meeting were important, so was security. Ambergris Caye was an island accessible only to private transportation. Representatives of the Sorentino had picked up the Perez family at the airport in San Pedro and whisked them away by private car and then brought them here by private boat.

Perez turned to the woman at his table, having mulled over her proposal for almost a full two minutes without speaking. "You have to understand," he said in English, with almost no trace of an accent, "the job you are asking me to do is difficult. I would have to enter the United States and make many preparations. While I have some excellent contacts there, the target you suggest would not be easy. The Americans have greatly tightened their borders over the last decade, as well as their ability to pursue people on their wanted lists."

"I would think a man of your ingenuity would have no trouble getting into the United States," the woman said.

"Getting *out* would be the challenge. I have many friends in the underworld in the U.S. Russian, Latino, Mafia, Irish. Political underworld as well as criminal enterprises. Word travels quickly. Presumably a massive 'unofficial' reward would be posted for me if my work were successful. I would be hunted worldwide."

The woman opened her mouth, but Perez raised a polite hand to silence her.

"I also have," he resumed pleasantly, "many ethical issues about striking targets in the U.S. I have some affinity for the Americans and do not dislike them. I have worked for Americans, as you know. I have many friends there, some who do not even know the nature of my second business, some who do. Though it may surprise you, I do have a conscience. I'm not sure that I would want to bring the attention of American authorities upon me. Right now, they may have a vague notion of who I am. I'm not so certain I would want the extra attention." He paused again. "Worse, the job would have to be undertaken in New York City," he said. "That would draw even more attention." He shook his head. "None of this is good."

"Then you're not interested?" she asked patiently.

As they did so often when he was deeply contemplative, Perez's eyes returned to the sea. Then they returned to his family, three little girls who continued to splash in the surf, a beautiful wife whom he doted on, flanked by the pretty young Maria in a two-piece suit, which sometimes made him think thoughts he shouldn't.

Another minute passed. Perez sipped more tea. Idly, he rubbed his right kneecap. There was some swelling today with the heat. Nothing incapacitating; the discomfort never was. He had some prescription painkillers with him. He would chew one later in the day. But certainly not in front of his guest. A weakness, a tiny flaw of any sort, was never to be revealed. Even Nicoleta didn't know how much the knee sometimes vexed him. But then there was much that Nicoleta didn't know.

The woman at the table understood enough to remain silent. Out of habit, Perez looked over his shoulder and saw Antonio standing exactly where he should be, by the door, arms folded, watching everything, and even keeping an eye on a couple of American blondes on the beach. Everyone who knew Tony knew that blondes could distract him for a moment or two. Everyone joked about it. Fortunately, Nicoleta was a brunette and Antonio kept his priorities in order. If only, Manuel Perez thought to himself, everyone were as dependable as Antonio.

Perez's eyes drifted back to his children. Images of his own childhood came into focus. He could remember the squalor of a cement-block home, the blazing summer heat of Mexico, running barefoot in the streets as a young child, and the horrible car accident that had injured him. Rich people speeding through his neighborhood. The driver who had hit him never stopped. Why would anyone stop after hitting a slum kid? Who cared? The knee injury had prevented him from joining the Mexican Army, but it had never had any bearing on his ability to use a rifle. So it never cost him the chance to join a foreign army as an expert marksman. And the ability to use a weapon had acquired for him what a normal body and an education never could have: wealth, enough to start his own company. Wealth, enough to marry a woman of the caliber that he could only dream of as a teenager. And power. Now he had power, the type that comes from an impressive bank account, and ancillary respect that flowed from the shooting end of a rifle.

Now he had what he had always longed for. And he was close to making that final big play that would cement it all and make it secure for him. He looked at the resort as the memories of an impoverished boyhood faded. One needed to have an unspeakable amount of money to afford to live like this. He turned back to her.

"May I add some details?" she asked.

"Of course," he said.

"We already have people in place in New York. Through our various corporations and shipping interests, we own an impressive portfolio of real estate, including one building that would afford you an excellent shot at the target. We would give you secure access to a rooftop, and we already have a construction project on the roof, which would provide the proper cover to shoot from. We can give you keys to everything. All you would need is to secure your own weapon and take your shot. Or shots."

"One is usually enough," he said. "But two or three could be a pleasant luxury."

"As you would have it," she said.

Perez thought further. "Sadly," he said, playing his hand carefully, "I don't think anyone will pay what I would want to make a hit like that in New York City. So for this reason, I might never accept a job such as the one you describe."

"Name a figure," she said. "If I can pay it, we'll speak further. If it's unconscionable, I'll get up and leave and not waste any more of your time."

He named an astronomical figure.

The woman settled back into her chair.

"I think we can do business," she said.

THIRTEEN

Saturday arrived. Alex spent six hours in the office. She and Ben had dinner together that evening, Hastings again. At first there was tension between them, but then it dissipated. The subject of a romantic relationship never came up.

On Sunday, Ben prepared a brunch for Alex at home, and then he stayed in and watched the Yankees, while Alex, dutifully, put in more hours at the office. Ben used the afternoon to pack, since he was heading back to Washington that evening. His interviews had gone well, and he was convinced that he would be hired for an internship starting in June.

Ben was set to depart at 6:30 p.m. on yet another pleasant spring evening. Alex went down to the street with him. He carried a large valise slung over a strong right shoulder and looked for a taxi to take him to the Amtrak Station on 33rd Street.

As he stepped off the curb to hail a taxi, Alex was sorry to see him go. Part of her wanted to reach out to him and ask him not to go. She had an urge to do something to reverse the direction in which she had sent things.

Okay, she suddenly thought. I don't want to let him go. He's too good a man and there aren't enough good men around. I saw him first and I want to keep him. She wondered whether she was rejecting romance simply because she was scared of being in love—and possibly losing love—again. A wonderful man had presented himself to her, hers for the asking, and she had driven him away.

Wake up! a voice inside screamed to her. She was sending him away to another woman who would presumably be smarter, wiser, and do everything in her physical and mental capacity to make him happy and keep him.

He found a cab. It pulled to the curb, and before she could say anything, he tossed his bag into the backseat. Alex stepped up to him. "Ben, listen, I— "

"It's okay," he said, interrupting. "Don't worry. Really, it's okay. We're friends and I value that a lot."

Before she could protest, he embraced her and kissed her. It was a sexy kiss, right on the lips, and it stunned her, although it shouldn't have.

He stepped back and gave her an affectionate wave. Then he slid into the backseat of the cab and closed the door. Her final image was how handsome and strong he was. Then the taxi pulled away from the curb. She watched until it disappeared among the other vehicles moving down Seventh Avenue.

FOURTEEN

American Airlines 777 from San Juan, Costa Rica, eased downward, ten miles east of the Statue of Liberty. Manuel Perez glanced around the cabin. He hated to fly. Killing didn't make him nervous, but the sound of landing gear being extended sometimes did. As it descended toward New York, the plane hit a pocket of bumpy air. The turbulence rattled him. Then the aircraft moved through a layer of clouds, and suddenly a crisp view of New York City appeared: Manhattan, the majestic skyline above the rivers, fronting on the harbor, and the five boroughs connected by bridges. For a moment, in the brilliance of the early June day, everything looked clear and clean, like in a movie.

They flew above Central Park. Perez loved this city. He hoped to come back with his wife soon, take the kids to the big zoo up in the Bronx, maybe even to the new Yankee Stadium. His little girls loved *béisbol*, and his wife was fluent in English, just as he was. Nicoleta had worked in New York when she was in her twenties and still loved the place.

Maybe they'd even buy an apartment here a few years down the road. Still, he hated this current job. Hitting a target in the United States was definitely not something he would have wished to do.

To Perez's right, in the distance, he could see the Statue of Liberty presiding over the harbor. The aircraft shifted into its final descent over Queens.

In another twenty minutes, he had picked up his single bag and proceeded to immigration, where he now stood quietly as the American immigration officer scanned his passport. The officer read the name on his Costa Rican passport. Orestes Piñero. The agent switched into Spanish. *"Buenos dias."*

"Buenos dias."

"Traveling here on business or pleasure?" the officer asked.

Since 9/11, these people asked irksome questions. Perez knew what to expect and had already memorized the details of a pharmaceutical buyers' convention that was in progress at two of the midtown hotels. So he handled the nosey questions well. He had even booked a hotel to cover his stay and his ID.

The immigration officer waited for something on his computer screen. His brow furrowed. Perez remained calm. But was this whole thing going to blow up right at the start? He was entering the U.S. illegally on a freshly forged passport. Were the Americans one step ahead of him? To get pinched here at the airport over something minor would be catastrophic. His cover story would unfold eventually, fingerprints could lead to something in a database somewhere, and—

"¿Hay problema?" he asked. The peon of an immigration officer was looking at the screen too long ... much too long. It went through Perez's head: someone somewhere squealed. He was walking into a trap. He turned and scanned the room. Security people all over. Nowhere to escape.

The immigration officer frowned. He was a nice-looking Latino in his thirties. Probably a Puerto Rican, Perez guessed. Clean cut, olive skinned. He looked a little like a cop. He refused to smile. His brown eyes slid from the computer screen to meet his. He then scrutinized the passport once again. "New?" the immigration officer asked in Spanish, looking back up.

"New what?" Perez asked.

"The passport?"

"Yes. Just issued. My first trip."

"Uh-huh," the customs man said. Then he smiled. "Enjoy your visit," he said. The immigration man closed the passport and returned it.

Within ten minutes, Perez had found a taxi and was on his way into Manhattan, still unwinding, promising himself that never again would he do this. The risks were too high.

FIFTEEN

The next morning, Alex arrived at her eighth-floor office at 8:23 a.m. and walked through the metal detector into Fin Cen's suite. "You might want to go into the chief's office as soon as you can," Stacey said when Alex approached. Stacey handed Alex the morning message slips. Then she mouthed the initials *FBI.*

"What?" Alex asked.

Stacey shrugged and repeated.

Alex gave her a nod. "Okay. You haven't seen me yet," she said.

Alex stopped in her own office long enough to put down her attaché case. FBI was always a mixed blessing. Couldn't work with them, couldn't work without them. Alex did a quick scan of her emails. There was one from Christophe Chatton at Credit Suisse; Federov's check had cleared. The two million dollars was available and bearing interest at a rate of eight hundred fifty dollars a week. It was an excellent example of the wealthy getting wealthier, though Alex would never have called herself that. Wealth, to her, wasn't measured in dollars.

She riffled through the message slips. No biggies. Back to the present: FBI — Frat Boys Investigating. What was *this* about? Typical that they would turn up unannounced and crash into everyone else's schedule. She strode from her own office to De Salvo's corner suite. The chief's secretary, Elsa, sat guard outside as usual. Elsa already had Alex in her gaze by the time Alex's eyes found hers.

"Go on in," Elsa said. "Looks like a war party."

"Great," Alex muttered.

Alex opened the door and stepped in. She could tell right away — it was trouble. De Salvo sat at the center of his wide mahogany desk, but to his right, on various chairs, sat two men she didn't recognize and one woman, Leslie Erin, whom she did. De Salvo stood up and the other two men shot to their feet twice as fast.

"Hello, Alex," Leslie said, standing also. "Sorry about this, but everyone agrees there's urgency here."

"Okay," Alex said. "No one looks too happy. What's going on?"

Alex took the only vacant chair. Leslie did the introductions. Special Agent Jorgé Ramirez, very tall, maybe six-four, Alex processed quickly, very dark in a sharp suit. He greeted her with a solid handshake. He was fit and between thirty and thirty-five, Alex reckoned. He looked as if he could pick up a desk and throw it across the room, complete with whoever was sitting at it. The second Fed was Special Agent Walter MacPhail. He wore a boxy khaki suit. He had thick graying hair, an uneven single brow above dark eyes, and a proprietary air that suggested that he was the lead on this case even though he was six inches shorter than his associate. He made up for the extra six on the waistline, however.

"Alex," De Salvo said, "these gentlemen are homicide investigators who operate within an anti-terror unit of the FBI. They're based in Florida and focus on issues involving the security of U.S. citizens."

"Well, that means you must be busy," Alex said. "I'm honored."

"Your chief speaks glowingly of you," Special Agent MacPhail said. "We're honored as well."

"Alex," De Salvo said from his desk, "we've been chatting. Our associates here know what Fin Cen is about and what we do. Quick learners," he said with a smile. "I was just starting to explain that Párajo is an operation that targeted Panama and the surrounding area, which was an obvious choice, and that you were put in charge earlier this year."

Looking at De Salvo, MacPhail responded, " 'Obvious choice' — why?"

Alex took over. "First, Panama's a major 'transit' country for contraband. Narcotics and money are the two most insidious, with weapons not far behind."

Both Feds, as if on cue, flipped open netbooks and began typing. De Salvo leaned back.

"For example," Alex said, "last year Panama interdicted more than sixty tons of cocaine. That's the highest number in Central America. Keep in mind, given the geographical nature of the Panama's Caribbean coast and its remoteness, most of the cocaine trafficked from Colombia to Central America and Mexico passes along this route. Take the city of Turbo in Colombia. Turbo is a banana export center located on Colombia's Caribbean coast. The banana boats, however, run interference for the cigarette boats that head straight for isolated destinations along Panama's Caribbean coastline where they deliver their cargo. The Atlantic coast, from Colón to Costa Rica, is the most active. Physical geography is a great facilitator. Remoteness makes these routes attractive to smugglers. The stretch of land that connects Panama with Colombia is a dense jungle and a haven for narco *contrabandistas*."

MacPhail, the older agent, exhaled a low whistle, looked up, and shook his head. "The Darien Gap, right?" he asked.

"Correct."

"You know your stuff," Ramirez said to Alex.

"I wouldn't be in this job if I didn't," she answered.

"I had an operation that took me to the Darien Gap six years ago," MacPhail said. "We were chasing down some stolen aircraft and crossed swords with some bad guys from Cali in Colombia. The Darien Gap is a hell hole. We lost two agents."

MacPhail looked back at Alex. "George, that's Jorgé, and I both speak Spanish and have spent time in Central America. We're familiar with what goes on in Panama. The area presents dozens of options for front businesses and money-laundering operations. Those are your targets?"

"Correct," Alex answered. "Here's an overview: Panama gives Colombian drug traffickers a culture they can blend into.

Colombian-owned businesses also make up the majority of Panama's most successful companies, most, if not all, located in Panama City. Many Colombians own vacation land or plantations in Panama and make up part of the billions of dollars Colombians invest in Panama. A lot of the money is legitimate, but a hefty percentage isn't. Look. If U.S.-bound cocaine starts in Colombia, the key transit link is Panama. You know this as well as I do. While we can make regular interdictions, we're hard-pressed to combat the sheer number of options Panama City and the rest of the country offer to criminals. So we go after the big shots."

"The Dosi family," MacPhail said.

"Correct."

"They've been arrested?" Ramirez asked.

"They're in hiding. Possibly in South America somewhere as of this morning, looking for a sanctuary state to escape to. That's between us, of course."

Leslie spoke up from a visitor's chair. "Here's the issue, Alex. The Dosi family's planning a counterattack."

"A counterattack?"

"They've hired someone to kill you," Ramirez said.

Alex tried to wrap her mind around this. Then she sighed. "Threats are nothing unusual in cases like this," she answered. "People talk, they get angry, they threaten. Carrying through is something else," she said. "I have a scar and a pain in the left shoulder that reminds me every day that I've been shot at before. There's always blowback from these Central American hoods when there's a successful operation against them. And macho oversexed thugs that they are, they probably like it even less when a woman is leading the charge against them."

MacPhail produced a manila envelope. From it slid a photograph.

"Take a look," said Ramirez. "This is Manuel Perez. Ever seen the face?"

Alex looked at the picture. "No. Haven't seen him, don't know anything about him, and have never heard or read the name before."

"Consider this," MacPhail said. "Four months ago, the Mexican judicial minister, Nelson Sanchez, who was involved in financial fraud and money laundering, was at his beach-side villa on Mexico's Pacific coast, just south of Zihuatanejo. The whole place was cordoned off by army and local police. There were two navy speed boats in the bay in front of him, protecting him while he was there. He was sitting on the beach with his mistress when two fifty-caliber bullets came at him. One of them hit him in the forehead, the other in the chest. The final report said the shot came from a boat half a mile out at sea. The sniper had fired long range and escaped."

Ramirez picked up the narrative.

"Now put that in the back of your mind, Alex, and consider a more recent case when a similar sniper fired on a motorcade driving Ramon Inezia, the chief of Colombia's national anti-narcotics squad, to the airport. Inezia's car was armor plated and thought to be bulletproof. But the sniper had a new bullet that was ahead of the glass technology used by Mercedes Benz. Three bullets hit the car. One got Inezia in the neck. The other got him in the head. The third hit the vehicle's fuel line and killed the driver when the vehicle exploded. Quite an efficient bit of shooting from about four hundred meters at a fast-moving car. There's television footage available. Sort of Zapruder-style. You can see the Mercedes speeding along, first with an impact point and then the whole back window blows apart, as does the late Sr. Inezia's head a nanosecond later. We can arrange a viewing if you like."

"I'll take your word for it," Alex said.

"Then take our word for the rest of it too," Ramirez said. "We have staff people who get paid to correlate these things. There's one smart girl who works with a computer in the Miami office; whenever there's a hit of any notoriety in the world, she throws all the possible links into it. Then we play back all the links, things of substance, rumors, whatever. In both of the above cases, as well as several older ones, we believe this Manuel Perez was the gunman."

"Only a few people in the world can work a rifle like that," MacPhail said.

"Now, both Sanchez and Inezia had a lot of enemies," Ramirez said, taking up the dialogue. "But both of them had locked horns with the Dosi organization and both were involved in preparing indictments against them and their empire."

Alex listened carefully.

"Perez is someone we track as best we can. We tend to know where he's been and try to have a projection about where he'll be. We have several hundred high-profile shooters in our files. Most are Russian or Middle Eastern these days, but the ones associated with the Colombian and Mexican gangs are in our database too."

"Plus a few of our own, I'm sure," Alex added.

"We know Perez was in Colombia the week of the Inezia hit. And he was in Mexico for Sanchez." He paused. "Do you think Señora and Señor Dosi knew that your operation was on the verge of striking against them?" he asked.

"I'm certain they were aware of Párajo," Alex said. "We speeded things up and made arrests sooner than we'd hoped. Word was getting around, and we were worried that the Dosis were going to travel to Israel to get beyond extradition."

"True enough," MacPhail said. "Our source in Panama told us that last week and added that Señora Dosi had interviewed a professional shooter in Belize. Big man, spoke Spanish. Arrived by private plane with his family, left the same way. Our surveillance film got the visit. Physical stature works for Perez, but we didn't get a face. Anyway, the rumor gets better. Said she paid him a big-time sum of money and that he was on a new assignment. The assignment's in New York. And the target's a woman."

"So," said Ramirez, "put it all together. The bottom line is, you organized a massive operation against the Dosis, and your work is costing them millions of dollars and, if you're successful, their freedom."

She fingered the photo and stared into the black eyes of her would-be killer.

"So is he in New York?" Alex asked.

"We doubt it," MacPhail said. "Our spotters think he went to Mexico City first. But then there's the issue of our borders with Mexico. Fact is, he could be anywhere."

"Do you have a security system at home?" Ramirez asked.

"No. I can take a hint. I'll get one."

De Salvo leaned forward. "We'll have it in place by tomorrow, Alex," he said. "We'll take it out of our Rodent Fund. Also, we'll need to put some interior bullet proof glass in as quickly as possible, unless you're willing to move very quickly, which is actually what we'd prefer. Temporarily, of course."

Alex sighed.

"You have a gun?" MacPhail asked.

She reached to her hip and showed off the baby Glock. "Of course, I do," she said. "Several if you want to know."

"The FBI doesn't have enough free personnel to protect you," MacPhail said, "but we've spoken with the U.S. Marshal Service. They can put a few agents on this to act as support for us, at least until we get Perez — or at least neutralize him. Would that work? The marshals have already been assigned and should be in your building by midnight. And until we get Perez, you don't ride the subway, you don't walk anywhere, and you don't run in Central Park. While you're at it, you don't leave your window shades up either."

"He's a long-range sniper, Alex," Ramirez said. "Or at least that's how he usually works. This isn't something to take too lightly."

"Why aren't the marshals in place already?" De Salvo asked. "What's the delay?"

"Just logistics," said Ramirez. "Getting agents off one assignment and onto another. It has to happen in the real world, not cyber space. Listen, *we* just came in on this a few hours ago."

Alex leaned back in her chair, unhappy.

"How do you know so much about this Perez?" she asked.

They looked at each other. There was a long pause.

"We trained him," MacPhail said.

"He's U.S. Army, retired," Ramirez added. "We know everything about him — except where he lives."

"The thing is," said MacPhail, "we have a wonderful opportunity here to bring several cases together at once — as long as he doesn't shoot you first."

"Thanks," she said. "I'm happy about that." She looked back and forth at them.

"If the marshals start tomorrow," she said, "what am I supposed to do tonight?"

Ramirez smiled. "That's why we're here," he said. "Consider us your escort service for the rest of the day."

"I'm honored," she said.

SIXTEEN

MacPhail and Ramirez led Alex from the elevator to the parking garage beneath her office building. It was past six in the evening, but the garage was still busy. Her bodyguards walked her to a Lincoln Navigator. Black. Tinted windows. Bulletproof. Alex slid into the backseat. MacPhail took the wheel; Ramirez slid in beside Alex.

"Tough day, huh?" MacPhail said.

"I've had worse," she said.

"We all have, I guess," he said. "You okay, Jorgé?" he asked.

Ramirez gave a thumbs-up gesture.

"Hey, look, Alex," Ramirez said. "I can call you 'Alex,' right?"

"Sure," she said.

"We got this," he said. "Gets us through more than a few days." He motioned to a small compact cabinet between the seats. He opened it to reveal a compact mini bar as the SUV started to move. "We can't join you; we're on duty. But you can unwind."

"Have one on the taxpayers," MacPhail said. "They'll never know."

Ramirez was helpful, pulling some ice out of a small chest. There was an array of half-size liquor bottles—Irish, Scotch, Canadian, Vodka, and gin—and soft drinks, water, and mixer.

"Mineral water would be fine," she said.

Ramirez poured her a glass.

"Taxpayers' money?" she asked, motioning to the bar.

"Sure. But they don't know," Ramirez said.

Then the vehicle left the ramp and crept into the Wall Street traffic. Alex drew a breath and eased back. She looked out the window and longed to be one of the normal people, with a normal job, not someone with a target on her head.

The SUV accessed West Side Highway and began the crawl uptown through the rush-hour traffic. If she could choose, she thought to herself, she would have donned a pair of walking shoes and hiked. The exercise would have done her good. But not today, she told herself. What about tomorrow? How long was she going to be under informal house arrest?

She opened her laptop to distract herself. More documents from work. Various agencies from South and Central America were sending her information that she already knew. She clicked the first one open and scanned.

> The Government of Panama should continue implementing the reforms it has undertaken to its anti-money-laundering regime in order to reduce the vulnerability of Panama's financial sector and to enhance Panama's ability to investigate and prosecute financial crimes, including money laundering and potential terrorist financing.

She moaned. She went on to the next. More bureaucratic claptrap:

> Colombian narco-traffickers are perhaps the most adapted and prepared for work in Panama. They thrive on the ability to constantly change routes, members of their network, and technology, such as cell phones and other communication devices.

"Really, Einstein?" she grumbled silently. "I never would have known."

At a red light, she glanced out the window. They were on Eighth Avenue at 45th Street, west of the Broadway theater district. Down 45th she could see the glowing marquees of the theaters. She realized that what she really wanted to do more than anything was to tell her driver to pull over so she could jump out and run over to the TKTS booth on Broadway and score a ticket to anything.

Another thought. Two million clams in the bank. Did she *really* need a job where she could get zipped any minute? She tried to go back to work, bury herself. More bull from some South American police agency:

> While Panama offers a wide range of options for smugglers, geography is only a fringe benefit. Colombian boats that pass through Panama must stop along the route to refuel or transport the shipment from one boat to another. This practice invariably requires that individuals in other Central American countries become involved in the race to move drugs from Colombia north and money and guns south.

Man's greed and nefarious nature could always trump the good that other men and women were trying to do. Two centuries earlier, over the same routes, it was slaves, rum, and molasses. Now it's coke, guns, and contraband currency. Maybe she was just being a fool to think she could make a difference. *A fool, a fool, a fool.*

> Nicaragua is the next stop for drug shipments moving north along the coast and has a plethora of guns left over from a lengthy civil war. Guns make for perfect currency. And like Panama, much of Nicaragua's Caribbean coast is a semi-autonomous area with little to no government presence. Small towns like Bluefields, Nicaragua, have become perfect stop-off points for Colombian traffickers, who bring with them not only the bounty of what local fishermen have begun to call the "white lobster," but also the devastation of addiction that comes with it.

Great. And indicting the Señora and Señor Dosi was going to stop that? Whatever had possessed her to go into law enforcement? She smelled career change. It's not like she needed to work for a few years, maybe a decade. Federov had seen to that. But what would God have her do? Mission work? Where? The answers didn't come easy.

Traffic ground to a halt near Columbus Circle. On impulse, she grabbed her cell phone. For reasons she couldn't explain, she felt like talking to Paul Guarneri. Not Ben, but Paul. Maybe because he had grown up around violence and greed. Maybe because she sensed, in a funny sort of way, that he grasped the world better than she did.

Older? Wiser? More cynical? All of the above? None of the above? Who knew?

As the car broke free from congestion, Alex dialed Paul's cell phone. Two rings, three. Then it kicked to voicemail.

"We're here, Alex," Ramirez said.

She looked up and saw the canopy of her building. She cut off her phone call and left no message. She dropped the phone back into her purse.

SEVENTEEN

Unlike Alex, Paul Guarneri had had an excellent day.

He had used his contacts at the New York Police Department to find a woman to accompany him to Cuba. She was a city detective on leave, named Ramona Gálvez, Puerto Rican by ancestry, fluent in Spanish, adept with weapons. She could easily pose as his wife. He had interviewed her that day and was inclined to make an offer. Ramona was tough. Five-eight, a hundred and fifty pounds, much of it brawn. She looked like she could throw people through walls and that could be an asset for this kind of trip. So Guarneri was pleased.

Alex remained his first choice, but it was evident that that wasn't going to happen. So all that remained was for Guarneri to phone Alex, withdraw his offer, and explore things further with Ramona. Sometimes, he told himself, second choices work out well. Sometimes even better. Anyway, he mused, you have to play the cards life deals you. His father, the casino guy and occasional philosopher, used to tell him that.

At his home on Long Island, sitting in his den, he wanted to give it a few more minutes of thought. He glanced at his watch. Normally, Alex worked late. Should he call her at her office or at home?

Home might be better, he figured. Or, for that matter, her cell. His housekeeper would be serving dinner soon. Better make the call sooner rather than later.

He reached for his cell phone and realized it was turned off. When he clicked it back on and allowed it to boot up, he looked at the calls he had missed and recognized Alex's number. Strange, he pondered. What did *she* want?

EIGHTEEN

Eleven stories above 62nd Street, Alex unlocked her apartment door and then stepped aside. Special Agent Ramirez drew his weapon and entered. She waited in the corridor.

Ramirez threw on the light, stopped, and listened. He went to the bedroom and looked. No one. He checked the closets. He returned to the living room, moved swiftly through the dining and kitchen area, then moved to the extra bedroom that Alex used as a study and guest room.

He checked every closet and any other place someone might be hiding. He looked for any signs of tampering or disruption. He saw none. It was a quick eyeball search, but he was good at it. He placed his gun back in its holster and went back to the front door.

"All clear," he said. "Welcome home."

Alex and Special Agent MacPhail stepped in. MacPhail looked toward the window. "Nice view of Manhattan," he said, "but I need to drop the blinds. Can never be too sure."

Alex had too much reading to keep her mind off work, but at least the ride home had relaxed her. "Right," she muttered. Then, "Hey," Alex said, "those blinds are tricky. I'll get them."

"No, no," MacPhail said. "You stay back. I'll get them."

She put down her purse and her laptop. She cut off MacPhail and walked to the window.

NINETEEN

Three hundred meters away, across several Manhattan rooftops, Manuel Perez stiffened and frowned. He could not believe his eyes. The light that had just gone on in Alex's apartment was the first signal that his moment was at hand. But then someone, a man who looked like a bodyguard, had come in first and gone from room to room, as if looking for something. Pieces of a puzzle flew apart and scrambled in his head. If police were searching her apartment, and if she was right there — as he could see she was several seconds later — then somehow the secrecy of his assignment had been compromised. Somehow the Americans had found out about the hit and were taking steps to prevent it. That being the case, and he quickly surmised that it was, he either took his shot now or he might never get another chance.

There seemed to be some discussion at the doorway. One of the agents was pointing at the window. His target, the woman, was already approaching. Quickly he realized that if a security ring was being dropped around her, this would be his only shot.

He cursed. He had never had a development quite like this before. But he stayed calm. He was good at quick shots and could launch a barrage if he had to.

His eye went back to the friendly *O* of the scope, and he moved the crosshairs and the little laser dot toward its target.

Head shot? Body shot? Body, he decided. Upper torso.

Then, at the last second, he decided he had more confidence than that. He would go for the head. Get any piece of it and he would have a kill.

Ancillary question: What about the bodyguards? He pondered for a second. Get them too?

Yes, he would. Seal the room with three dead people in it. It would give him more time to get away from his perch. He smiled. He had never missed. As he squinted, aligning the rifle perfectly, he could even see the color of her lipstick, the hoop earrings she wore. Pretty, he thought. What a shame. Well, nothing personal. She had her job and he had his.

He ran the crosshairs around the room, came back and found Alex. The nose of the rifle came up a millimeter. Head shot. She made things easy for him, walking toward the window. He eased his breathing down and prepared for his first shot.

TWENTY

In his study on Long Island, Paul Guarneri pressed the last two digits of Alex's cell number with his thumb and hit Send. There was a moment's delay as the signals shot around cyberspace, then beamed back down to earth on the west side of Manhattan.

On the other end of the line, the phone rang. Once, twice, three times . . .

TWENTY-ONE

Alex remained jumpy. When her cell phone rang, she jerked her head to the left. Almost simultaneously, she heard a deafening explosion as half of the plate glass window that overlooked Seventh Avenue shattered. Shards, like little knives, flew everywhere, followed by the whack of several follow-up slugs hitting the floor behind her and then ricocheting up against the wall.

It took less than a second for the situation to sink in, but when she looked back toward the open space where her window had been, there was no question. And the noise was drowned out by the voices of the men behind her.

"Down!" MacPhail screamed.

Alex was already on the floor, hard and flat. Ramirez hurtled across the room to push her flush against the wall beneath the window. Then he snaked to the side and reached upward, caught the blinds cord with a sharp yank, and dropped them.

MacPhail called out. "Anyone hit?"

Alex answered. "I'm all right!"

Ramirez followed. "I'm good."

By then the unseen attacker poured shot after shot into the room, hoping to claim a victim in the chaos and in the dark. Five, six, and then seven more shots came in until the remaining bits of plate glass had been blown out and collapsed in a flood of shards and splinters. Alex heard most of it hit the floor but knew that much of it fell outside the building, raining down eleven flights onto the sidewalk below, onto anyone who had the misfortune to be passing by.

TWENTY-TWO

The next afternoon, Andrew De Salvo sat at the head of the conference table, waiting, a glass of water in front of him on the twenty-seventh floor room at 26 Federal Plaza in Manhattan, FBI Headquarters. The blinds were always drawn.

De Salvo stood when Alex came in, escorted by George Ramirez and Walter MacPhail. She had stayed in a midtown hotel overnight. De Salvo reached to her and gave her an embrace. "Good to see you up and around," he said.

"Good to be up and around," she answered. "Good thing that guy can't shoot straight. Must have missed by a combined three inches with two of those shots."

"Good thing the phone rang," Ramirez said, "or we'd be using the word *homicide* this morning."

De Salvo returned to the head of the table. Alex sat to her boss's left, two empty chairs between them. MacPhail and Ramirez sat across from her. It was after lunch and Alex had spent the morning with the New York City police, detailing what had happened.

"Okay, the first problem," MacPhail said, "is simply to keep Alex out of the crosshairs. That means keeping her out of her Fin Cen office for a while—and maybe out of the city completely. How's that for starters?"

"Brutal but understandable," De Salvo said.

"For how long?" Alex asked. "Away from everything?"

"Until we know the threats against you have been negated," Ramirez said.

"Are we talking years?" Alex asked, her indignation rising. "Someone takes a shot at me and misses, and it puts me out of business? Then the other side has succeeded? I don't like it."

"They haven't succeeded," De Salvo said with sudden defensiveness. "The arrests are continuing, the investigations as well, the indictments ..." He paused. "Someone else will pick up your files and not miss a beat."

"What about the Dosis?" Alex asked. "Anything new this morning?"

"Still fugitives," De Salvo said. "We're checking all flights to Israel as well as nontraditional venues in South America."

"Do we know what passports they'd be traveling on?" Alex asked.

Silence around the room, which meant no.

"Alex," De Salvo said. "You're going to have to let go for a time. Your safety is the paramount issue now."

"They nearly kill me and I'm supposed to let it go?" she snapped.

"No," De Salvo said, "but you're better off letting other people handle it."

She turned to MacPhail, who spoke before she could. "We approach these things thirty days at a time," he said. "We get you out of this office, hopefully this city, for a month. After that, we'll see where we are."

"You make it sound simple."

"We've never lost anyone in our custody yet," Ramirez said.

Alex couldn't resist. "You nearly did last night."

MacPhail sighed. "Look, not to separate the flea feces from the pepper, but you weren't technically in administrative custody yet. You were in — "

"My own home and my head nearly got blown off," she said, "because you guys were a few days behind the guy assigned to whack me! That doesn't inspire a lot of confidence, gentlemen. I don't feel myself bonding here."

"Look, I can put Alex on protective administrative leave," De Salvo said. "This happened one other time in my memory. That's what we did and it worked."

"But where do I *go*?" asked Alex. "I'm not sure I have faith in the system you're presenting to me."

"Where would you like to go?" Ramirez asked. "Within reason."

She considered it. "What are we talking about? Short-term witness protection?" she asked. "Something 'flyover'? Arizona? New Mexico? Grand Rapids, Michigan?"

"Something like that. There's a lot of latitude."

"I'm not buying into this, gentlemen," Alex said. "Part of me says I could go underground by myself and survive just as well." She thought of the two million dollars in the bank. "Maybe even better."

"Than what?" MacPhail asked. "We can't help without your cooperation."

Silence rolled around the room like a fog. Finally, "Well, maybe you should make that trip to Cuba, after all," De Salvo said as a joke.

"Maybe I should," Alex answered, not as a joke.

MacPhail and Ramirez glanced at each other. "What trip?" MacPhail asked.

"One that's not going to happen," Alex said.

Another uneasy silence rolled around the room. Then, "If you have something good, we need to hear about it, okay?" MacPhail said. "Cuba? Can you talk about this?"

Alex glanced to De Salvo, who threw her a shrug. She looked back to MacPhail and Ramirez. "Can I talk about it?" she asked her boss.

De Salvo opened his hands and nodded.

"This goes back to a previous operation," Alex began. "A friend of a friend has unfinished business in Cuba. Goes back many years. He's looking for someone to go to Cuba with him. A woman."

De Salvo looked to Alex. "Give them the back story," he said.

She did, in a five-minute mini-clinic, running from the catastrophe in Ukraine to the most recent dinner in Brooklyn.

"How long would the trip to Fidel's socialist paradise take?" De Salvo asked.

"Maybe a couple of weeks," Alex said. "A month at most. That's what Paul was talking about."

"Paul?" MacPhail asked.

"Her quasi-organized crime guy who's running this," said De Salvo.

"He's not OC himself but he knows people," Alex answered. "We don't have anything on him except where he was born and who his old man was."

"Sometimes that's enough," MacPhail said. "But no matter. Maybe we can use this." He paused, then asked, "You're on a first-name basis with this guy? Good work."

"Don't make more of it than it is, all right?" she answered sharply.

"A trip to Cuba would get her off the New York streets for a time while we wrap up Manuel Perez," Ramirez offered.

"*Far* off the streets. No one would ever look in Cuba, I got to say. On that score, it's brilliant. And the beaches are great, I hear," MacPhail said. "I know Canadians. And Germans. They go snorkeling and scuba diving every February. It's cheap."

"He means drinking and fornicating, most likely," Ramirez said.

"Gentlemen, let's bring it back to our immediate problems, okay?" De Salvo said. "Is this a possibility?"

"Yes, it's a possibility for us if it works for you," MacPhail said. "And there's one other iron that we might be able to get in the fire. Want to hear it?"

"Go ahead," Alex said.

"Okay, look, I hear things," MacPhail said. "Caribbean desk. They often use freelance people in Cuba. What are you going in for? What purpose specifically?"

"My friend seems to think that a sizeable amount of money is stashed somewhere. He wants to go grab it. At least that's what he's telling me, though whether he's telling me *everything* is another question," Alex said. "Some of what he says doesn't wash. But I feel he's got credibility on the money angle."

"Okay," MacPhail resumed. "What are *you* supposed to do on this trip?"

"Pose as his wife where necessary and watch his back."

"So he could help you on an operation in return for you helping him, correct?" MacPhail asked. "And all of this would be off the books? No one would even know ... that's what you're saying?"

"In essence, yes," Alex said.

"We could put her on leave," De Salvo said. "There'd be no official record of where she is."

MacPhail settled back. "Let me run a name past you," he said. "Roland Violette." The name drew blanks from Alex and her boss. "Nothing?" MacPhail asked.

They shook their heads.

"Roland Violette was a CIA employee in the 1950s and 1960s," MacPhail said. "Turned out he was a Russian agent. He ratted out several CIA operatives in Central America to the Soviets in the '70s, then defected to Cuba in the '80s. He's been there since."

"So?" Alex asked.

"He's been making noises about coming back to the U.S.," MacPhail said. "Says he's got a packet of Cuban intelligence goodies to bring with him. We could use someone to go in, check out the situation, and get him on a covert flight out if he's worth it. Interested?"

Alex glanced to her boss, then back to MacPhail. "Might be," she said.

"We're dealing with him through the Swiss Embassy in Havana," MacPhail said. "If you can get yourself onto the island, we can get you off ... maybe seven to ten days later. Would that allow you enough time to keep your *capo* happy also?"

"Don't know. I can ask."

"Why don't you *tell* him, not *ask* him?"

"That might work too," she said.

"Why don't you do that?" MacPhail asked. "We can work within a time frame that will cover the next thirty days. See when your friend wants to go into Cuba, when he wants to get airlifted out." MacPhail glanced at De Salvo. "What do you think? How crazy is this?"

"It might work," De Salvo said. He turned to Alex. "I can have someone step up and run your operations for you, we can clean up the Perez mess, your Mafia guy gets his payback from the Federov operation, and you get out of town."

Alex turned back to her boss.

"If I'm going to do this," she said, "I'm going to need some quick background. I'm not going to a place like Cuba cold. I need to know what I'm doing."

"I can arrange it," De Salvo said.

TWENTY-THREE

Late that afternoon, Alex's guards took her to a townhouse maintained by the FBI on East 38th Street between Lexington and Third. The building had six apartments. Two NYPD guards sat in the lobby, which was concealed from street view behind two locked doors.

Alex was given a three-room apartment on the third-floor rear. It was pleasantly appointed, clean, and safe. The Feds also sent a housekeeping team over to her home on West 61st Street. The housekeepers retrieved clothing and everything else she requested and moved her in by that evening at 9:00 p.m. She settled in, knowing that she would be moving again within a few days, if the Cuban mission received a green light.

De Salvo came by that evening. He had files on flash drives for her and a fresh laptop. They had a working dinner over Thai takeout.

"So," Alex asked at length, "what can you tell me?"

"Almost everything you need to know is on the drives," he said. "Hope you don't mind some heavy reading."

"I don't," she said, "but I want to know what *you* know. You've been on Central America and the Caribbean your whole career. What stands out?"

"Well, here's a tidbit you won't hear from anyone else," De Salvo said. "As Americans fled Castro's takeover in 1959, people with connections to the U.S. Embassy dropped off a lot of stuff for safekeeping. Valuables like jewels, furs, stock certificates, antiques, even boxes of money. It's still there to this day. The 'U.S. Interests Section,' located in the old U.S. Embassy, is technically part of the Swiss Embassy. But it's fully staffed by American personnel and is an embassy in all but name. That this is a part of the Swiss Embassy is just a mutually convenient legalism, both for us and the Cubans. Everything is in a room that's been kept locked ever since 1960. It's so sensitive that the stuff has never been inventoried. No one knows what kind of identification accompanies the items. I doubt if there's anyone alive who was physically on the premises to take the items in. Couple that with the fact that most of the people who dropped that stuff off are dead. The ultimate fate of such property? Who knows? Stuff like that is going to make your buried money look like an easy case."

"All we have to do is dig and skedaddle," she said, making a joke of it.

But De Salvo remained serious. "Look, Alex," he said, "I'll ramble a bit and tell you this: the United States is going to have to bite a few bullets and prepare for a reasonable transition in Cuba. We don't have a lot of good intelligence coming from the island to guide us. That's why someone like Violette could be important; that's why I'm guessing the people at Langley want you to ride shotgun with Guarneri. Fresh eyes on the island. You remember how Russia and Eastern Europe crashed into 'gangsterism' after the fall of Communism in the 1980s? Well, imagine the Mafia returning to Cuba and doing business with the *narcogobiernos* of Mexico and Colombia. The U.S. would quickly find itself with the Latin American drug wars ninety miles off the coast of Florida. That would be a whole lot less convenient than a bearded old Bolshevik in an army uniform trying to hang onto the last gasp of his Commie dream."

"The American mob pretty much ran the island before Castro, right?"

"Absolutely," De Salvo said. "That's why Fidel had popular support. The brutal dictatorship under Batista was completely on the payroll of the American Mafia. Meyer Lansky was the key guy. The mob wanted to establish the Cuban government as a fully owned subsidiary of their interests. They had plans to make Havana the Monte Carlo of North America. Anything you wanted that was illegal in the U.S., you could get legally in Havana. Drugs. Women. Sex shows. Gambling."

"And the mob lost all its interests when Castro took over in 1959?"

"Absolutely," De Salvo said. "The big shots got out of Cuba fast. A lot of their middle- to lower-level people ended up in jail or in front of firing squads."

"Which explains why the U.S. government enlisted the mob to help kill Castro, right?"

"Absolutely right again. I was a young kid working at the Justice Department when a lot of this stuff came to light in the '70s," De Salvo said. "Fresh out of law school and two years working as an assistant U.S. Attorney in Chicago. The attempts on Castro's life from the United States go way back to Eisenhower. Ike set up 'Operation Mongoose.' The CIA had several hundred people working on this project, including anti-Castro people who were left-behinds in Cuba. The CIA trained a paramilitary guerilla force inside Cuba to remove Castro. But Fidel was enormously popular on the island, at least back then. So the idea was scrapped by Ike, and the job was left to Kennedy. That was the first time the Mafia was hired, during the Kennedy years. The mob wanted its businesses back and JFK had friends in the mob. So it all made sense. If Castro were killed by the Mafia, the CIA could wash their hands of the job. So you had this back-alley spectacle of the FBI working with the Mafia, offering a certain amount of immunity for a bunch of hoods in the U.S. in exchange for the death of Castro."

"Much like the way my acquaintance Yuri Federov got his tax breaks," said Alex.

"And much like the way Lucky Luciano got parole after World War II — for helping the United States Navy with the invasion of Sicily," De Salvo said. "When the CIA was planning the Bay of Pigs invasion, the agency asked their contacts in Cuba to assess the chances that an invasion would set off a popular uprising. The CIA also asked the mob to identify the roads that Castro might use to deploy troops and tanks in meeting attacking forces. The wiseguys asked their old contacts who were still in Cuba to set up a network of spies. Idiotic idea. The CIA at its worst. They were dealing with a bunch of crooks. The contacts told the CIA exactly what it wanted to hear. They claimed that they'd found that an insurrection was in the works, but of course, it never came off. Still hasn't. And you didn't need spies to tell you about the roads near where the Bay of Pigs invasion was planned. There was only one road to the beach, and any local sugar cane farmer could have told you where that was. We were flying spy planes at low altitude over the island all the time, and the single road was visible from the air. It was the road the Cuban army used to beat back the invasion."

Alex shook her head.

"If I remember correctly," De Salvo said, "the whole concept of 'Operation Mongoose' went completely haywire. JFK put his brother Robert, the Attorney General, in charge of getting rid of Castro. They hatched out a new program called 'Operation Freedom.' That's when it went from dumb to dumber to dumbest. During a United Nations meeting that Castro attended, some CIA dupe slipped a poison cigar into Fidel's cigar case. The CIA thought it would be a certain way to knock him off, but someone inspected the cigar case and figured it out before Fidel lit up. The same CIA agents had originally planned to give Castro a cigar with a mini-bomb in it. That never went to fruition either."

De Salvo was shaking his head and laughing now. So was Alex, laughing from the absurdity of it all.

"Another plan was to slip Castro a cigar spiked with LSD," De Salvo said. "The plan was that after he smoked it, he would be an obvious head case and everybody would think he was nuts. Castro was also fond of scuba diving. So the CIA sprayed a scuba suit with tuberculosis bacteria. They gave the suit to an American lawyer who was going to Cuba to negotiate for the release of prisoners from the Bay of Pigs. At the last minute, they chickened out, saying that even if it did work it would be too obvious and would cause a national embarrassment to the U.S. Another half-wit idea was to set a trap at one of his favorite diving spots. The trap would be an exploding conch shell. This one wasn't carried out because planners thought it would be far too difficult to prepare."

De Salvo's fingers fiddled with some paperclips on his desk.

"When one of Castro's bodyguards turned against him and offered to kill him, the CIA gave the guy a fountain pen full of poison. It worked like a syringe, shooting poison out of its tip. That didn't work either."

"Why didn't they just go the normal route?" Alex asked. "Guns. Assassins."

"Oh, they tried that plenty of times," De Salvo said. "The CIA sent Cuban exiles into Cuba with telescopic rifles, but Fidel was too smart. He knew what had happened with Trujillo in the Dominican Republic ..." De Salvo paused. "And what had happened to Kennedy. I mean, read all that JFK assassination stuff, and the words *Mafia* and *Cuba* surface almost every other sentence."

"So I recall," she said.

"Last time I checked," De Salvo concluded, "there'd been more than seven hundred plots to kill Castro, mostly involving the mob, hatched out of the United States. Imagine the odds. Seven hundred different plans against the man — and *not one* worked! In spite of everything, Castro lived into his eighties and ruled for more than forty years. Amazing." De Salvo frowned. "Did you talk about any of this with your Guarneri pal?"

"Not in any detail," she said.

"Detail," he said repeating. "You know what they say: The Devil is in the details. You can imagine how many devils there are in the Cuban details."

Late that evening, around 10:00 p.m., Alex phoned Guarneri.

"Hello, Paul," Alex said. "We need to talk."

"Always a pleasure. Talk now."

"About that trip. Cuba. Is the role of your wife still open?"

There was a pause. "I think I have someone," he said. "Why?"

"Looks like I might be able to do it. If we do it soon."

"Soon would work for me," he said. "That's what you wanted to talk about?"

"Yes, but I was thinking we should talk in person," she said.

"That works too. When?"

"Tomorrow?"

"Excellent. What about tomorrow evening?"

She drew a breath. "Paul," she said, "a sniper took a shot at me yesterday. Rooftop to window. They *just* missed."

It was his turn to pause. Then, following a charming expletive, he said, "Yeah, I saw that on television. That was *you*?"

"I'm keeping a low profile until they catch the shooter. I need to stay out of view. My boss suggested I make the Cuba trip. They can tie it to one of their assignments. I'd need to be in and out of Cuba in a week to ten days. Still want me?"

"Yes," he said, "of course. I was about to hire another woman, but—"

"Don't do anything yet," she said. "It's hypothetical until I get an official okay."

"Where are you now? I can send a car."

"I've got bodyguards," she said. "FBI. They know how to drive."

"Feds, huh?" He laughed. "Want to come over to Brooklyn tomorrow night? My family's here, part of it anyway. My sister. Two of my kids, who've lived with me since my divorce. We can talk over dinner. We have a few guest rooms. You could stay a night or two. I'll even put up your Feds."

"I'll be there for dinner. How's that?"

"Perfect," Paul Guarneri said.

At 11:15 that night, another shoe dropped. Special Agent Walter MacPhail phoned with a small report on his evening's activities. He had had his minions run Paul Guarneri's name through their computers. Guarneri may not have been perfectly clean, as

Alex had suggested, but he wasn't dirty either. He was a usable asset. He even had a family history of anti-Castro activity, which gave him a perverse pedigree with the CIA. Better still, as recently as eight days earlier, the one-time defector, Roland Violette, now in his late seventies, continued to make noises to his Swiss-American contacts about wanting to "go home," about finishing his life in America, and being buried in American soil. It was, Violette maintained, his final wish.

If Guarneri could get himself and Alex into Cuba, CIA contacts and sources from off the island could get them out. So unofficially, the proposed trip had a green light. But like anything else involving American operations overseas, it had to be a quick hit: in and out fast or it would inevitably end in disaster.

Also, Alex learned, New York City Police and the FBI were scouring the city for Manuel Perez. So far, they'd come up cold. The man knew how to disappear when he had to.

TWENTY-FOUR

Paul Guarneri's home was a Federal-style red-brick townhouse on Cranberry Street in Brooklyn Heights, a mini-estate behind an unobtrusive façade. MacPhail and Ramirez delivered her there by 7:30.

Guarneri, wearing a blue button-down shirt and khakis, emerged to welcome his guests personally. He and Alex's guards sized each other up, and Guarneri offered a handshake, which the Feds accepted.

"Normally when you guys are out in front of my place it's for a wedding. You show up to write down license-plate numbers and take pictures. I have to send my brother Sonny out to smash cameras."

The Feds looked at Guarneri, then at each other. Then they all laughed.

"Why don't you guys come on in for some dinner?" Guarneri asked. "You're supposed to keep watch on Alex. You can sit at the table and watch her that way."

It violated no rules, so they accepted.

The building was from the 1920s but had been renovated recently. The entrance area was a great rotunda with twelve-over-twelve windows. On the right, it led to a pine galley with original paintings. Beyond that, Alex could see a den. On the left, the rotunda led to a living room and a formal dining room.

Dinner was at a long table. There were introductions all around. The oldest of Guarneri's children, Lisa, was away at boarding school in Massachusetts. "The same place one of our nitwit presidents went," as Guarneri explained it. The other two children were at home, however; daughter Lauren, twelve, sat next to her brother, Joey, who was eight.

Guarneri's housekeeper, a Guatemalan woman named Florence, cooked and served the dinner. Guarneri conversed with her in Spanish, as did Alex and Lauren. Rounding out the attendees was Guarneri's sister, Diana, who lived in Glen Cove, farther out on Long Island. She often served as a parent-in-absentia for the children, Paul explained, while he was away on trips. Diana was mid-forties, childless, and divorced.

"Diana will be here when I'm in Cuba," Guarneri said, "however long my absence may be." Guarneri had no trouble speaking with the FBI agents present. After dinner he offered them cigars from his collection. They went outside to smoke a couple of San Cristobols while Guarneri led Alex into a den so they could talk privately.

"So," he said, sitting in a leather arm chair, "someone took a shot, huh?"

"Right when you phoned," she said. She settled into a plush chair across from him and distantly wondered what it would be like to live in such a lavish home. The home where she had grown up in California would fit into a quarter of this space. Yet it had been honest, warm, and happy. Her thoughts bounced back to the present. "I turned to pick up the cell phone and the bullet missed. It was your call."

"That's why the bullet missed you?"

"That's the way I see it. Thanks for the call. Sorry I couldn't take it," she said.

"Great timing, huh?" he said.

"Providential," she said. "I'd like to think there's something I have left to do here on earth and so God kept me in the game."

"You religious?" he asked.

"More than most people," she answered. "Less than some others."

"I'm a lapsed Catholic myself," he replied. "I have more questions than answers. Isn't that often the case with thinking people?"

"Often it is," Alex said.

"Anyone know who fired the shot?" he asked.

"There are some credible leads," she said, "but nothing I can discuss."

"I understand," he said.

The room was dominated by a large-screen television on one side, some New York Yankees memorabilia on the other. Two large leather chairs and a matching sofa over plush wall-to-wall carpeting. A man's lair. In one corner was a bag of golf clubs thrown up against some fencing equipment, including an assortment of epées and sabers.

"Can Florence get you coffee?" he asked. "An after-dinner drink maybe?"

"I'm fine, thank you."

Then Paul was on his feet. "I'd like you to see something," he said. He went to a drawer and found a passport. He opened it, then walked to Alex and handed it to her.

"My ID while I'm traveling to Cuba," he said. "I hope this isn't a deal breaker."

The document was Canadian, or appeared to be. She opened it. It bore the name of Richard Valenteri of Toronto, an identity as fictitious as the passport itself.

She glanced up at him, partly in dismay, partly in admiration as she turned the pages. "This is rather good," she said. "It has a nice well-used feel, neither too full nor too empty. Ever used it before?"

"No."

"Of course," she said. "I suppose officially I don't know about this," she said. She closed it and examined the binding. "I can't find a flaw in it," she said. "Very professional. I won't even ask where you bought it. Expensive?"

"These things are," he said, taking it back. "It won't stand scrutiny at a port of entry to the U.S.," he said, "but it'll protect me in Cuba." He put it away in the same drawer and remained on his feet. "I'll be back in a second," he said. "I want to see if the kids are doing their homework." Then he was out the door.

She surveyed the room. The bookshelves on the wall were bulging, mostly with histories and biographies. A few empty spaces were marked by bookends and small statuettes, frequently those of New York Yankees players: Mantle, Reggie, Guidry, Mattingly, Jeter, Posada, A-Rod. One set of bookends was marked with the coat of arms of Cornell University, while another set was a reproduction of the New York City Library Lions, and there was an impressive statuette of Rodin's *The Kiss*.

After a minute Guarneri reappeared, looking cross, carrying a bottle of water. "My girls are my students and my son is my terrorist," he said. "Lauren's studying. Her sister's at prep school, so now she wants to go away to school too. Joey's into *World of Warcraft*. Can't get him to open a book."

"Sounds like a typical American family," she offered.

His expression changed. He smiled. "Maybe," he said. He closed the door. "Can't say I blame Joey for wanting to have his fun," he said under his breath. "Kids should be able to enjoy childhood. I never had many games when I was a kid. We lived a Spartan existence: a two-bedroom in Hempstead. My mother got money from my dad but was always afraid it would end, which it did one day in 1973."

"The day he was murdered."

"Correct," he said.

"Joey's named after your father then?" Alex said.

"No, Joe DiMaggio," he said. Then he grinned. "Yeah. He's named after my dad," he said. He sipped the bottled water. "Sure I can't get you a drink?"

She declined again and he sat.

"How did you land at Cornell?" she asked.

"My father had a funny attitude toward formal education," Guarneri said. "He didn't have one himself. He was an illegal immigrant from Naples in the 1930s. Jumped ship in Miami, eventually got mobbed up. His education was the waterfronts, the bars, the brothels, and eventually the casinos and racetracks. So he figured I should have a real education — the best he could find. He was street smart and wanted culture; I got culture and wanted street smarts. But the old man named the tune. So I got sent to tough parochial schools on Long Island. My dad always said, 'You get an education; no one can ever take that away from you.' So he was on my case all the time about studies. Bless him. I was his only son, at least that I know of. He steered me away from his sordid world. He did a lot of things wrong, but he did some things right as well."

"And yet, in a way, you're steering back," she suggested.

"What do you mean?"

Alex wondered if she had touched a nerve. "Well, Cuba. That's a trip into your father's past. On one hand you say you're glad you moved away from that, and yet you want to reach out and touch it again."

"You have a point."

"Unless it's just the money," she said.

He laughed. "It's never just the money, Alex," he said. "Not for any reasonable man or woman."

"Then what is it? In your case?"

He leaned back in his chair, his hands folded behind his head. "Family. Destiny. Promises once made. Timing." She thought he was ready to say more, but didn't. "May I let it go at that for tonight?" he asked.

"You may."

A thoughtful pause, and he added, "No one's completely bad, are they?"

"I'm not following the question."

"My father," he said. "Giuseppe Cristoforo Guarneri, though he was Joe to those who knew him. Nineteen twenty-eight to 1973, somehow by the grace of God. Joe from Napoli. Joe the gangster, who was on the payroll of Lucky Luciano of Murder Incorporated. Was Joe a bad man?" he asked. "That's my question."

"It might be your question, but I can't answer it," Alex said.

"If he was, am I a bad man for honoring a bad man's wishes?"

"Depends on the purpose."

"Evil fascinates me. Maybe more than good does. Name an evil man," he said. "Completely evil."

"Hitler? Stalin?" she tried.

"Point taken," he said. "Want to add Castro and Fulgencio Batista to your list?"

"I'll let you do that," she said.

"I just did. Yeah, yeah, I know," he said, musing. "The apple doesn't fall far from the tree, does it? That was part of it. It took many years for my father's execution to wear off. I was in denial for a decade and a half. Then I wanted to know more. About him. About the events of the time. Hell, it's where I came from. If dad hadn't had an eye for the chorus girls, I wouldn't have been born."

Alex laughed out loud. "That's an odd way of looking at it."

"It's a realistic way of looking at it," Guarneri countered.

"So you want to sneak into Cuba, and yet you're an expert on Cuba?" she said.

"An amateur expert," he corrected. "A lay expert."

"What can you tell me about the Bay of Pigs?" Alex asked.

He laughed slightly. "Quite a lot. I can tell you two things," he said: "the invasion was a disaster, and my old man was there."

"Your father was part of the force that invaded Cuba?" she asked.

"Yup. He went to Miami and trained with the invading force. Then he went in. He was captured on the beach. Lucky he wasn't killed. Spent time in a Cuban prison camp before the U.S. made a deal to get the men back. It was the only time my father ever spent time in jail."

"So he had CIA contacts?" she said.

"Sure," Guarneri said, "but don't make too much of that. The CIA was going crazy back then trying to get rid of Castro. They'd play ball with anyone. My dad's contacts probably were not any better than five thousand other people's."

She looked at him to ferret out the truth. "Or at least that's what you're telling me," she said.

He snorted slightly. "Why would I lie to you?" he asked.

"I don't know. Why would you?"

"I have no reason to," he said. "None. The CIA, they'll lie to anyone. Me, you. The press. The president. Santa Claus. Anyone." He paused. "I hate them," he said.

"It's hard to figure you out sometimes, Paul," she said.

"Why's that?"

"I don't know. I get in here in your home. Books. Fencing. Library. Kids. Not what I expected."

"What did you expect? A blend of DeNiro and Joe Pesci?"

"Maybe," she said.

"Well, that's me in a nutshell, isn't it?" he said. "Half in one place, half in another. I'm Cuban, but I'm Italian. I'm Italian, but I'm American. I'm a thug and a mobbed-up guy, but I'd be happy at home reading a history book. I hate violence, but I own guns. I'm divorced, but I'm a family man." He shrugged. "Go figure."

"I'm trying to," she said, "but don't change the subject."

"Did I?"

"You did."

"Then ask me whatever you want," he said.

"What do you know about the Bay of Pigs from your dad?" she asked.

"From my dad? Not a thing. He never talked about Cuba. Oh, he acknowledged what his business was there, who he had known. And I knew he was in the invasion and was captured because he disappeared those years, then came back, fuming about Kennedy, the CIA, and everyone involved. He probably hated the people who were on our side as much as he hated Castro."

"But he talked about it enough to tell you that there was some money stashed."

"Sure." He paused. "Joseph Guarneri was an old-fashioned guy. What you'd call a 'sexist pig.' I was his only son. He had two daughters with his American wife. He always said he would let me know later, we'd 'have a talk.' I believe he was thinking that I, as his son, should be the one to know more, to go back, to settle things. Follow?"

"I follow."

"He said he would tell me everything when I was twenty-one. When he was whacked, I was eighteen."

"Ever talk to your half-sisters about him?"

"A couple of times. They know nothing. And they married non-Italians. They want nothing to do with this. Your parents still alive?" he asked.

"No. Neither," she said.

"So we have that in common too," he noted.

Alex agreed that they did. "Your mother became a U.S. citizen?" Alex asked.

"Oh, yeah," he said. "Very quickly. That way she wouldn't be deported if things went the wrong way." Paul went to the bookcase. He picked up an eight-by-ten portrait in a silver frame. It was a black-and-white of his mother, a pretty Latina in a gown and a mink coat. Behind her was the finish line and pari-mutuel board of a racetrack.

"This was taken at Oriental Park Racetrack in 1958," he said. "My mother liked the horses, same as my dad. She liked to put a few dollars down here and there. See, the horses ran during the day. Both my parents were busy working at night with the clubs and the shows. So the daytime was when they could be together." He laughed. "I wouldn't be here without certain lazy afternoons in Havana," he said.

"I understand," Alex said with a smirk.

Guarneri gave the photo a final glance, then walked it back to the shelf and carefully returned it to its place.

Alex glanced at her watch. It was past eleven. She said, "The other day, you said you could leave quickly if you had to. Is that still the case?"

"Yes."

"I'm willing to go with you to Cuba," she said. "I need time to accomplish my own assignment, but we can go together. If you'll do it, I'll do it."

"What's your assignment? May I ask?"

"The return of a CIA defector. He wants to come home. The Cubans won't let him. So I'm supposed to rendezvous and bring him back."

"Does he have a name?"

"I can share information only after we land," she said. "Sorry, that's the deal."

"Fair enough," he said. "I don't really care anyway. I'll help you as much as I can if you'll help me."

"Hopefully, we'll come out at the same time."

"Hopefully, but one never knows," Guarneri said.

"What does *that* mean?"

"Men make plans; God laughs," he said. "With a trip like this, who knows what's going to happen? Everything goes according to plans until the first shot is fired."

"You expect shots to be fired?"

"I hope not. It was a metaphor."

"Could you be ready to leave in four days?" she asked.

He thought for a second, then nodded slowly. "I can set it up," he said.

"Then do it," she said. "Set it up. We have an agreement."

"Not quite yet," he said. "There's one other thing I need to tell you."

"Go ahead," she said. Then she waited.

"I'm not exactly a virgin going into Havana. Yuri Federov used to go in for me and make some contacts, do some business. And twice I went with him."

She was stunned, then suddenly angry. "Then you *have* been there before! Not just when you were a kid but more recently!"

"That's right."

"So you lied to me?"

He shrugged. "Yeah, yeah," he said. "Unfortunately, I did. I'm sorry. Once in 2006 and then again in 2008. Okay? So I know the island a little better than I let on. There was a security issue surrounding those trips, both mine and for those who helped me go in and out. So I honestly couldn't tell you until now. And now I'm telling you point blank in case you want to bail. Then again, you've got your own business to attend to also. And I know you're not telling me every aspect of that either. I know because those CIA people always put you up to something. Even when you're *not* working for them you *are*. Right?"

"That's correct," she said.

"So we understand each other? We find ourselves in a similar situation?"

After several seconds she said, "We do." "I think we finally understand each other. But don't ever lie to me again."

"Are we still going to travel?" he asked.

"We're going," she said.

He smiled, came to her, and clasped her hand with both of his. "Excellent," he said. "Excellent!"

Half an hour later, Alex sat in silence as the SUV crossed the Brooklyn Bridge and reentered Manhattan. With the midnight skyline stretched out in front of her, she rode in silence, knowing two things. The first was that the voyage to Cuba was going to happen. And the second was that Paul Guarneri had come within a hair's breadth of sharing with her his real reason for going to the island but had stopped short. Why, she wondered. Something she had said? Or was he just not trusting her enough? Or was there a strain of dishonesty in him that she hadn't picked up on yet?

The SUV eased into the traffic on the East Side Drive and then headed uptown. Several minutes later, it pulled to a stop in front of the safe house on East 38th Street. MacPhail and Ramirez jumped out first. They scanned windows and the street, then allowed Alex to step out.

"What did you think of that guy, Paul Guarneri?" she asked.

They both shrugged. MacPhail spoke. "He is what he is," he said.

"You have access to FBI records, don't you?" Alex asked.

"How many years?"

"Thirty-six," she said.

"Sure. We got those."

"See what you have on Paul's father," she asked. "Who killed him, how he was hit. Anything. Can you do that?"

"Might take a day or two," MacPhail answered.

"See you tomorrow," Alex said. Her guards waited till she was in the door before they, in turn, concluded their own very long day.

Before drifting off to sleep, Alex made a mental note. Tomorrow, she would call an old acquaintance named Sam Deal, her own expert on Central America and the black arts of espionage. Sam had been of assistance on background with previous cases. Now Sam was making an honest living, sort of, in retail security in midtown Manhattan. She knew Sam would be up for a drink, a sexy flirt, and some conversation. The value of the latter, she knew, would offset the nuisance factor of the previous two. Without doubt, Sam Deal was the most disreputable man she knew. And for that reason, he was of infinite value.

TWENTY-FIVE

Ironically, Tío Antonio always felt safe in lawless Mexico. As the Perez family bodyguard, he liked the place, the people, the family he worked for, the food, and the *chicas*. The truth was, he preferred Mexico to a quiet place like Belize. Oh, he could ogle the wealthy American and European women on the beaches, but even that had its limits. They were beyond his reach, after all. So now it was good to be home, keeping an eye on the Perez family while his boss was away again on assignment, this time in America.

This morning, he had escorted Señora Perez to the school, where they dropped off her children, and then to her job at the pharmaceutical company. Now, in his Mercedes, he had arrived back at the gates of the family compound in the southern suburbs of Mexico City. Time for relaxation. He could watch soccer on satellite TV until he had to pick up the children in the afternoon. He had to bring them home, and they would stay with the housekeeper, Maria, behind the locked gates until it was time to pick up Señora Perez. On most days, this job was pretty easy.

In his car, he pressed the remote and waited for the two locked gates to open. There was no movement. He tried again. Still no movement.

He muttered to himself. The electricians had been here twice in the last ten days to fix this infernal electronic gate, and once again their fix hadn't lasted. Time to fire them. That was one thing that he didn't like about Mexico—chronic incompetence. *Mañana* was a popular religion, in addition to *No es mi asunto*—"it's not my thing."

He stepped out of the vehicle. No one around. Good. He went to the brick pillars that supported the steel gates, still sighing about Mexican workmanship. He blinked in the bright sunshine.

He put on a pair of sunglasses. He tried the key that would bypass the electronic system. He jiggled it. The keyhole was resistant to his touch too, which started to make him suspicious.

Then he heard the familiar crude click and a metal bolt withdrawing from a clasp. The giant latch that held the two steel doors in place had given way. Much better.

He walked to the spot where the two wide gates met. He gave them an aggressive push with his foot. With the usually noisy, rusty, aching creaks, the doors gave way and slowly opened, just the way they had so many times before. He put his shoulder to one and leaned hard, pushing it so that it swung wide. Then he pushed the other one the same way. He now had room to drive through into the Perez compound.

From somewhere nearby came the sound of bicycle tires and then a gentle skid. He turned at the same time that he heard a woman's voice, young and sexy.

"¿Señor?" a girl asked.

He turned, slightly startled. A girl on a bicycle, a pretty blonde, had stopped. She wore short shorts, a snug T-shirt, a helmet, and shades. He had seen her in the neighborhood for the past few days. She was in her early twenties and probably lived in the gated compound up the road where a lot of foreigners lived, wealthy people who worked in Mexico City for big corporations. She apparently exercised by biking around the neighborhood, always in tight black bike shorts and a red and yellow shirt. Plus the helmet. There was no way Antonio or any other male in the area could miss her. She was sexy. Some man was lucky. Or was she someone's daughter? She had smiled at him and waved in gratitude as his car gave way to allow her a lane to ride.

But he also reminded himself that he must have been slipping. Pretty *chica rubia* or not, where had she come from? He hadn't seen her this time until she had rolled to a stop. His mind processed quickly: well, did it matter where such a pretty girl had come from? Then again, people who appeared all too quietly set off alarms for him.

He pocketed the key and smiled. *"Buenos dias,"* he said curtly.

"Buen día," she chirped. She smiled back. *"¿Tiene aqua fría?"* she asked. Cool water. That's what she wanted. She did have an accent. Probably American. That made sense. Most of the wealthy people up the hill were American.

He stared at her in surprise. Why was she asking him about cold water? Why didn't she just carry some of her own? On the other hand, the house was empty. If he could entice this *chica* into the hacienda, well, it wouldn't be the first time he had had some extracurricular fun during the daytime hours.

She held up her water bottle, laughed, and shook it upside down to show him that it was empty. Then she shrugged and giggled, helplessly and flirtatiously. He assessed her carefully. Well, he had some cold bottled water in the car. The Perez family always kept some. They could spare some. *"Momento,"* he said.

He motioned with his thumb to the hacienda. Yes, she was coming onto him, he decided. The girl was probably the trophy wife of some nasty Yankee businessman who didn't have the physical stamina to keep her happy. He had seen this before among American women in the neighborhood. They'd go on the prowl during the day, looking for a local *toro* to take care of them.

Well, he decided, why not? He gave her a nod. She dismounted from her bike, swinging one lithe leg over the other. She was, he noted, absolutely spectacular.

The wooden baseball bat that came from behind Antonio was aimed straight at the back of his knees. It smashed home with a sickening crack, followed by another bat that came from his right side and whacked his arm just above the elbow with an even louder crunching sound.

At the same time as Antonio bellowed in pain and groped for his pistol, the woman with the bicycle quickly charged him. From behind him, helmeted men in the uniform of the Mexico City Police swarmed. They grabbed him and hit him hard again from behind. Then they shoved him down onto the pavement. Antonio fought like a madman. Despite the searing pain in his legs, he threw his powerful elbows at the men behind him. His broken right arm pulsated with pain and flew wildly at obscene angles. But he caught one of the men in the jaw and one in the gut. He clenched his good fist, threw a backward punch at one of the men, and caught him in the center of his face. The man howled profanely and loosened his grip.

But one of the men hammered at Antonio's right knee again with the bat and caught it dead on. Antonio screamed again and cursed even more profanely in Spanish. He groped with his left hand for the gun he carried under the left armpit of his jacket. His hand touched the weapon, but one of his assailants grabbed his wrist with both hands and forced it back and up. Another forced Antonio's thumb backward so hard that it felt as if it were about to snap.

Then the blonde girl slipped a quick hand under his jacket and yanked his gun from him. She threw it away. Other hands were on his throat and fingers were in his eyes.

One of the intruders had a police club and seemed to enjoy using it. He walloped Tony on the left side of the collarbone, then thrust the club butt first into his groin.

On the ground, Antonio retreated into a shell, trying to protect himself. The fight was over, and he knew these people were probably here to beat him to death. He felt his hands yanked behind his back and cuffed. His mouth was hot. Salty little shards of a tooth floated on his tongue. There was no fight left in him now.

The bicycle girl knelt and leaned over him like a death angel, a hypodermic needle in her hand. Everything hurt. He could barely see, but he then managed to catch a glimpse and the sounds of something nearly surreal.

"Should I give it to him now?" the female calmly asked in English.

"Yes, do," came the response, also in English.

Antonio felt the jab as it came through the seat of his pants into his left buttock. That was followed quickly by a tingling iciness radiating down in his backside, from the middle of the left buttock outward. Within seconds, the iciness exploded into a warmth that enveloped his whole body. Antonio had tried opium once and the sensation was similar. Suddenly, nothing hurt as much. Suddenly nothing mattered much at all. His vision blurred. All hands seemed to be off him now, and he lay in one big puddle, his own wrists manacled behind his back. He felt as if the sun was only a few feet over his woozy head.

The young woman stood. Then his eyes widened. An angel, he thought to himself in his incipient delirium. The blonde had come to deliver him, but he couldn't decide whether he was to be delivered to death or to somewhere else. That was his final thought. The whiteness exploded like a couple of big steel gates slamming shut. Then everything went black.

TWENTY-SIX

Alex met Sam Deal in the vast street-level floor of one of Manhattan's biggest jewelry emporiums, a fortress of a building on New York's 57th Street. Alex arrived a few minutes before 2:00 p.m. and slowly wandered among the display cases, one eye on the diamond rings and the other looking for Sam.

She spotted him as he emerged from one of the elevators east of the lobby. The store employed him as one of their heads of on-site security.

Sam was burley and had an eager bounce to his gait as he approached her. He was wearing a suit. He was pink-faced and glowing. He smiled when their eyes met.

"Alex, right?" he said. "Beautiful as ever."

"Hello, Sam," she said.

MacPhail and Ramirez lurked in the background. Sam noticed them right away. "What's with Sonny and Cher?" he asked, jerking his head toward them.

"I got backup today," she said. "I'm on a case. They're watching my back."

"Lucky you," he said.

"Not a problem, is it?" she asked.

"No. Shouldn't be. We sit at one table, they sit at another, right?"

"That's how I pictured it, Sam," she said.

"Okay, that's kosher," he said. "I'm doing a late lunch. We're getting out of here, right? You want to talk?"

"Absolutely," she said.

"I know the place," he said. "Come on."

For years, Sam had been the presumed head of an unofficial group of CIA-financed operatives known as "the Nightingales."

They worked out of Miami, focused on Latin America, and were far too disreputable for Alex's tastes. But they had their uses. For years they'd handled hit-and-run jobs that were too dirty for the CIA to touch directly. They knew things, they knew people, and Sam, now in his late sixties, was the poster boy of the whole operation.

Semi-retirement agreed with him. He seemed busy, content, and eager to display the dark knowledge he had accrued over a lifetime. He let Alex go through the revolving door first; then they were on Fifth Avenue. Ten minutes later they were seated in the back of a small, noisy delicatessen on West 56th Street. A waiter, without being asked, placed a Corona directly in front of Sam. Alex declined. MacPhail and Ramirez settled into a table close to the door as Sam started his oily schmooze.

"You should have been a model, Alex, really. You got the face, the legs, the figure. You wear clothes as if they were invented for you. Why did you choose to get into our scummy line of work when you could have been sitting by a pool in Malibu having your picture taken? Answer me that before I answer anything for you."

"Just crazy, I guess, Sam." In spite of herself, flirtatious Sam made her laugh.

"Yeah, yeah," he snorted, "aren't we all?" He sipped directly from the green bottle.

"So who you work for? I know it's government. It always is unless it isn't, right?"

"Fin Cen, New York."

"Oh, yeah. Financial crimes. Money. You're down on Wall Street, right?"

"Nearby. Right," she said.

"Yeah. That's right. You got brains too. That'd disqualify you from modeling. Wall Street, huh? Plenty of financial crime there. The whole place is a financial crime. Banks. Stock markets. Convertible debentures. Predatory lending. Bailouts for people who shouldn't even be out on bail. They should all be in jail, but I don't run the world. Plus, I wouldn't put them in jail; I'd just have them shot. Anyway, what's on the plate today?"

"For starters, does the name Paul Guarneri mean anything to you?" she asked.

"No. Should it?"

"Probably not."

Sam thought for a moment. "Mafia guy?"

"Connected family," Alex said.

"New York?"

"The city and Long Island."

"I don't know him," Sam said. "Does he say he knows me?"

"I never asked."

"Then don't. He's probably connected. Italian. If he's on some list of yours and he's Italian, he's connected. I'm Italian, did you know that?" Sam asked. "All Italians are connected to the Mafia in some way, large or small."

"Really?" Alex asked, bemused.

"No," Sam countered. "But why you asking me?"

"Because I want to pick your brain about Cuba," Alex said.

"Ha! What about it?" Sam asked.

"I heard you've been there," Alex said.

Sam sipped more of his beer and smiled. "You're a clever little fox, Alex," he said. "You going to Cuba?"

She remained silent. She winked.

"Enjoy your trip," Sam said. "The rum is *fabuloso*."

"You were around for the Bay of Pigs in '61, weren't you?"

"I was a kid. I was around for the aftermath. So what about it?"

"I'm a newbie on Cuba, Sam. Impress me with your inside knowledge."

It was just the encouragement that Sam needed. He laughed.

"What do you want to hear about?" he asked. "The really bad old days of the '40s, when Lucky Luciano came back to the island after exile in Italy, or do you want to hear about how Sinatra used to be a courier for money from the American mob to the Havana casino operators, then would sing at private performances for his mobster friends?" Sam laughed again. "Or how about when JFK was a U.S. Senator and a hood named Santo Trafficante set up an orgy for him at the Hotel Comodoro?"

"Start with JFK, but skip the rest," Alex said.

Sam smirked. "That's the best part. But I'm not surprised. Get down to business, no fun and games with you, Alex LaDuca."

"Why don't you take me to the Bay of Pigs?" she said. *"Playa Girón.* That's what they call it in Spanish, isn't it?"

"Yeah, that's it." Sam shrugged. "But I don't know too much more than anyone else," Sam said. "Kennedy was president by then because Mayor Daley in Chicago stuffed all those ballot boxes and tipped Illinois to the Dems. Anyway, it's a year after the election, and JFK rushed an invasion plan into play on the idea that Castro would later acquire a stronger military capability and be able to defeat it. Fact was, Castro already had that capability. The CIA also told the president that Castro only had an obsolete, ineffective air force. The agency said they weren't in combat condition and had no communications in the Zapata Swamp area and had no forces nearby. That's where the *Bahía de Cochinos* is, the Bay of Pigs. Everything about the intelligence was wrong. They expected mass defections among Cuban military, and none materialized. The Cuban air force had Lockheed T-33 jet trainers, the same planes the U.S. had given to Batista to fight the rebels. We figured they didn't have pilots, but we were wrong. They were more effective than predicted. Then Castro's army moved to the beach and crushed the exiles with greater efficiency than any estimate had anticipated. In fact, the Cuban jets were largely responsible for the exiles' ammunition losses. Kennedy, having approved the plan with assurances that it would be both clandestine and successful, quickly discovered that it was too large to be clandestine and too small to be successful. Ten thousand exiles might have gotten it done. Twenty thousand would have walked over the Cuban force. But fourteen hundred? Forget about it. There. That's the front half."

He paused. Sandwiches arrived. They fell silent. When the waitress was gone, Alex asked. "What's the back half?"

Sam continued, "The Bay of Pigs had every element for a perfect disaster, and that's what it turned into. Then the suits at the CIA flipped around and claimed Kennedy had betrayed them when they had set him up with implausible intelligence."

"They came in at dawn, right . . . ," Alex asked, "the invasion force?"

"Yeah. And that was a problem too. The brigade relied on a nighttime landing through uncharted reefs in boats with outboard motors. South shore of the island. Even with ample ammunition and control of the air, the brigade couldn't have broken out of its beachhead or survived much longer without substantial help from either American forces or the Cuban people. Neither happened." He shook his head and continued. "The invasion was intended to provoke an uprising against Castro. Instead, it gave him a military victory and a permanent symbol of Cuban resistance to American aggression. Great move, JFK. Way to go, CIA. Idiots!"

"Do you still have contacts on the island?" Alex asked.

He took several seconds to answer. "Not really," he said. "It's been a long time. There have been so many other fish to fry in the last few years. Colombia. Venezuela. Honduras. Nicaragua." He shrugged. "I could make some phone calls if you want. I used to know a guy named Gilberto in Old Havana. Used to sell postcards and rum to tourists — and guns, Argentine passports, and black-market dollars to people who wanted to leave the country. I have no idea if he's still alive. If he is, he'll talk to me; if he's dead he probably won't. I could do some asking."

"If you would, that would be nice," Alex said easily. "And look, maybe you could run the Guarneri name past a few of your old Playa Girón contacts," she added.

Sam laughed and grabbed the notepad in front of him. "What's the full name?"

"Joseph Guarneri," Alex said. "G-U-A-R-N-E-R-I," she continued, spelling it as Sam's pudgy hand quickly wrote. "He could be down as 'Giuseppe.' Born in Italy."

"Why don't you throw the name past your friends, the Feds?" he said, throwing a glance at MacPhail and Ramirez. "Or did you do that already?"

"I always like to check the official version against the unofficial version," Alex said. "That's why I'm here. Can you blame me?"

"No. Call me in a week," Sam said.

"I don't have a week."

"Ah. I get it. Then I'll put some zip on it. I'll phone you when I have something. You working on a CIA assignment?"

She was silent again. Another wink.

"Foxy fox, aren't you?" Sam said. "I like it. You got great legs too. Did I mention that? What do you do? Run? Swim? Gym? Tight shorts and a muscle T-shirt. I bet you look hot."

"Can I try another name on you?" she asked.

"Don't let me stop you."

"Roland Violette."

Sam instantly knew the name. "Whoa. *That* snake! He's been down there Havana-way doing his señorita and drinking rum for twenty years. That's what I hear."

"Twenty-*six* years."

"I hear the man's crazy," Sam said. "Complete loony tune. Of course, he was always dealing with a deck that only had forty-nine cards. He's vermin, you know. Ratted out a lot of good CIA people. Why's his name in play?"

"A little birdie told me he wants to come home," Alex said.

"Ha! That shows you how crazy he is. The CIA has a price on his head. There's bad, bad blood there. Be careful."

"May I speak off the record, Sam?"

"*Everything's* off the record. You see any record? There *is* no record."

"Violette is claiming he has a bag of goodies that he filched from the Cuban government," Alex said. "He might be looking to trade them for a ticket out."

"Might be, eh? Who wouldn't?" Sam snorted.

"Do you think Violette was ever in a position to score some good intelligence?" she asked. "Does his story wash?"

Sam pondered. "It might." Sam then said, "Violette had access, if that's what you're asking. Who knows what he might have swiped?"

"Thanks," she said.

"Don't thank me. Thank Violette." Sam had a faraway look, then came back to earth. "Bloody Cubans," Sam said. "They deserve better. As much as I hate Castro and his whole red crew, I can't say he's worse than Batista. It's like Russia. Who was worse? Czar Nicholas II or Lenin?"

"Depends which Russian you were."

"Yup. Just like it depends which Cuban you were. If you were mobbed up or the owner of a sugar plantation, Batista was your man. What did they call him? *El Mulato Lindo?* If you were a peasant in Santiago or if your sister had been turned into a prostitute by fat American tourists, then Fidel or Che were your guys." Sam lightened. "My kid came home with a Che T-shirt when he was twelve. I ripped it off him and threw the lousy thing away. I said, 'Che? You want to know about Che?' Che performed the same role for Fidel Castro as Felix Drezhinsky performed for Lenin and Himmler did for Hitler. Guevara was Castro's chief executioner. Under Che, Havana's La Cabana fortress was converted into Cuba's Lubianka. Know your Russians and Russian history, Alex?"

"Reasonably well."

"Che was a Chekist: 'Interrogate your prisoners at night,' Che told his goons. 'A man's resistance is lower at night.' I knew this Cuban prosecutor in the '60s who defected: José Vilasuso. José estimated that Che signed four hundred death warrants the first months in La Cabana. I knew a Basque priest named Iaki de Aspiazu who did final confessions and last rites. He said that Che ordered seven hundred executions by firing squad during the period. Some Cuban journalists who later defected claimed Che sent two thousand men to the firing squad. Ever heard of a CIA guy named Felix Rodriguez?"

"No. What about him?"

"He was the Cuban-American CIA operative who helped track down Che in Bolivia. He was the last person to question him. He says that during that final talk, Che admitted to a couple thousand executions. But he shrugged them off. Said they were all imperialist spies and CIA agents. That's your heroic Che."

"You have your point of view, Sam," Alex answered.

"Well you came to listen, right? And to learn?"

"I did indeed, Sam."

Sam finished his drink. He glanced at his watch. Ten minutes before three. "Hey. I got to scram," he said. "I'll ask around about Guarneri. My man in Havana. Wasn't that a book?"

"*Our Man in Havana*. Graham Greene," she said.

"Yeah. Brit writer. That's it. I liked that one. Do you read a lot?"

"When I have time," she said.

"Yeah, you look like you might. Your brain's as sharp as your body."

They walked back along 57th Street, with MacPhail and Ramirez trailing behind. The sidewalks were crowded. Sam took a cell phone call but quickly dispatched it. When they reached the southeast corner of 57th at Fifth, Sam stopped again before going back to work. "There's a couple of things that'd be good for you to remember."

"Go ahead."

"First," Sam said, "it's my personal feeling that the Kennedy assassination was organized by Castro. From the early sixties on, the CIA had tried to have Castro assassinated and had hired goombahs from the American Mafia to do the job. Bobby Kennedy was deep in it and so was the president. The Kennedys were trying to get to Castro, but Castro got to the Kennedys first. Payback. Oswald spent time in Cuba, remember?"

"I know the theory, Sam."

"What do you think? Am I nuts?"

"Like all the JFK assassination theories, it has its merits and its imperfections. What's the other thing?"

His dark eyes fixed on a point in the middle distance. "You know," he said. "I forgot." Then the meeting was over. Sam bounded through the doors of his retail employer and was back to work.

Later that day the other zapato dropped.

Señora Perez was in the lobby of her office building in Mexico City when three men in police uniforms approached her. They explained that there was some threat against both her and her husband and they'd been sent to protect her.

Her first question: *"¿Donde está Antonio?"* Where is Antonio?

"He's gone to the airport to join your husband," they said.

"His flight's probably in progress as we speak," one of the men in uniform said.

"May I call my husband?" she asked.

"Of course."

They waited. The call was unsuccessful.

"Very well then," she said.

They escorted her to a pair of waiting Mexico City police cars. They then proceeded to the children's school. Only after that second pickup did these men reveal that they were not police officers. Señora Perez also learned that her husband had lied to her over many years. He was involved with a business beyond the import and export of fruits. She also learned that she and her family were in custody, as was her bodyguard. What she had no way of knowing, however, was who her captors were.

TWENTY-SEVEN

The next morning, the Department of Treasury approved Alex's mission to Cuba. She advised Paul Guarneri, and they made tentative plans to meet in Miami before continuing on to Havana. He gave her an address in Miami where they would rendezvous. MacPhail and Ramirez's duty would be to get her that far and probably to the sea launch to Cuba as well. After that, she was at the mercy of fate and the man with whom she would be traveling.

"I'll make arrangements to get us to Cuba by small plane and boat," Paul said. "I've had a scenario set up for months. Now I just need to put it into effect." He worked with some smugglers, he said. Not the most upstanding of citizens, but efficient people who got the job done.

In the afternoon Alex went out for some air. Walter MacPhail accompanied her. They carried weapons. Ramirez walked about twenty feet behind. They stayed around Third Avenue and the Thirties. "We'll be driving down to Washington tomorrow morning," MacPhail announced as they walked. "You'll have a conference at the CIA in Langley about Roland Violette. We'll be in D.C. for one overnight, maybe two."

"Makes sense," Alex said. "Got anything yet on Guarneri's old man?"

"Nothing yet. Still trying. Bureaucracy, you know ..."

"See if you can kick-start the request," she said. "It's not like a year from now will do any good."

"I'll make another call."

Later, Alex went back to the table that supported her secure laptop. Clad in jeans and a T-shirt, with the baby Glock on her hip, she clicked into her secure email account. Two items had arrived in the last hour.

The first was an FBI summary on Paul Guarneri's father, Joseph Guarneri. He had been born in Sicily in 1928, confirming what Paul had said. He had jumped ship in 1944 to remain in the U.S. Records were hazy, but two younger brothers eventually followed him to Cuba. This casual tidbit had been annotated many years earlier, presumably by an agent long since retired or deceased:

> Examiner's note: Salvatore Guarneri, 1931 - 1959, was a pit boss and trainer of dealers at Meyer Lansky's Riviera Hotel; Giovanni Guarneri, 1942 - ??, last known as an active but no longer influential member of the Cuban Communist Party. SpAg P.S.D., 10/17/1973.

Noting the conflicting politics within the family, Alex continued to read. Joseph Guarneri, the file said, maintained houses in New York, Miami, and Cuba while Batista was in power and, it was believed, had two families, one official, one unofficial. The latter was obviously Paul and his mother.

Guarneri controlled criminal operations in Florida, Cuba, and Puerto Rico. He maintained links to the Bonanno crime family in New York but had been more closely allied with Sam Giancana in Chicago. In Guarneri's day, the east coast of Florida and Cuba had been a tight conglomerate of New York family interests with links to Meyer Lansky and Benjamin "Bugsy" Siegel. But Giancana, a former Capone associate while in Chicago, also had his fingers in the pie. So Guarneri had operated under Mr. Sam's umbrella. This organization traced back to 1929 in Cuba and the outset of Prohibition in the U.S. Paying off members of the Gerardo Machado dictatorship, which had preceded Batista in Cuba, the New York underworld built huge rum factories on the island and contracted with Cuban sugar refineries to guarantee an endless supply of molasses, the main ingredient in rum. Upon such a firm foundation did a vast criminal enterprise rise to prerevolutionary glory.

A separate Treasury Department document also indicated that Joseph Guarneri's business interests had included parts of several legal casinos in Cuba, laundry and catering services to those casinos, a Havana drive-in movie theater, shares in *La Sirena Gorda* restaurant in Miramar, where Hemingway and the literary set liked to knock back booze, a racetrack in Havana, a catering service in Havana, and several other restaurants and bars in Tampa, Florida.

Alex read the concluding sections carefully:

> Joseph Guarneri was frequently arrested on various charges of bribery, bookmaking, and loan sharking. He escaped conviction all but once, receiving a two-year sentence in 1954 for bribery of a judge, but his conviction was overturned by the New York State Supreme Court before he entered prison . . .
>
> In 1959, Castro's revolutionary government seized the assets of Guarneri's Cuban businesses and expelled him from the country as an "undesirable alien." Thereafter, Guarneri came into contact with various American and expatriate Cuban organizations that opposed Fidel Castro. He later served in the military brigade that invaded Cuba at the Bay of Pigs in 1961. Captured and held as a prisoner after the failure of the invasion, he was ransomed by the United States. Guarneri either lost his taste for underworld life in later years or was forced out of his businesses and settled in Florida and New York . . .
>
> A fan of thoroughbred and standardbred horse racing, Joseph Guarneri would, when in Manhattan, have his driver stop in front of

the sprawling newsstand that once stood at New York's Times Square. Guarneri would emerge from the rear door, enter, pick up his reserved copy of *The Morning Telegraph*, hand three dollars to the clerk, climb back into his car and proceed to either Aqueduct or Belmont ...

He focused on real estate in his later years but still retained some old enemies. His execution took place one night when Guarneri was coming home from Yonkers Raceway in the New York suburbs. On the porch of his house, he was ambushed by three gunmen; two opened fire with pistols, a third with a shotgun. The hit was particularly brutal and was an exception to organized crime's own rules about not hitting a victim in or near his home if he had family ...

An additional quirk: even in the New York underworld, there was consternation over the hit. No one knew who had arranged it or who had set it up, especially since Guarneri was believed to have been retired at the time. Yet, for a man with such a career, it wasn't entirely incredible to have an enemy step out of the shadows of the past, bearing a grievance, either real or imagined, and effect a day of reckoning. The homicide inquiry was never resolved ...

Alex further noted a short addendum:

Examiner's note: FBI picked up the trail of a known Cuban operative named Julio Garcia who had covertly entered the United States in May 1973 with a Honduran passport. Garcia was a known "verdugo" or executioner for the Cuban

Intelligence Services. The FBI lost his trail in New York and had no record of him leaving the U.S., but he was believed to have been in the U.S. when Joseph Guarneri was murdered. Garcia was last known to be in Cuba as a member of Cuban State Security in 1981 and remains a member of the Cuban Communist Party ... Notes between FBI and CIA were never compared or correlated at the time. SpAg J.N.H., 07/19/1993.

Julio Garcia, Alex mused. How many Cubans had that name? Five thousand? Ten thousand? She proceeded to the next email. This one, from the CIA, was a series of briefs on Roland Violette. Alex made some coffee, then spent an hour reading the reports and reviewing surveillance photos, the most recent taken fifty-six days earlier.

She noted that Violette had been stationed in Washington, then Madrid, which rang some loud bells for her. Within the last year she had worked out of the U.S. Embassy and the CIA office in the Spanish capital. She wondered if her contacts from those operations might be able to tell her things that might not be in the official summary.

"Okay," she told herself. Bringing Violette out of Cuba was the assignment. *Can do, can do, can do,* she told herself. As she started to ease into her new assignment, however, she realized how shaken she still was from the sniper's near miss. Shock and trauma were like depression, she concluded; you don't realize how bad it is until you're past it.

She wasn't the only one whose brains felt like scrambled eggs these days, she realized. She read a pair of blurbs from a CIA contact with a Honduran passport who had encountered Violette in Havana by chance six weeks earlier.

Examiner's note: HW File 7-TF, 05/14/11: Roland Violette sits in Juanita's Café on the Calle San Rafael ... and he tells the old stories over and over. They frequently have no appearance of reality and bear not even a faint resemblance to the truth.

But he has told them so often over his morning daiquiris that it's obvious he's come to believe them himself. Sad. His head has turned to mush with a destroyed spirit and body to match . . .

This was followed by another examiner's note from within the last two weeks.

Ronnie the Violet, also known as Ronnie the Deep Purple Red [some recent sorehead had written while reviewing the file] remains a rat bastard. May he burn in hell forever over what he did to this agency in the '70s and '80s.

She reread that one-line entry. It was fascinating that Violette still elicited such strong feelings. His defection had been a full quarter century earlier, and the damage that he had done went even farther back. But she was intrigued, too, that someone else had preceded her through this file within the last few days. She could feel someone's hot breath on it. Were the fingerprints from this present operation or some other?

Then she recalled that if Violette was looking to return to America, the file had undergone a Lazarus effect. It was back from the dead. She decided to do a little water testing of her own and threw a few keystrokes onto the computer, trying to make her own comments on the file. But the file was closed and refused to receive any new amendments. She looked at the initials following the examiner's notation: *HW.*

She didn't know an HW, but she would now look out for one. HW was clearly senior enough to add his or her own notes to the file, which meant that HW carried some weight in the CIA.

And since the file was closed to her but not to HW, that told her something too.

Okay, she would double check this herself. Her fingers worked the keyboard. Via secure email, she fired an inquiry to a colleague she had worked with in Madrid. She asked for anything the Madrid office might give her on Roland Violette and his defection. He had worked at the CIA office there in the 1980s, she noted, and the office had been on the top floor of the embassy. So surely Madrid had files. And surely they could share, even if the files didn't officially exist. Since she wouldn't have time to read through entire documents, she asked for an overview.

Then, for good measure, she sent the same dispatch to her old friend Gian Antonio Rizzo in Rome. Alex had worked with him on various occasions in the past, including the Madrid assignment. He was a retired municipal policeman who continued to moonlight for the CIA. Rizzo always had his ear to the ground, always had some odd bit of pertinent information. If nothing else, he was always amusing.

If she were lucky — and often she wasn't — she would be able to compare the three responses. By the time she finished, it was ten minutes to five. She was so deep in thought, searching for implications and inferences, that at first she didn't hear the three low rings of her cell phone. She stared at it in an unfocused way. It sounded a fourth time before she answered.

"It's 'no go' on Gilberto, beautiful," Sam purred. "I told you I'd try to call him, since he was my old informant in Havana, but he died seven years ago. His store folded, his son works for the Castro government out in the Sierra Maestra, and another family runs a bodega out of his storefront."

"So you don't know anyone else on the island?" she asked.

"Gilberto was my best guy and he's gone," he said. "Sorry."

"But do you hear anything?" she asked. "Unofficial or otherwise?"

Sam shrugged. "Just some low level stuff. The U.S. diplomats are teed off because Cuba gets a free pass on human rights abuses from most of the world's democracies. Diplomatic visitors from Canada, Australia, and Switzerland never criticize the Castro regime or meet with dissidents while they're on the island. A friend showed me a confidential diplomatic cable sent to the State Department from Havana. The cable was transmitted in November 2010 and was signed by the top American diplomat in Habanera town. It said there were economic motives behind the suck-up approach. But if so, these countries weren't getting much in return. The rewards for acquiescing to Cuban sensitivities were laughable: over-pumped dinners and for those who bowed lowest a photo-op with drooling old Fidel or dithering old Raul. Big fat deal, huh? And that's all I hear, other than the fact that all the Cuban dissidents supported by Washington for decades were old, out of touch and so split petty squabbles that the United States needed to look elsewhere for future leaders. Like Miami, maybe."

"I appreciate your insights," she said. She wondered if someone had gotten to Sam in the hours since they'd seen each other. She rejected the notion. Sam was his own man these days.

Then Sam interrupted her thoughts. He said he had also made a few other calls about Paul Guarneri's father and found an old contact who'd known Joseph Guarneri during the 1961 invasion. The old man had been a good soldier and a stand-up guy to his comrades-in-arms, Sam's unidentified contact said. And he had been hip deep in a number of anti-Castro endeavors in the late sixties.

"CIA stuff, Sam? Do you think?" Alex asked.

"More than likely," Sam said. "You can just about take that to the bank."

"Here's the funny part, Sam," Alex said. "I spent two hours going through Joseph Guarneri's FBI file this afternoon. It mentioned all the racketeering, the family, the contacts, touched on the anti-Castro stuff — but it uttered not a peep about the CIA. The CIA wasn't even mentioned in Guarneri's file. What do you think?"

Sam laughed. "Typical. The CIA would never share information with the FBI, and the FBI is too dumb to discover it on their own."

"Should I make something of the omission?" Alex asked.

"In an FBI file?" Sam said. "No. Forget it. When it comes to the FBI, never attribute to duplicity what can be attributed to laziness, pigheadedness, or stupidity," Sam said. "They miss the big picture all the time. They probably missed it here."

"That or they're keeping a second file they won't let me see," she said.

"There's always that," Sam said philosophically. "Anything else I can do?"

"Keep my cell number handy if you think of anything else. And I'll keep yours."

"God bless," Sam said, then, "Oh, I remember the other thing I was going to tell you," he said. "Thought of it right after I got back inside the fortress."

"What?" She was almost starting to like Sam. Almost.

"A travel tip. Havana has two million people," he said. "And one million of them are police. So be careful. Don't get pinched by the Cuban cops. It'll take you years to get out." Then he rang off.

TWENTY-EIGHT

At his hotel in Manhattan's East Fifties, Manuel Perez ran his room card through the slot in the door above the doorknob. The little green light came on. He pushed the door open. His hand was still on the knob when a blackjack smashed across his temple above the right ear. The blow staggered him. A second intruder, crouched behind the door, came from the left with a baseball bat and took out Perez's knee from the left side. A second harder blow to the lower back dropped him to the floor.

Perez threw his elbows at the men on top of him. He caught one in the center of the face. The room resounded with crashes, thumps, and profanity. Perez clenched a fist, threw a massive backward punch at one of his assailants and caught him in the throat. The man staggered and loosened his grip. But there were five of them, Perez now realized. He was outnumbered and out-muscled. From the blow to his head, blood flowed into his eyes. He could barely see.

Two men started to yank Perez's hands upward behind his back. One of them shoved a Taser to the base of Perez's neck and unleashed several seconds of current. He was aware of the numbing pain and the buzzing, zapping sound. His body convulsed. He howled again, then gagged. At the same time, the two men worked his hands upward and handcuffed him.

Perez lay on the hotel carpet, stunned but still not unconscious. Someone grabbed him by the hair, lifted his head, and slammed it down again. He was breathing hard, more blood flowing from his brow. He wondered how he could have walked right into this trap.

He could hear someone unleashing a strand of tape with a ripping sound. From behind, someone wrapped the tape firmly across Perez's mouth. Then they sat him up on the floor. One of the assailants, a burly man with a gray crew cut, pushed a gun to Perez's throat, and the Mexican was convinced that he had less than a few seconds to live.

"You're coming with us, Manuel," the man said in Spanish. "If you resist, we kill you. If you cooperate, you live to work again. How's that sound, *amigo*?"

Perez barely had the stamina to give a nod, but he found enough to do so.

"Get him to his feet," the leader said.

His legs throbbed where he had been hit, and he stood with great difficulty. Then he heard the hotel door open again. A shaft of light from the hallway burst into the room and into his eyes. Someone dropped a black hood over his head, prisoner-of-war style, and they pulled him out into the hall.

At first he thought these men were police, but now he realized they weren't. They were something else, but he didn't know what. They frog-marched him down the hallway. Then, another note of absurdity: they spoke to each other in a language he didn't understand, an Eastern European language of some sort, Czech, maybe, or Polish or Hungarian.

Where was he being taken? Out of the country? Had some foreign intelligence service grabbed him for their own inventory? Or worse, did this have something to do with the shots he had fired a few nights earlier? Was it payback for some previous mission, in Croatia perhaps ... or Afghanistan or Russia? He heard an elevator door open and he was pushed inside. The doors closed, he staggered again. Strong arms on each side of him held him up.

The elevator reached the ground floor. He felt cool air, air conditioning. The sound of automobiles. He sensed one pulling close to him. Vehicle doors opened. There was a hand on his head, and he was forced into a backseat. He could barely breathe. He was pushed low at first, then fixed upright. He guessed the windows were tinted. No one could see in. He had previously done operations like this himself, but he had never been on the receiving end. Until now.

By the sound of the tires, he realized that the vehicle was outside the garage and on the city streets. Then suddenly the hood was lifted. He had fewer than five seconds to notice the inner trappings of the van. A huge fist came directly into his face with a rag in it. The rag stank like kerosene, but he knew better. It was ether. He resisted it out of instinct, but his efforts were to no avail.

He felt himself starting to slump, then lost consciousness, having no idea who these people were or where they were taking him. And once everything went black, he no longer cared.

TWENTY-NINE

Toward 7:15 the next morning, Alex emerged from the townhouse on 38th Street. Two black Cadillac Escalades with tinted windows were waiting. Alex's bodyguards ushered her to the first one. She climbed into the backseat, and Ramirez, the looming gunman, slid into the seat on the other side. MacPhail rode shotgun up front.

They had a young driver today, a young blond man with a crew cut. He signaled to two other men in the second Escalade, and they all started to roll. Soon they were cruising through the morning traffic in the Lincoln Tunnel, and within half an hour they were barreling down the New Jersey Turnpike.

Alex attempted small talk with Ramirez and MacPhail, but they weren't talkative. She got the impression that they'd been out late. So she retreated into a book, a fantasy ghost story called *Cemetery of Angels*, then shifted to her iPod for the next few hours. Wary, but also sleepy, she managed to nap for part of the ride. When she opened her eyes, the Escalade was crossing one of the bridges from Washington, D.C., into Virginia.

Being back in the Washington area brought back a flood of memories, some of them happy, others bittersweet.

They arrived at CIA headquarters in Langley shortly after noon, passed security, and took a light lunch with a case officer who'd been assigned to babysit her until her meeting at 1:30. His name was McAdams. He was cordial, talked a lot, but said almost nothing. Alex knew that the important talk would be held behind closed doors.

She returned the small talk through lunch and waited.

The meeting was in a conference room on the second floor, east. Her babysitter led her to the door, but her bodyguards were asked to wait outside. Alex entered and waited.

Inside was a rectangular table with six empty chairs. The walls were light green, normal CIA decor, with, surprisingly, a window that overlooked an inner courtyard. Near it was an American flag in a stand. In less than a minute, Alex heard voices. The door opened and three men entered. All three wore dark suits, ID badges in plastic holders dangling across their neckties.

"Agent LaDuca," said the leader, extending a hand. "I'm Maurice Fajardie, Assistant Director/DCA, Central American Affairs, Caribbean Division. These are my associates who will also be involved in this case." He then introduced her to Curtis Sloane, in charge of overall covert intelligence pertaining to Cuba, and Tom Menendez, whose title told her that he oversaw pursuit of fugitives in the eastern Caribbean.

After handshakes all around, they sat at the table.

"So, Alex," Fajardie began, "I hear someone took a shot at you. How are you holding up?"

"The good news is they missed," she said.

"We've all been briefed on what's going on," Sloane said.

"You're quite a trooper," Menendez added with admiration.

"I feel more like a head case than anything ... that or Bambi in deer season."

There were faint smiles. She looked around the table. The two associates had their eyes fixed on her, like a couple of foxhounds waiting for a bugle.

"It was a long drive from New York," Alex said, "so let's get to it, shall we?"

THIRTY

Fajardie began, "The powers-that-be feel we can coordinate you into a fluid situation we're having right now in Cuba. Part of the plan is to keep you away from whoever might be sniping at you while putting you to work in an operation." Fajardie glanced to the others. "What do we hear from the FBI in New York?" he asked. "Anything on Perez?"

"They have a trail," Menendez said.

"Hot? Cold?" he asked.

"Getting warmer by the day," Menendez said. "I talked to someone on major cases just before lunch."

"Good," Fajardie said and turned back to Alex. "Meanwhile, we need to keep you safe and get you out of the country." He paused. "We've read the background on Paul Guarneri. There's plenty on his old man, but not much on him. He thinks there's a pile of dough sitting somewhere in Cuba, huh?"

"That's what he says."

"Hard to imagine that it's still sitting there after all these years," Menendez said. "Fidel's probably already spent it for him."

Alex shrugged. "I'm just along for the ride as far as Guarneri is concerned," she said. "My assignment is Roland Violette. I saw some initial briefing documents. I know he's a fugitive who wants to come home. That's the extent of my knowledge."

"How much do you know about Cuba?" Fajardie asked. "Politics. Background. History."

"My boss in New York brought me up to date. And I've got my own personal opinions that the embargo on Cuban goods has done more harm than good, particularly to the Cuban people. But that's just me, and I have some unpopular ideas."

"That *is* an unpopular idea around here," Fajardie volleyed back. "I think the island deserved the embargo for going Commie. But we're here to discuss something else. Fugitives. Turncoats. Traitors. That's the order of this bright day in June, isn't it? We're also in the territory of these two gentlemen. So Curtis will give you the background on fugitives in Cuba in general, then Tom will bring you up to date on a dismal excuse for a human being named Roland Violette." He paused. "We'll give you a hardcopy file and some secured flash drives to take with you, but you can only apply them twice. You're traveling with a laptop or do you need one?"

"I have one."

"Secure?"

"I wouldn't be using it if it weren't."

Another short beat, then, "Okay," Fajardie said softly. To his left, Menendez was looking at an open file, glancing up and down intermittently, while to his left, Sloane sat stiffly in place.

"Sorry," Fajardie said. "I have to ask you to sign these."

He handed her some confidentiality bonds. She looked at the documents, scanned them, and pulled her silver Tiffany pen from her purse, the one with her name on it. She signed and laid the pen on the table. She handed the documents back to Fajardie, who then turned to Sloane and said, "Okay, Curtis, amuse us."

Sloane cleared his throat, consulted his notes, and began. "By our count, 258 fugitives from U.S. law currently reside in Cuba. Our numbers are approximate because we don't have that many eyes on the street in Cuba, and some of our files go back forty, fifty years. People die, they disappear, they get off the island and disappear to other places. Like Mexico or Honduras or Guatemala."

"Even Panama?" she asked, bemused.

"Even Panama," he said. "Particularly Panama. But every once in a while one of these individuals wants to repatriate. For whatever reason. They're sick, they're ailing, they want to see a parent before they die. Change of heart even."

"All of which factor into Violette's case, from what I know," she said.

"Possibly," Sloane said. "We'll get to him in a minute. Take a recent template for his case though. Luis Soltren. That name mean anything?"

She racked her brain. A light went on. "A highjacker, right?"

"Very good!" Sloane said. "Luis Armando Peña Soltren. Age sixty-seven. Soltren surrendered to U.S. law enforcement in October 2009 after arriving on a flight from Havana. He'd been in Cuba since 1968 when, in November of that year, he and three other men forced their way into the cockpit of a Pan Am flight and diverted it to Havana. Smuggled weapons on board in a bag of disposable diapers. Such hijackings were frequent at the time, with thirty successful or attempted diversions to Cuba in 1968 alone. Anyway, there are scores of other Americans living in Cuba outside the reach of U.S. law enforcement. Most have been there for decades. Some are in plain sight; others live deep underground. The best-known American fugitive is the former Joanne Chesimard. She's sixty-two now and was a member of the radical activist organization called the Black Liberation Army. She was found guilty of first-degree murder in the shooting of a New Jersey state trooper in 1977. She escaped from prison in 1979 and was last seen in Cuba in 1984."

"Chesimard is definitely one of the top people on the list of fugitives," intoned Fajardie. "If you pick up any scent, you'll want to report it."

"She's been living in Cuba for decades under the protection of Castro," Menendez added. "In the beginning, the fugitives were treated well. Fidel used them to flip a finger at the U.S. As years went by, he got tired of them. Most were common criminals, and even the political ones were troublemakers."

"Most of these men and women have been there for a long time," said Fajardie. "Worthless bunch of losers, if you want to know. Many of them, like Soltren, hijacked planes, sought refuge, and have been living there ever since they escaped the United States. Some were members of Puerto Rican separatist groups or black nationalist organizations."

"So there's no extradition treaty?" Alex asked.

"That's a laugh," Fajardie said. "Cuba and the U.S. have had an extradition treaty since the 1920s. In 1971, the two countries signed a pact that dealt specifically with extraditing hijackers. But the U.S. hasn't extradited anyone back to Cuba, so Cuba hasn't extradited anyone back to us. The biggest fish of all was a guy named Robert Vesco. Heard of him?"

"Sure. Financial crimes are my turf, remember?" she said.

"Vesco fled to Cuba in '82 after a series of charges were brought against him in the U.S. and throughout the Caribbean," Fajardie said. "He stole $200 million from investors in the 1970s. After receiving the protection of the Cuban government, Vesco was sentenced to prison in Havana in 1996 and died from lung cancer in Havana in 2007."

"The majority of fugitives just tried to lay low," said Menendez, "hoping that when the Castro brothers finally drop dead, relations will improve. But there's not much in the way of statute of limitations for most of these people. Murder. Air piracy. Fraud. They're looking at prison time if they come back here." He paused. "Then again, they get old and start to think. The right to die on one's native soil. That's a pretty strong pull. You wouldn't think it would be, but it is."

"On the contrary," Alex said, "I would think it would account for a lot."

"And that brings us to Violette," Fajardie said. He turned to Menendez. "Tom, talk to us."

"Roland Violette," Menendez began. "Soviet mole. Traitor and first-class CIA rat."

"I second that," Sloane said.

Fajardie said, "And me, three, and Alex, four. Now run with it."

Menendez threw a stack of surveillance photos onto the desk. "Here's the ugly story," Menendez said. Alex listened as she looked through the photos. "Roland Violette was nearly born a CIA agent. His father spied for the CIA in Venezuela, Bolivia, and Colombia during the '50s and '60s, so as a kid he learned Spanish like a native. Mixed race, by the way. His father was part-Haitian, part-Anglo, but his mother was something darker. Very pretty woman, a quarter Martinican, a quarter South American Indian of some sort, the rest Spanish. Pretty volatile mix if you ask me."

"I didn't, but go ahead," Alex said.

"In 1957 Roland went to Camp Peary in Virginia. He was born in 1940, so he was seventeen at the time." Menendez steadied his gaze at her. "You know about Camp Peary, right?" he said.

"The Farm," she answered, "as it's called by those who know and loathe it. It's the CIA training facility in York County, Virginia, the one whose existence the CIA has never admitted. Specializes turning misguided, maladjusted individuals into misguided, maladjusted CIA officers."

Nods all around, some laughter, six eyes on her, two-and-a-half smiles: Fajardie was less amused than the other two. "That's the place," Menendez said.

"I even know why they call it 'The Farm,'" Alex offered.

"Okay, why?" he asked, testing her.

"During World War II, beginning in 1942, Camp Peary became a stockade for special German prisoners-of-war. Most of the POWs at Camp Peary did farm work within the camp during the war," she concluded. "Hence, the name. But back to Violette."

"Well, despite his family tree and years on The Farm," Menendez said, "Violette was one of the most damaging moles in CIA history. Starting in 1974, he sold out every spy the CIA and FBI had in Central America. He began at the CIA, recruiting locals in South America to spy on their own governments, but he didn't have much talent. Luckily for him, his assignment was with a Cuban military attaché to Honduras named Rafael Figueredo. Figueredo had already been convinced to spy for the U.S., but he wasn't useful until he was transferred to Violette's CIA department. In Violette's hands, Figueredo, who was code-named Vesper, was reassigned to the Cuban Foreign Ministry. There, he went to work and routinely photographed sensitive documents and files. So even though Roland Violette had never successfully recruited a single spy, his handling of Vesper earned him a promotion. He became the counterintelligence branch chief of Cuban operations, where he had access to information on every aspect of U.S. operations in Central America, Cuba in particular. So that brings us to 1977. Violette ran into skirt trouble."

"Imagine that," Alex said. "A man with skirt trouble."

"Violette was having an affair with a wealthy Costa Rican woman named Rica. He brought her to D.C., and it wasn't long before she started making trouble. She must have been one tropical storm in the bedroom, because she immediately demanded that Violette divorce his wife. Instead of dumping a troublesome mistress and cutting his losses, he did what Rica asked. You know what divorces are like: it nuked almost all of his savings and his assets. Yet Rica continued to spend money as if she and Violette were printing it at home, which, by this time, Violette was probably wishing he could do. His Costa Rican cutie quickly dug Violette into nearly $50,000 of debt. He became so desperate for funds that he borrowed from every friend he could tap, maxed out all his credit cards, and even considered robbing a bank. But then he remembered that the Soviets paid $75,000 for the identity of American spies working in their country. He arranged a meeting with Sergei Vassiliev of the Soviet Embassy in Washington. They met at a bistro in Georgetown, negotiated, and Violette gave up three CIA spies working in Moscow and one in Warsaw. Three men, one woman. In exchange for this information, Violette received $200,000."

"When I was at the university, or maybe even earlier," Alex said, "I learned the multiplication tables. Four times seventy five is three hundred thousand."

"The Russians bargained him down," Menendez said. "What do you expect when slimeball meets slimeball?"

"What happened to the blown spies?" Alex asked.

"Shot, three of them," Fajardie said, interjecting sharply. "That was the men. The woman was raped by several members of the Polish KGB. When they were finished with her, she was hanged by a piano wire at the Mokotów Prison in Warsaw."

Alex drew a breath. A deep, involuntary shudder of revulsion went through her. God help any Western woman who fell into the hands of such brutal enemies. Then a second wave of disgust went through her, one for Roland Violette and his various paths of betrayal, followed by a third wave, which had to do with the occupants of the room. She wondered, on a personal level, whether anything was worth a piano wire around the neck or a bullet in the back of the head.

"So who was Violette working for?" Alex asked. "The Russians or the Cubans?"

"Both," Fajardie said. "As well as himself. But face it. The Cubans were just the paw of the Russian bear. The *cubanos* didn't do anything big without the consent of their Russian masters."

There was a pause. "So, go on," Alex said. "I'm sure there's more."

Menendez continued. "Violette's tale might have ended there, except for the arrest in 1979 of another turncoat, U.S. Navy Warrant Officer Thomas Gosden, who was caught selling surveillance information to the Cubans. Violette was so afraid that Gosden would rat him out that he decided to go for a final score. He contacted his Cuban handlers first, said he wanted to go for that big grand salami to end the game. The Cubans turned him over to the Russians. Vassiliev came across with a suitcase full of dollars. A big suitcase. Maybe a million. Cash. In return, Violette squealed out every 'human asset' the CIA had in Russia that he could finger. Violette also snitched out an Italian spy and turned over twenty pounds of photocopies of documents he carried out of CIA headquarters in his briefcase. For his 'good work' in the Evil Empire days, he was privately awarded the Order of Lenin and given a bonus of another $250,000. Final total, Violette named three dozen spies. All were apprehended by either Soviet or Cuban authorities, and at least eighteen were executed. Meanwhile, the CIA transferred him to its office in Madrid."

"Been there," Alex said with detached irony. "Nice office. Right in the embassy. I know some of the people."

"You've been around, haven't you?" Fajardie said.

"You could say that."

"Just curious," Fajardie said to Alex. "How many languages do you speak?"

"English, Russian, French, Italian, and Spanish. And I fake Ukrainian."

"No Icelandic?" Sloane asked as a mild tweak.

"Not yet," she answered. "Ask me again in six weeks."

"Ever had a notion to come work for us directly?" Fajardie asked. "Don't you get bored crunching numbers at Treasury?"

"Not when bullets come flying through my window and I have to get smuggled into the only Marxist country in the hemisphere just to keep the rifle sights off me."

"Good answer," Fajardie shrugged.

He glanced to Menendez to indicate the latter could continue.

"Violette felt Rica would be happier in Spain, language and all," Menendez said. "He also wanted to distance himself from all his felonies and make things easier if he needed to make a break for an escape. He did not, however, distance himself from the greenbacks the Russians were paying him. He and his Costa Rican broad lived lavishly. His CIA salary was $80,000 a year, but Violette wore a $20,000 Patek Philippe watch on his wrist and drove a maroon Mercedes Benz 450 SL to work. And Rica, she could always find a way to burn more money. She started smoking these little gold-tipped cigarettes. Not gold paper, mind you. Tipped with gold leaf. No filter. She had them specially made by a tobacconist in Madrid. It only took the CIA five years to notice that something didn't add up. They started looking at him cross-eyed in 1982, and the crap hit the fan in '84. Arrest warrants were issued for both Violette and his wife."

He paused. Then he continued. "Somehow, however, Violette got wind of it ahead of time. They cleaned out their bank accounts and caught a plane to Tunisia, just hours ahead of the Spanish police. Everyone expected them to head to Moscow, but they had fake Bolivian passports stashed for a rainy day—and it was starting to drizzle. So they used them to fly to the Dominican

Republic from Tunisia. From there, they continued on to Havana via Mexico City. Arrival: November 1984. Same day Ronald Reagan got reelected."

"And they've been there since?"

"As far as we know. Both went underground — one in one way, the other in another." Menendez paused. He smirked. "There were stories that Rica had left him, threw him over for a Frenchman named Jean Antoine who ran a restaurant in Havana. Jean Antoine was one of Violette's friends but apparently stole his wife. Or maybe just rented her. She wasn't seen with Violette for several years, but if she had a fling, it didn't last. She came back before she died. Our reports are that Violette forgave his friend. Other reports say that he didn't. But he did take his wife back before the little gold-tipped cancer sticks killed off Rica in 2004," he said. "She's buried in the Cementerio de Cristóbal Colón in the Vedado neighborhood of Havana. She's got her own mausoleum. Violette paid for it even though his money was running out."

"I'm surprised he didn't have her stuffed and mounted," Sloane said. "You know? Like Juan Perón did for Evita and Roy Rogers did for Trigger."

"Knock it down a level, would you?" Fajardie said.

Alex looked back to Menendez. "Okay. So then where are we?"

"Violette's making noises about coming back to the United States," Fajardie said. "This you know, and this is where you come in. We got several messages through the American-interests section of the Swiss Embassy in Havana," Fajardie said. "He's seventy-eight years old, cuckoo, and his wife's dead. He has an aging mother here in the U.S., a brother, and a sister. We get the idea his health isn't good. He's ready to make a deal and come home. He's been gone for a quarter century. A little more, actually."

"That's not so long ago in terms of the intelligence community's memory," Alex said. "I notice that some people would still like to have his head on a plate."

"Three of them are in this room," said Menendez, "not just for what he did but to serve notice to anyone who does something similar in the future. A roulette wheel has no memory but this agency has a long one."

"I follow that part," Alex said. She turned to Fajardie. "But how do you know Violette really wants to defect back? Maybe he's just teasing. Or he's got some final double-double game going."

"American-interests section of the Swiss Embassy," Fajardie said. "As I said. They assess it as serious, although everyone agrees that the man is completely unstable. One day he wants to come back, next day he's not so sure. So he needs enticement."

"He's been negotiating a deal," Menendez said.

"I understand that," Alex said, "but how do you know he really wants to defect back? Maybe your information's wrong. Dare I say, it often is."

"It isn't," Fajardie snapped. His tone was frosty. "It isn't, and we want him back. If we can coax him onto a plane, we need to do it." He paused. "We're told that he still has an eye for the ladies. So what better way than to send someone like you, Alex—good-looking, obviously in our employ, versatile in English and Spanish—to entice him onto an aircraft off the island? Bringing with him," Fajardie added in conclusion, "any goodies he might have for us. Anything he's toting would be just a bonus. Much appreciated, but a bonus." He paused. "So if you could drop in on a meeting with him and get him onto the small aircraft that we're going to arrange to lift you and him and your Mafia pal out of there ...? Well, that would be a wonderful thing for everyone, wouldn't it?"

Alex watched the eye contact between the three men shoot around the table, like the ball in an old arcade game. Pinball wizards, all of them. The Who's deaf, dumb, and blind kid would have loved this trio. But in the eye contact, she wondered what she wasn't being told. What and how much.

"What are you going to do with him once you get him back?" she asked. "Take him out to tea? Pin a medal on his chest? Push him out a window?"

"Don't be silly," Fajardie said.

"I'm not being silly. I'm asking. I know it's unusual for someone with a sense of ethics to be sitting in front of you, but that's what you have here. So maybe you could answer my question?"

"There's not much we *can* do if he sets foot on American soil, Alex," Fajardie answered. "He's worked out a deal through lawyers in New York. I'm not even a party to it, but I do know that if we violated it once he's back, we'd be looking at criminal and civil suits for a decade, from him or his dear relatives. He's not worth it, Alex. We're just trying to button up some old business."

Alex was about to ask more when Sloane resumed. "It's all in the file we're going to give you. Everything that we know. Take it with you. You'll move toward Cuba the day after tomorrow."

"We want Violette before he changes his mind," Fajardie said, "which he changes as quickly as he changes his underwear, assuming anyone has spare underwear in Cuba these days."

"And you're sure the man you're dealing with is the real thing?" Alex asked. "Ronald Violette?"

"There are some correspondences," Sloane said, easing slightly, "handwritten. Violette's proposals to us via the Swiss. We had the handwriting analyzed. It's him. We know that." He paused. "There are scans of the letters. You can take a look."

"Just curious. Are they in English or Spanish?" she asked.

"English. Does it matter?"

"No," Alex said.

"Good," Fajardie said. He plopped a bound file on the table between them, plus a smaller envelope containing the flash drives.

"Take a look at this stuff tonight," he said, "and call me with any questions. Meanwhile, tomorrow morning, the agency will outfit you for your trip. Passport. Weapon. Money. After that, you're on your way."

Fajardie eased back for a moment, appearing as if he was proposing to say something further. Alex held onto the silence.

Finally, Fajardie uncorked. "Ronald Violette," he said, "the shrinking Violette. He won't be forced, Alex. He must be nursed along. Prodded and cajoled, charmed, tricked, or bamboozled. He flirts with leaving the island, then never does. But the time might finally be right. So he needs to be goosed, juiced, reduced, deduced, or seduced — or anything to get him onto that aircraft. Clear? Opaque? Transparent? That's your assignment, Alex, and you'll probably have one roll of the dice over his morning shot of rum. Anything. Just get his filthy traitorous butt on that plane out of there in any way you can. Fun, right?"

"Fun," she said.

"Which reminds me, if you can get us some Havana Club or a handful of Cohibas or Bolivars, it wouldn't be a bad thing, either."

"I thought you disagreed with the embargo," she said.

"I do. But I have my own personal needs as a drinker and a smoker, all right?" He winked. She eyed the file, her mind a warren of doubts. Then, for some reason, her own brief career flew before her mind's eye, as well as that of Roland Violette. What did she have in front of her, sandwiched between the covers of a manila envelope, other than a testament to an aging man's life?

How should he be seen, and how should she see him if she found him in Cuba? As a man who had set out to achieve one set of goals but then had worked toward the opposite? A man who had betrayed others? Or, in his bizarre fidelity to his lifetime companion, Rica, was he a man who had found a higher loyalty and been true to that instead? For a moment, she tried to push ideology aside. Surely, Violette could see through capitalist values much the same way she could see through Communist ones. She wondered what it could have been like to make such a step of loyalty to one's partner that one was obligated to spend the back end of one's life in a place as isolated as Cuba.

"I'm still not buying this completely. If Violette is so widely hated here, why bring him back at all?" she asked. "Other than to prosecute him. Why cut him any sort of a deal?"

"We make deals with people we hate every day," Fajardie said. "Plus, if you want me to be ornery, it's not your job to wonder about such things. It's your role to either accept the mission, argue out of it, or resign. The choice is yours."

"I figured you'd explain it that way," she said, thinking about the two million dollars in the bank, then thinking about the bullets that crashed through her apartment window.

"Is there any other way to explain it?" Fajardie asked graciously.

"None at all," Alex said with a sigh. "I get where you're coming from." She reached forward and accepted the files, and with them the assignment in Havana. "Okay," she said. "I don't like it, but okay."

"That's kind of my attitude every morning in this place," Fajardie said. "Why should you be living a different life than I am?"

"No reason I should," she said. They missed her sarcasm.

Fajardie turned to Sloane and Menendez. "Thank you, gentlemen," he said. They rose and were out the door in another minute. Alex would have followed, but she felt Fajardie's hand on her wrist. Then he released. He glanced back to the table and indicated she should sit again.

"A final detail or two, Alex," he said. He moved to the door and closed it.

It was obvious to Alex that Fajardie had something significant to add. She sat.

"A couple of creeps those guys," he muttered of the duo that had just left.

"Imagine *that* in this agency," she said.

"Yeah, right," he agreed. "And now I'm going to be one too."

"Want to spit it out?" she asked.

"I'm going to tell you your *real* assignment in Cuba."

Alex stiffened slightly.

"There's a larger issue there," Fajardie said. "Potentially a huge one. It will most likely develop on your visit, but it's absolutely at the top level at this moment. Well beyond the purview of those two clowns who just left."

"Wait a minute," Alex asked. "Is the Violette operation genuine or not?"

"Absolutely," Fajardie said, "and it's the perfect cover within the agency for your second task in Cuba. There is, in fact, a second defector, a much more important one, who is holding a top-drawer bag of goodies for us. 'Figaro,' we're supposed to call him, until we learn more. *I* am not even sure who he is, but the package he's selling is quite impressive. Potentially a first-rate defector with two eyes on the future, whereas Brother Violette is of the third-rate variety with one bleary eye on the past. Follow?"

"Vaguely. This Figaro — is that his cover name or one our side gave him?"

"His, I believe. Why?"

"A theory of mine," she said, warming to the subject, "which has been borne out in recent times. The more one conceals an identity the more one reveals it."

"And what does 'Figaro' tell you?"

"Well, what are the associations? The original Figaro was a character in a pair of eighteenth-century French plays, who then became a character in an opera by Mozart and an opera by Rossini. Figaro was a barber — the "barber of Seville" — who was a subversive against the ruling class. If a Cuban took the name, it suggests an unusual affinity for European culture. Unless, of course, it means nothing."

"The Figaro issue began about two years ago. There was some sort of flap involving a Spanish passport," Fajardie said. "I saw that part of the file. Not my department, and I'm not the case officer. I'm *your* case officer but not Figaro's. I don't suppose that connects to anything, does it, the Spanish passport?"

"It might," Alex said.

"How?"

"I spent some time in Madrid last year. I suspect you're referring to one of the provisions of *Le Ley de Memoria Histórica*. Several thousand Spaniards fled Spain during the 1936–39 Civil War, as well as during the Franco regime, and settled in Cuba. Only a handful are still alive. But they, their children, and grandchildren now hold legal rights to Spanish citizenship. It's part of the reconciliation process put forth by the current Spanish government. Seville, by the way, is in Spain, so there's a subtle subtext with your Figaro. He's not the Tailor of Saville Row in London; he's the barber in Spain."

She looked at Fajardie and wasn't sure if she was connecting.

"So you think he's a barber?" he asked.

"It's always possible, but how would an ordinary barber have access to anything important? More likely he has an affinity for opera. Or Spain."

"Could be," said Fajardie.

"Before we overthink the point," she added, "I'll also point out that Figaro was a kitten in Pinocchio, and it's also a chain of pizza joints in Los Angeles. So I'm as wary of overthinking as you are, okay?"

"I'm told Figaro was supposed to get a Spanish passport but didn't," Fajardie said, expanding. "That's unofficial."

"If a Cuban got Spanish citizenship and a Spanish passport, he — or she — could leave immediately," Alex said. "Sounds like the Cuban government prevented this individual from getting a passport and exiting."

"Only one reason they'd do that," Fajardie said.

"Sure," Alex said. "If he worked for the government or in defense or in anything sensitive, the government wouldn't *want* him to leave."

"That jibes with the scuttlebutt. He wanted to vamoose and they wouldn't let him. The *they* in my sentence is the Castro government. And they'd have to be watching him pretty closely. So he had to be waiting for the perfect moment to slip his leash. He's probably looking for someone from our side to contact him. He wants to find us. That's where you come in. If he makes the wrong move at the wrong time, they'll shoot him. And anyone helping him."

"How do you know Figaro's a man?" Alex asked.

Fajardie shrugged. "We don't, but we've assumed it from the information."

"Might be a foolish assumption," Alex said. "You never know about the demure middle-aged woman who's been a party functionary for years. She's quiet and outgoing, but seething beneath the surface and ready to clean out the vault."

No response. Then, "Maybe," Fajardie said with absolute certainty, "our Figaro has already slipped us some engaging tidbits. Apparently, Figaro worked as part of a high-level Cuban delegation to Iraq in 1991. He says that, based on intelligence from a Russian spy facility at Lourdes in Cuba, the delegation had tried to convince Saddam Hussein that he could not win a war against the U.S. He claims to have met Saddam on several occasions. Do you know the name Arnoldo Ochoa?" Fajardie asked.

"No."

"General Ochoa was the commander of Cuba's intervention in Angola in the 1980s. He was scheduled to take over the most powerful and important command in Cuba after Angola. But he began speaking against Cuban *colonialismo* in Africa and in favor of *glasnost*, the new openness of Soviet President Gorbachev. Soon afterward, Ochoa was convicted of narco-trafficking. He was executed in 1989 with Fidel Castro's permission. With his death, as when Che Guevara died in Bolivia, a popular and powerful potential rival to the president was eliminated. The real reason Ochoa was executed was political. We never knew that." Fajardie laughed. "What does that tell you about Fidel and his regime? Fidel was pleased when Che died and pleased when Ochoa died. He is a low-budget Stalin who would never tolerate his Trotsky."

"This is news?" Alex asked.

"The people on the sixth floor crave this stuff. What can I say?"

"So? What am I supposed to do about Figaro?" Alex asked after another moment.

"Keep your eyes and ears open. Be prepared to think on your noble feet, and if anything comes up while you have your boots on the ground in Cuba, rope him in. Bring him to the U.S. Getting Violette up here would be a home run. Bringing in Figaro, I'm told, would be a grand slam."

"I assume I don't mention any of this to my travel companion," she said.

Fajardie laughed. "Absolutely not!" he said. "The only one you mention this to is me. And the aforesaid Figaro if you meet him."

"If I'm lucky enough to find him," she said.

"No," Fajardie said in conclusion. "There's no chance that you will find him. As I said, Figaro will find you—or it doesn't happen at all."

THIRTY-ONE

MacPhail and Ramirez checked Alex into Washington's Madison Hotel that evening. The two agents sat outside her door, waiting to be relieved overnight by agents from a local office. Even the room service waiter had to pass a security check.

After 8:00 p.m., Alex opened her laptop. She had a soft drink on ice after changing out of her meeting clothes into a T-shirt and jeans. Might as well be comfortable. Tonight, the Madison was the crown jewel of the American protective-custody system. Five floors below, along 15th Street, traffic rumbled along. As her computer booted, Alex walked to the window and pushed back the curtain.

Was she still in danger? she wondered. Was another sniper preparing to pick her off? Maybe the same sniper? But she felt like a fugitive. She used to live in Washington and, by and large, enjoyed her time here. She used to move around freely as a younger woman. Restaurants, clubs, the gym.

She had a man in her life back then, someone she loved. She enjoyed her various promotions, the career excitement. Then abruptly the disaster and tragedy in Kiev struck. Now, more recently, there was the promotion to her job in New York. Yet fate and emotions kept pushing her back down. Tonight she felt overwhelmed and lonely. She thought about the two million sitting in a bank account for her in New York. She drew a long breath. Why did God allow her to get that money?

But as long as that sniper was out there, she couldn't lead a normal life. Most other women her age had families, husbands, or steady relationships. What, she asked herself, did she have to show? She had the burden of a job in which she could get her head blown off. So why did she keep doing it? What if God intended for her to use that money to get away from it all?

She continued to gaze out the window, making herself a target as she stood. She watched couples, presumably happy, going to movies, bars, and restaurants. Right at this moment, Alex would have traded places with any of them.

Then her thoughts tripped a mental landmine, one of sadness and longing, one of still painfully missing her late fiancé. The memories set off a worse wave of loneliness within her, one she fought almost every day for at least a few moments. Intellectually she had accepted what had happened in Kiev, but emotionally she hadn't.

She let the curtain close. She didn't feel like working. She didn't feel like praying more. So, dragging herself back to the laptop, she accessed the flash drives the CIA had given her and poured through the files that Maurice Fajardie had provided. It was tedious stuff, poorly organized and repetitive. It added nothing to what he had presented to her in person. But she plodded through it.

Roland Violette came off as the loosest of cannons. She read copies of his most recent correspondence to the CIA, frequently struggling with Violette's drifting handwriting—and his reasoning, which drifted even more obliquely.

> The cold war ended in 1986, but the true struggle lies before us ...
>
> The socio-economic exploitation of the population of Central and South America has exceeded anything Karl Marx could have imagined ...
>
> I love America and its ideals very deeply ...

And, almost inexplicably,

> Even if greedy America were knocked out of the game by heroic Islamic fundamentalism, the price of fish in Lima, Peru, would hardly be altered.

The latter was the opening salvo in a wandering five-thousand-word essay that tortured Alex's ability to read.

After more than an hour, she had read enough and seen enough to understand the assignment. She went to her cell phone and called her friend Ben, who lived just a few blocks away.

The phone rang once, twice—

"Well, I can leave him a message," she thought to herself. "He's probably at the gym playing basketball. Or maybe he's with his girlfriend."

Three rings. A fourth.

"Maybe we could chat later when—"

Then Ben picked up.

"Hey," she said, almost in surprise.

A pause, then, *"Alex?"*

"Really," she said. "Your favorite head case. The one and only."

"What the—! What a nice surprise!" He paused a little awkwardly. "How are things?"

"Oh, they're okay," she said. "Hey, listen ..."

"Yeah?"

"I'm in Washington."

"You're what? *Now*?"

"I'm in town," she said, rallying. "Passing through. One overnight and—"

"And you didn't tell me in advance? I'm hurt."

"It happened suddenly. Part of a case I'm on," she said. She hesitated. "But I've got a little time later. Want to talk?"

"Where are you?"

"At the Madison Hotel."

He laughed. "Slumming, huh?"

"Right. At the taxpayers' expense. Listen, I only called to talk and—"

"So let's talk in person," he said.

She turned and glanced at her door and pictured her guards beyond it. "Oh, I don't think that would be possible," she said, "but—"

"Come on, Alex," he said. "You're here in town. Let's get together."

"Ben, it's complicated," she said. "I'm on an assignment. I'm dealing with some bad people, okay? That's why I'm passing through quickly and — "

Her voice wavered for a moment as memories came flooding back. She remembered the night Ben had convinced her not to commit suicide and saved her life. She remained quiet as she regained her composure.

"You there?" he asked.

"I'm here. Hey. Wait for a second, okay?"

"Of course."

She thought for a moment, rose, and went to the door. She opened it. MacPhail and Ramirez were sitting outside, playing cards.

"Hey . . . ," she said, putting a hand over her phone.

MacPhail looked up. "Problem?" he asked.

"Listen, guys. I know I'm under some form of high-rent house arrest," she said, "but do you mind if I have a friend come over?"

The Feds looked at each other. "We're not supposed to let anyone in the room with you unless we're there, Alex," MacPhail said. "Those are the instructions. Isn't that going to cramp your style?"

"Not in the slightest."

"Oh, it's a 'friend' friend?" MacPhail asked.

"That's what I'm trying to get across. So how about the restaurant downstairs? Can I meet a guy for a drink?"

"You buying for the four of us?"

"No. You are, Walter," she said.

The Feds looked at each other again, back and forth. "We got to go with you and watch the door," MacPhail said. "You know that. Unless you're in that room by yourself we can't take our eyes off you."

"That's fine. In fact, I appreciate it. So how about the bar?"

Ramirez shrugged. "Sure," he said.

"Good," Alex said. "We'll do it."

"Go for it," Ramirez said.

She gave her bodyguards a thumbs-up and went back into her hotel room. She closed the door.

"So?" Ben asked.

"Be at the Madison Hotel in ninety minutes. Fifteenth and M Street."

"I know where it is," Ben said.

THIRTY-TWO

Alex settled in at the far end of the bar and waited. The room was sleekly modern, an offshoot of Palette, the adjacent restaurant. The counter was light wood, and the cylindrical hanging lamps echoed the shape of liquor bottles. Tall, comfortable stools flanked the bar.

MacPhail and Ramirez took up positions near the door that led to the lobby. Alex scanned the room. It was moderately busy. She saw at least one congressman and a gaggle of lobbyists. She waited.

Alex saw Ben before he saw her. She lifted an arm and gave a subdued wave. He spotted her. He was in jeans and a polo shirt and looked fit and happy, with only a slight limp. He came directly to her and didn't even notice when she gave a nod to her FBI babysitters to indicate that this was her friend and he was okay.

"Hey," he said in greeting.

"Hey," she answered.

She slid off the stool into his embrace. It was longer than it needed to be, but she went with it. She felt his lips linger on her cheek. Then he released her, and she installed herself back on the barstool.

"No hard feelings?" she asked.

"From what?" He eased onto the chair next to her.

"I didn't like the way we said good-bye ... in New York."

"Nah." He waved her off. "It's forgotten. We're friends."

"You're okay with that?"

He shrugged and winked. "I'm allowed to keep hoping that something might change, right?" he said, gently teasing. "I mean, no law against wishful thinking, right?"

"You're allowed," Alex answered.

The bartender appeared, and Ben ordered for himself and Alex. Alex glanced over at MacPhail and Ramirez. Ramirez gave her a goofy grin and a thumbs-up. She scowled back just as Ben turned back to her.

"So?" he asked. "What sort of trouble you in now?"

She blew out a long breath. "I'm making a trip out of the country. That's all I can tell you. It's against the rules even to say that much. I'm nervous and scared, and I need someone friendly to settle me down."

"Okay," he said. He put his hand on hers. "I'm here."

"Thank you. That means a lot."

"Between us, there were threats against me in New York. So I'm dropping off the radar and taking what might loosely be called a short-term foreign posting, also known as keeping my head down and trying not to get killed. If I seem blasé about it," she concluded, "that's a huge feint, because I'm nervous as a dozen scared cats, but you're the one person I can bare my soul to. How's that?"

"Lousy," he said. "And I know you well enough to see how shook up you are."

"It's that obvious?"

"To me," he said. The drinks arrived. Ben continued, "You going alone?"

She hesitated. "I can't tell you that."

He looked at her strangely. "Someone you work with?"

"No. Someone I know. I can't tell you the name."

As he tried to decipher the situation, Alex began to feel the whole conversation was going the wrong way. "Someone you're involved with?" he asked after a long pause.

"No," she answered immediately. "And, Ben, don't ask questions like that."

"Why not?"

"Because I asked you not to. Please?"

"Okay, okay," he said.

"Ben, I need a friend right now. I need you to be that friend, to have a strong shoulder, and to believe in what I'm doing. Without asking questions. Can you do that?"

"Maybe," he said. "I'll try. It's just that . . . you come to D.C., I see you, I think I'm over you and can accept the way things are, and I take one look at you, and it all goes in another direction. I'm *not* over you. *That's* what."

She steepled her fingers in front of herself. She didn't know whether to cry or scream. She should have known this was a bad idea. Out of the corner of her eye, she saw her two FBI guards. It was 11:00 p.m., and they were watching ESPN's Sports Center more carefully than they were watching her.

"How long have you known this guy?" Ben asked.

She quickly calculated. "Just shy of a year," she answered.

Ben leaned back on the stool. He seemed to stretch slightly, then settled again. "Wow," he said. "That explains a lot."

"What does it explain?" she asked, turning the conversation around.

"Why you were never interested in pursuing anything with me," he said. "There was someone else. You might have at least told me. Or mentioned it."

"Ben, I don't need this right now. It's not why I asked you to come over. And I'm not involved with Paul. It's a professional assignment."

"Yeah, right, okay," he said sullenly, hearing but not listening. "We'll just be buddies. I'll listen to what you have to say. I won't get mad, and I won't tell you how much I burn with envy and jealousy over the guy you're traveling with."

She put a hand on him, but he seemed unreceptive. In the back of her mind, a voice told her that she should have left him alone this evening.

He looked down into his drink.

"I asked you over as a friend," she said.

"Sure," he answered. "But you just play around with me, you know that? Just play around." He looked her squarely in the eye. "I'm in love with you. You know that."

She was unable to respond.

"There," he said, "I said it. It's in the open. Do you think that's meaningless? Does it bother you? Don't answer any of this," he continued quickly, "because anything you say will make things worse." He paused. "But I've given you plenty to think about, haven't I?"

"I already had plenty, Ben," she said.

"And now you have more," he said. He leaned over and kissed her on the cheek.

"There," he said. "That makes me happy and probably makes your FBI guys happy as well, or it would if they were paying any attention. The only person it doesn't make happy, I'd guess, is you. But at least I told you. If you don't come back from this trip, wherever you're going, at least I got to say it once."

He stepped from the stool and downed the end of his drink.

"Good night, Ben," she said.

"Good night, Alex."

She watched him in the mirror behind the bar as he disappeared out the door, his limp more pronounced than when he arrived. She stayed, in frustration. A lonely businessman at the far end of the bar sidled over to her and attempted a clumsy late-evening no-one-is-ugly-after-midnight pickup.

She indulged him with conversation for a few minutes, then went upstairs by herself. By then, the night team had relieved MacPhail and Ramirez. In her room, she lay awake, wondering what had just happened — and why.

Then she slept.

THIRTY-THREE

Alex woke up early the next morning and opened her laptop. There were documents in her secure email. Nothing of much importance from Rome. Gian Antonio Rizzo had managed to cadge a few files — a half dozen official ones plus one extra from his private stock. They reaffirmed what she already knew about Roland Violette. At least there were no glaring discrepancies. In his email, which was dated the previous evening, June 7, he sent these seven items along with a funny, literate, affectionate, flirtatious, mildly obscene and thoroughly decadent note in Italian. *"Mia Carissima Alejandra,"* he wrote in Italian,

> As you continue to contact me for sources and the deep dark background of these sordid matters, I conclude that you have chosen me to serve as your personal Mephistopheles. Elated at the anointment, I note that Mephistopheles first appeared in the Faustian legend as one of the seven princes of hell. There are seven deadly sins in the Bible. A Roman, I come from the city of "i sette colli"—the seven hills. Today is the seventh of June. Coincidences, Alex? I believe not! Hence, I forward these seven files to you, my wicked, divine, beautiful American friend, with only one regret—that they are transmitted electronically and not on seven ragged fragments of human skin, upon which they deserve to be. May these seven items bring you better luck than they brought to those discussed therein . . .

Rizzo then proceeded to regale her with personal news. He had apparently lost both his heart and the final vestiges of his common sense to his young associate Mimi, a girl one third his age, and one of his best code breakers in Rome. They were heading off on holiday together to Vietnam, stopping in Los Angeles on the way so they could both go to Disneyland. He noted in closing that he was booked on an Alitalia Boeing 777.

What a world. And this was how Alex's *friends* behaved.

She was disappointed that Gian Antonio didn't have more, but at least he had made her laugh. When she closed out of that correspondence, she glanced at the time on her monitor. It was noon in Europe. Just now the U.S. Embassy in Madrid had sent their file on Roland Violette. It was from Peter Wilkins, her CIA case officer in Spain. There were some attachments of significant size.

Alex ordered breakfast from room service and scanned the new material. Breakfast arrived. She kept reading. One document considerably piqued her curiosity.

Soviet espionage efforts against the United States via Roland Violette

Document USSR/2007/10/12/cia- Esp.hg.7

On July 9th, 1983, the US Central Intelligence Agency intercepted a series of memos in Caracas, Venezuela, in which two Soviet consular officials discussed the contributions of a compromised intelligence officer who had been formerly assigned to Central American affairs in Langley. They mused about the possibility of obtaining confidential files generated by Secretary of State George Schultz vis-à-vis continuing efforts against (a) the government of Daniel Ortega in Nicaragua and (b) all upper-level government officials in Cuba, including Fidel and Raúl Castro. One of the Soviet officials had commented that they may get the letter from "Vortex," apparently a code name for the bribed CIA official in Langley, and belittled "Vortex" for his excessive and ostentatious display of personal jewelry, including a wristwatch that cost more than half his annual salary.

Examining officer's note: It has never been established when surveillance efforts actually commenced on Violette, but it is believed that attention settled upon him following the interception of the Cuban memos. He was tipped by the Israeli service he was supplying: GHL 01/23/05

Mention was also made that Vortex had married a Costa Rican woman with expensive tastes who was currently spending him into oblivion in "the best style of a devoutly capitalist Central American woman of a privileged family ..."

None of this was new. The memo only put an exclamation point on what Alex already knew, rather than to add question marks. The fact that Violette had been a renegade agent was history. But the memo, she noted, was the beginning of crazy Roland Violette's unraveling. It was curious that he had finally become undone by comments made by his Soviet handlers, rather than observation by his peers. In retrospect, to Alex's suspicious eye, the man had been off-kilter twenty-five to thirty years ago. Why hadn't anyone said anything, made inquiries, called in the attention of superiors?

Alex wondered who might have been protecting Violette, and why. Who had been the extra gardener for the corrupt little flower, if anyone? Under normal circumstances, she might have followed the flow of this and seen where it led. She made a mental note to examine this at greater length later on, if she ever had the time.

And yet, no matter what sort of nut case he had now turned

into, she was increasingly steadfast in her desire to bring Violette back to the U.S. The Madrid files added a few tidbits. Fifteen agents, possibly as many as twenty-one, lay in Cold War graves due to this man.

At one time there had been a plan to send some Miami Cubans into Cuba, grab him, and return him, Eichmann-style, to the U.S. But that plan had been nixed at the cabinet level during the administration of Bush 41. Rendition, which would gain favor with a later administration, was considered downright impolitic and incorrect in the pre-9/11 world. That nixed the abduction plan, as did the fact that Violette had a few doubles at the time, and it would have been a further embarrassment to the CIA to have broken every rule of international law and emerged with the wrong individual.

Must be a great package of goods he's planning to bring back, Alex concluded, if he's really planning at all. Tempers hadn't subsided over the years. There was an undertone of rage to almost all the notes on the case.

She was about to exit her email when another curious dispatch was smacked down in her account. It was a forwarded document from an anonymous sender within the FBI, a series of emails with names and addresses removed, forwarded to her as an "undisclosed recipient" from a sender who was equally undisclosed. It had to do with Paul Guarneri.

Overnight, some busybody—*MacPhail? Ramirez?* she wondered—had inquired from the U.S. Passport Service and subsequently the IRS—whether Paul Guarneri was eligible to leave the country, financially speaking. Did he have a valid passport, did he have any warrants outstanding, tax debts, civil liens, criminal investigations pending, child support overdue? Overnight, the gnomes of the IRS had been prowling, bureaucratic meddling and snooping at its finest. The inquiries stopped just short of investigating whether he had been good to his mother and was kind to animals. The inquisitors had failed to find anything. Paul Guarneri, in fact, seemed to have graduated from their probes with a certain fiduciary pedigree. He paid his taxes properly, had nothing derogatory lurking anywhere, and, from a quick assessment, was personally worth five to seven million dollars, while sitting astride a real estate empire worth several times that, even taking into account outstanding debt, which seemed to be minimal. In the end, the gnomes seemed to be on Paul's side, cheering him on, if anything. Aside from the associations of his birth, if Paul had come off any cleaner, he would have been squeaky.

She finished breakfast and closed the files. She packed up the flash drives and the hard copy CIA file. She showered and dressed.

MacPhail and Ramirez were in the hallway and wished her a good morning when she popped open the door.

"Sleep well?" she asked. "Feel good?"

"No," MacPhail answered.

"No," Ramirez echoed.

"Me neither," she said. "But I'm packed and ready. Let's get out of here."

THIRTY-FOUR

That afternoon at Langley, Alex again spent time with Thomas Meachum in the Technical Resources Division on the second floor of the main CIA building. Meachum was in charge of providing her documents and equipment. From a file in his office, he pulled out an assortment of documents, all with recent photographs of Alex. On top was the forged Canadian passport in the name of Josephine Marie LeSage, the name she had used in Cairo. Beneath it was the U.S. passport that she had used in Ukraine. Meachum looked at the two passports, compared the pictures, glanced at Alex, and raised a bemused eyebrow.

"Do you remember the name you used in Ukraine?" he asked.

"Anna Marie Tavares," she said.

"Very good," he said. "Date of birth? Place of birth? Remember what we did last time you were Anna Tavares?"

It took her a second. Then she recalled the formula.

"I think you took my real normal birthday, December twenty-fourth, and cut it in half. Twelve twenty-four became six twelve. And I was born in Los Angeles, right?"

"Good memory," he acknowledged.

From the folder, Meachum pulled a new item that the CIA had just concocted, using pictures on file. It was a Mexican passport in the name of Anna Marie Tavares, complete with a photograph of Alex.

"You're the same *chica*," he said, "but you're *mexicana* now."

"Muchas gracias," she said.

"De nada."

She examined the passport. It looked just like the standard Mexican government issue because it was. Like her ersatz American one, it had been backdated to reflect an issue of June 2007.

Entry stamps had been impressed into it from Ireland, France, and Ukraine.

"We continued the same persona that we created for you for Kiev," he said, "but we made you a year younger and changed your birthplace to Mazatlan. Aside from that everything is the same."

"That's fine," Alex said.

"Do you need to review the bible on your persona? We have it here."

"I'll take a look to refresh myself, but I think I remember."

"I'll add the usual precautions," Meachum said. "Don't bring any items with monograms. Same for magazines with labels or books with your name in them. If you want an address book, create a new one — or better yet, don't bring one."

"Uh-huh. I'll be traveling light," she said. "By boat. Hopefully we'll be in and out in five or six days. So I'm not bringing a library. Not even a Kindle."

He laughed. "Okay, notice those travel stamps," he said. "Ireland, France, and Ukraine. They're there because you've been to all three. Have cover stories for your trips, and note the days of entry and exit. Just in case you're quizzed by the Cuban police."

"A situation I'd like to avoid," she said.

"Yeah," he said, without expanding on the thought. "Please do. For everyone's sake, including your own. No Cuban police. Please."

Meachum began opening envelopes and pulling out supporting material.

There was a Mexican driver's license, valid, he claimed, which used another file photo of her. Then there were a pair of credit cards: MasterCard and American Express, plus an ATM card from Banco Azteca.

"These are both live credit cards," he said. "But only use the MasterCard. You can expense up to a thousand dollars on it, no questions asked, but be cautious. The Amex card is now a 'fly trap,'" he said. "If used, each card will function up to $200 but will issue an immediate alert that something has gone wrong. The ATM card will only work in a teller machine that takes photographs. If primed, it will send a picture immediately to the State Department as to the location plus the photo of the user."

"Even from Cuba?" she asked.

"Even from Cuba. The ATM card can be used as a distress sign. If we see you in the ATM photo, we're good. If we see someone else, that means trouble. Okay?"

"Got it," Alex said. "There must be a PIN number too."

"Today's date, day and month."

"Easy enough."

"I assume you'll want to carry a gun," he said.

"I have a Glock. Should I bring it?"

"No," Meachum said. "We'll provide one when you get to Florida. We're going to have an FBI agent meet your plane in Miami. His name's Frank Cordero. He'll have artillery for you. We don't want your personal issue going to Cuba."

"Okay," she said.

"I also have maps," he said, unfolding two. They were with the passport. "We're giving you a Havana street map and a map of the entire island. The maps are not waterproof, so no matter what happens on the boat, keep these suckers dry, okay?"

"Of course," she said.

There was a brief rap on the door. Meachum answered with a raised voice. The door opened. Maurice Fajardie stepped in.

"Hey," he said, looking at Alex. Fajardie shut the door behind him. He was alone today.

"Where are your two talking bookends?" Alex asked.

"Who?"

"Menendez and Sloane," she said.

There was a pause, a rueful grin. "On to other things," he said.

"Bigger and better?" she asked.

Fajardie took a place on the table, not at it but on it, sitting on the edge. "Just 'other things,' " he answered.

"I'm finishing up," Meachum said to Fajardie.

"Fine. Go ahead," Fajardie said. "I need a few minutes at the end."

Meachum turned back to Alex. "Now here's the best stuff," he said, opening a small box and bringing out a small plastic case that looked to be about six by eight inches. Out of it, he pulled three envelopes, also plastic.

The envelopes zipped open and shut. Indicating the first, Meachum said, "Money. Cuban pesos, about five hundred dollars' worth. This is the soft currency that's used on the island. No one wants it, but the captive population of the island has to take it." He went to a second envelope. "Mexican pesos, in keeping with your passport. About the same amount." He went to the third envelope and opened it. "American greenbacks. Lovely, huh. A thousand dollars, mostly fives, tens, and twenties. Everyone wants those."

"Including us," Fajardie said. "Bring back as much as you can and we'll party."

"Fat chance," Meachum said. "We're a bunch of tightwads these days."

"Darn," Fajardie said. "Not like old times."

Meachum put all three envelopes back into the plastic container along with the maps. He tucked Alex's new passport and bank cards in with them. They made a flat little package. There were straps on the case.

"You're going into Cuba at night on a boat," he said. "It could get wet, it could get rocky, it could get rough in more ways than I care to enumerate," he said. "So do yourself a favor. Strap this to your leg somewhere during the boat ride. You never know."

"Should I expect trouble?" she asked.

"You never know," Meachum said. "You might be greeted as a liberator. You might be shot on sight. Or both."

Alex turned on Meachum, displeased with his failed attempt at humor, and was prepared to react angrily. But Meachum didn't notice. Instead, he looked at Fajardie. "That's it from me," Meachum said.

Fajardie, seeing Alex's displeasure, took over the informal meeting. "Alex, you'll have a little trade craft that you'll need to master while you're on assignment," he said as she turned toward him. "Fortunately, the trade craft is simple. I'll run through it. Once you get to Cuba, get yourself into Havana," he said. "I think Paul Guarneri should be able to help you around. He's known to us and we feel he's dependable. Nonetheless, we're having some people down in Florida give him the same briefing that we're giving you, including a background cover story, where you met, favorite romantic movie, favorite restaurant, the works. I'd suggest you go over the cover story the night before you leave so you have it down. Later on, when you get to Havana you'll have the maps. Examine them before you set sail also. There's a list of dead drops in Cuba. Three of them. They're marked on the maps. Ten pin holes, plus numbers next to the holes. The numbers are one through twelve and marked with blue ink from a Sharpie. None of them are too far from tourist haunts so they should be safe, and the map could easily be for tourists if one didn't know better. Still with me?"

"Okay, so far," Alex said. "But what about the passports? We're husband and wife but the names don't match."

"The Cubans are used to that. Not a problem."

"How do you know his passport is secure?"

Meachum laughed. "We know its provenance. It's good."

"Third finger, left hand?" she said. "I'm a married girl, am I not?"

"Glad you reminded me," Meachum said.

He reached into his pocket, produced a ring box, and handed it to her. The wardrobe department had thought of the small details. She opened it and found an engagement ring and a wedding band. Gold and zircon in a breathtaking arrangement. Then the smaller details: She looked inside the band and found her fake initials joined with Paul's fake initials. With mixed feelings, she put the rings on and gave back the box.

"Careful what you wish for," Meachum said.

"Careful with your smart remarks," she answered.

"Continuing," he said, "once we know that you're on the island, we'll need to send a signal to Violette to let him know that you've arrived to 'bring him home.' We'll do this through the Swiss Interests Section once again. Nice lady named Elke, who has an American mother and favors khaki skirts from the Gap when she visits us in Washington. She does wonders for us, Elke does. The perfect Switzer lady: French charm with German efficiency instead of the other way 'round. She's from Minnesota. Thus, dead drop number seven. I'm told the location is the most convenient for Violette. Close to where he lives, on his regular path each day. *Convenient* means safest for him. He's got the big itch, you know. Senile paranoia. Who knows what he's going to do or who he's going to talk to if we don't get him off that island. So. Which drop number did I just mention?"

"Seven," she repeated.

Seven was easy for her to remember. Rizzo, her Roman consort, had paved the way with his dwelling on the number seven.

"Only holes six, seven, and nine are any good, by the way," Fajardie said, continuing. "The rest are dead ends for the opposition in case the map falls into the wrong hands. It'll buy a little time, at least while they chase their tails. Got that part?"

She repeated. She had it.

"You'll pick up a cell phone at the drop. Then once you have it, you'll enter a four-digit number: eight, eight, six, four, and hit Send. It will connect you to a voicemail. Just say, "I'm here." Violette will immediately double-check the active drop each day. If the phone is gone, it means you're clean and he'll call you within the next twenty-four hours. You be sure to speak first. What was the name you used on the passport that the CIA had for you in Kiev?"

"Anna Tavares," Alex said without hesitation.

"I'm told you'll be using a similar cover again. Is that right?"

"It is," Meachum said.

"It is," Alex confirmed. "The same cover, but a new passport. Mexican this time."

"Then identify yourself as Anna immediately when you answer the call from Violette," Fajardie said. "You'll be speaking Spanish to him, not English. No problem with that, correct?"

"Correct," she said.

"Your accent can pass for Mexican, right?"

"I'm fluent and it's from my mother and childhood," she said. "It's native."

"Violette's window for phoning will be between 4:00 and 6:00 p.m., Havana time, but he's erratic, we already know that, so he might call anytime. He'll arrange to meet with you at a rendezvous point. You'll have one go at it. One chance to sit down and talk him into coming to the U.S. with you. After you have him, you may need to babysit him twenty-four-seven if you have to; just get him to the aircraft."

"And where will that be?"

"Near the city of Cienfuegos on the south shore of the island. Cienfuegos. 'A hundred fires.' See if you can prevent it from being a hundred and one fires. The city is about forty miles southeast from Havana. There's an inlet another mile to the southeast. Your mob guy tells me he can arrange a driver."

"You talked to Paul?"

"Twice," Fajardie said. "In person. We know Paul," he said.

Alex was only mildly surprised. "That's interesting," she said. "How well do you know him?"

"He's dependable," Fajardie said. "If he says he's going to get something done, he gets it done. He's not one of us, if that's what you're wondering, but he's someone who has contacts in convenient places. We can work with him, hitch one of our operations alongside his. And that's good."

"So what happens when we get to Cienfuegos?" she asked.

"Your lift out will be a seaplane, limited seating," he said. "Four to six passengers plus the pilot. There's an army and naval base near Cienfuegos, and we'll be using an inlet and pier near there. It's no small task to clear the Cuban coast for a seaplane pickup, so there's not much room for error or change in schedule, and the smaller the plane the better for beating the radar. There's probably some U.S. Navy in the area for potential emergency help, but you can't count on that, and you don't want a distress call that the Cubans could follow."

"Much easier to sneak onto the island than off it," Meachum added.

"So it appears," Alex said.

"The aircraft, which will be coming from Grand Cayman, will take you to Yucatan in Mexico, then we'll airlift you back, or somewhere else if you still need to stay away from New York. But Violette comes back to Washington."

Alex continued to listen.

"The whole exit operation, the seaplane coming in and leaving," Fajardie said, "has to take place in under half an hour. The connection time will be 5:15 a.m. You'll be there ahead of time and hide out in a hut near the beach. I'm told you can't miss it. The hut will be flying a Brazilian flag because we have a contact there from São Paulo. Watch the southern horizon until you see the plane land and taxi to the pier. Got to beat the daylight, and you also have to beat the radar. When you see the plane come to the pier, the assembled passengers head for it, maybe ten feet apart, hands by your sides. If anything looks queer, the pilot turns and takes off without you. If you're not there and don't make the connection, it leaves without you and then who knows where we are? We'd have to reschedule and work another pickup and that is *not* the easiest thing to arrange. So let's avoid it, all right?"

Alex tried to process all of it. "I'll try to make things as convenient for you as possible," she said. "Seriously, if this thing falls apart, I'm in a Cuban jail and you're having beer and burgers in Georgetown the next day. I'd hate for you to feel bad over lunch."

"I would too," he said, going with it. "What's the numerical code for calling Violette?" Meachum asked.

"Bush Johnson," she said.

"What?"

"Bush was elected in eighty-eight. Johnson in sixty-four. That's how I remember these things."

"You're good at this," Meachum offered.

She smiled.

"Okay, today is June eighth," Fajardie continued. "You're going into Cuba tomorrow night, getting there the morning of June tenth. You're on your own getting in; Guarneri says it's a north shore landing between Havana and Matanzas. That's his arrangement for his personal part of the operation, not mine, so good luck. I'm setting up the airlift to get you *out*, along with anyone coming with you on June sixteenth. Questions?"

"A couple."

"Shoot."

"What if we have to alter the date of exit?"

"Ha! Please don't. It's hell to bribe a gap in Cuban radar." He paused. "But if you do ..." He pulled out his own cell phone. "Dial 7734 on the phone you will have. It will connect with me. Keep the call under one minute and call close to the hour on the hour. Okay?"

"Okay."

"What else?"

"What's the backup if I lose the phone?" she asked.

"There isn't one. Don't lose it."

"What sort of dead drops are we talking about?" Alex asked.

"One of them is a brick wall," Fajardie said. "Another's in a church. Iglesia de San Lázaro. That's the first place you should try. Go in, enter two rows to the left, sit down, and search under the pew. There's another one in a cemetery. You'll see it all in your notes, plus the map," he said. "Memorize everything because you shouldn't bring the notes onto the island."

"What's in it for you?" she asked. "For the CIA?"

"We're getting back a defector and turning him over to the Justice Department."

"I know that part, but what's in it for *you*?" she asked again.

"It doesn't make sense. Violette comes back to spend the rest of his life in prison. He's cut a deal somewhere with you, I'd guess."

"He'll be carrying a small suitcase," Sloane said. "He's managed to rifle some Cuban intelligence documents. Mostly political stuff. Shore defenses. Whatever. The deal is that we get him and his booty back to the U.S.; then we assess what value it has. If it has good value, he may serve less than five years and die a free man."

"With senile dementia?"

"All the more reason to get him back now," Fajardie said, "before he goes popping off to the wrong audience, if you know what I mean, and sells his bag of goodies somewhere else. At least if we have a collar on him, we can control him."

"He's cut a deal with you?" she asked. "Or someone has on his behalf?"

"Why do you want to know that?"

"Because I'm going to Cuba and have to sit down with him."

"A deal exists in principle," Fajardie said. "He's got one of the red lawyers from New York, one from the Brandeis/New School/Columbia axis of Maoist legal training, all right? Does that keep you happy?"

"Almost," she said.

"Look. He wants to come back, Alex," Fajardie said, his voice rising a notch in irritation, "and we're willing to take him. That's all. We're even arranging free pickup and delivery, rather generous, I would submit. What more could he want after the acts of villainy he's committed against this country?"

He settled down.

"So he can enjoy his old age and retirement in America," Meachum said.

"Like all the agents whom he caused to be slaughtered could never do," Fajardie added. "Further questions?"

"None for now, other than whether I should read your notes now while you're still here or look at them tonight."

"Suit yourself," he said.

She thought about it for a moment, then opened his packet. She read them and followed. "Okay," she said. "One final question. What's the Mayday scenario. What do I do in the case of complete disaster?"

"Complete disaster," Fajardie said, "is if you get arrested. And then there won't be an awful lot we can do for several months, if then."

"What if it's disaster and I'm still at liberty?" she asked.

"Remember the Swiss lady I just mentioned? Elke? Go to the Swiss Consulate. Not the embassy, but the Consulate. It's in Miramar, which is the upscale section of Havana where the embassies are. Ask to see Elke Bruhn. She's a political officer there. Use your Anna Tavares identification. Elke will take it from there." He paused. "Keep in mind, also, that if you're badly blown on an operation, that Cuban authorities — police, army, civil guard — will be looking for you in exactly that area. So be forewarned and be careful. Whatever you do, stay out of custody. They've got some military stockades in Camagüey and Santa Clara that are human roach motels. You go in, but you never come out. It's where they stash their toughest prisoners and most valuable captives."

"Okay," she said at length. There was an uneasy pause. "Is that it?" she asked.

"That's it," he said. "*Buen viaje*. See you in a week. We hope."

THIRTY-FIVE

The room was cold and gray, with concrete walls and soundproofed. Manuel Pérez was strapped to a steel chair in the middle of the room, his clothes filthy, his shirt soaked with sweat, red welts and gouges across his temple.

The first interrogator, the taller, younger, and leaner of the two men surrounding him, reached for the end of the duct tape across the lower part of Perez's face. He yanked it off with a sharp ripping sound. Perez responded by gasping for air, then with a torrent of obscenities in Spanish. Then the interrogator yanked a second tape off Perez's eyes, taking blotches of the prisoner's eyebrows with it.

"Buenos Dias, Señor Perez," the interrogator said. "It's so nice to meet you."

"Who are you?" Perez demanded.

"It doesn't matter, Manuel," said the interrogator. "You're our prisoner."

The hostage continued in Spanish. "Americans? Police?" Perez asked.

The two men laughed quietly. There was one stream of light in the room, and it came from directly above Perez. "What do you want?" he asked. "An admission? You get no such thing. I know American law. I want to see a lawyer."

"Manuel," the second man began. "We don't obey the law, and we're not in America. We wish to put you to work. We are going to put a proposition to you, and you will have to decide what you wish to do. Either we will pass you along for imprisonment—or possibly even execution—or we will restore you to your liberty in your beautiful home in Mexico. The choice will be yours."

A profound silence overcame Perez. He sat motionless, like a massive rock. His eyes followed his interrogators.

"It is true that the American police would like to discuss matters with you," the first man said. "They were a few hours behind us, ready to smash into your hotel room and put handcuffs on you. If that had happened, you would have appeared before a judge by now, and your picture would be all over American television. Then you would have had a long prison sentence."

There was a pause and Perez still held his silence.

"You're not going to deny that you were the sniper on West 61st Street the other night, are you, Manuel?"

Perez tried to move his ankles. He couldn't. They were attached to the chair by straps. His arms, he was now aware, were attached to the arms of the chair in the same way. He glanced to the floor. The front of his chair was bolted to the floor. He assumed the back of the chair was also. Still, he didn't speak.

"Do you remember Suárez, the Venezuelan? Gattino, the Italian? Brave men whom you served with when you were young. Do you know why you never see them or hear of them now? They were turned over to the filthy Islamics in the Middle East, whom they fired shots against. So naturally, they will never be seen or heard from again."

Finally, Perez spoke. "What is it you want me to do?"

"Be a sniper. Perform an execution," the first man said.

"The woman is either in hiding or has protection," Perez answered.

The first man smiled. "Oh, she is in Cuba," he said. "She is vulnerable and you will see her again. We will take you to Cuba. So why don't we discuss the details, what we need you to do so that we can send you home again."

Perez looked back and forth at them.

"How do I know I can believe you?" Perez asked.

"We keep our word," the second questioner said. "And we'll prove it."

"How?" asked Perez.

"We have your wife and your daughters in protective custody," he said. "And your bodyguard, Antonio, we have him too, in a different location."

Perez's eyes went wide, but he controlled his rage.

"We will let you speak with them," he said. "After you have spoken and agreed to finish this assignment for us, we will escort them home to your villa. We will allow you to speak to them again tomorrow. Then, once you complete your mission in Cuba, we will put you on a plane to Mexico City. And that will be that."

The first interrogator undid the strap that had held Perez's right arm. He handed him a cell phone. "Phone your wife, Manuel. She has been waiting with her cell phone for two days. She expects your call any minute. You can tell her that you will be home soon, or you can tell her that she will never see you again."

"The choice," the second man said, "is yours." As he spoke, he fiddled with a silver pen in his hands. It had Alex LaDuca's name engraved upon it. "Make the call and choose wisely," he said.

THIRTY-SIX

Alex flew to Miami International Airport the next day, still accompanied by MacPhail and Ramirez. They were met at the airport by Special Agent Frank Cordero and Special Agent Linda Rosen from the local office. They would serve as her new driver and bodyguard. With embraces, Alex thanked MacPhail and Ramirez, who had now completed their assignment. They turned around and headed to their flight back to D.C.

Cordero led her to a black Lincoln Navigator. Alex carried a small duffel with her personal effects. They were minimal.

The SUV was soon on the expressway that led to downtown Miami. Agent Cordero drove. He said little. Agent Linda Rosen sat in the backseat and was friendlier. She made some small talk about her dog and how the two of them, Frank and she, would be with Alex for the next day. "Pretty much till you hit the water for Cuba," she said.

"Water?" Alex asked, surprised they knew so much about her plans.

"It always starts with water, continues in the air, then ends on a beach. No matter which way you go."

"You send people in and out of Cuba frequently?" Alex asked.

"If it happened any more frequently, they could print a schedule."

Breaking his silence, Frank in the front seat laughed. But not for long.

Outside the Navigator, ninety humid degrees gripped Miami. Even the beaten-up cars on the expressway had air conditioning. Mere survival.

They passed the Orange Bowl and then the dull skyscrapers of downtown Miami. Cordero paid a toll. Then they took the causeway that led to Miami Beach.

"You know the address, right?" Alex asked to the front seat.

Linda answered. "Yeah," she said. "Frank's got it. We know the way."

On their left was an island set in a lagoon. Rising from it were mini-mansions. On Alex's right was the maritime channel, the exit for ships leaving the Port of Miami. The sight of them reminded her of Panama, and, with a shiver, the thought of Panama reminded her of the bullet that had come through her window on the west side of Manhattan.

The causeway led to Miami Beach.

Linda reached down to a shopping bag at her feet. From it she drew a cardboard box, the type that might contain six gourmet oranges. She handed it to Alex. "Here," she said. "Welcome to south Florida. Merry Christmas in June. Present from Frank and me."

Alex opened the box and examined the contents. The centerpiece was a Walther PPK 9mm short. Alex made sure it wasn't loaded. The pistol was slim and sleek and would carry well. It was small but could pack a lethal wallop if necessary. It came with a box of fifty bullets and a nylon holster.

"Thanks," Alex said, still examining it. She hefted it.

"Keep it low below the window levels," Linda reminded her. "I don't want other drivers to see it. It'd be a pain to explain to the Miami police what we're doing here."

"Of course," Alex said.

There was one more item in the box. An ankle holster that was in heavy waterproof canvas. Alex could hit the water, if necessary, or endure a rainstorm, and her ordnance would be secure.

Frank guided the vehicle up and down a couple of side streets, then pulled up in front of a deco-streamlined house in South Beach with the usual Miami pastel paint job, pink and blue on white stucco, four stories on a quiet street, windows curtained. Alex eyeballed it from her car. Frank parked.

"We're staying outside," Linda said. "Don't worry about us. We're babysitting you till you go on to Key West tomorrow," she said.

"You sure? You don't need to."

"We have our instructions," Frank said from the driver's cockpit.

"Got it," Alex said.

Alex moved her gun into her own duffel bag and closed it. She took the bag with her as she opened the car door and stepped out. Heat hit her. A lot of it. Plus a wall of humidity. Miami in late afternoon: thick, nasty air and low clouds.

She went to the door and drew a final breath. She knocked. Solid oak on top of steel reinforcement. Better to stop bullets, she reasoned. Better to stop a battering ram!

No response. She knocked a second time. Then she heard rustling within the house and the fall of latches from within. The door swung open and Paul Guarneri stood in front of her.

"Hey!" he said. "Nice of you to drop by."

"Wouldn't miss it," she said.

There was an awkward moment as they stared at each other. Then he opened his arms wide to embrace her. Against her better judgment, she fell easily into his arms and accepted a long hug.

THIRTY-SEVEN

The screened porch behind the house was long and low and overlooked a busy marina on the north end of Miami Beach. The screens were hung with net curtains, which made anyone sitting in the porch more difficult to see, much less be shot at, from the water. Alex and Paul sat at a small table, she on a sofa, he on a chair, over some cold fish salad, fruit, iced tea, and soft drinks. Frank Cordero sat smoking Camels on a patio that was below the porch. He watched the water approaches behind the house while Linda Rosen watched the front.

Alex sought to commit to memory the notes given to her by Maurice Fajardie at her final briefing, plus the brief instructions about Figaro. When she felt she had everything, she looked up and eyed her prospective traveling companion.

"Tell me about your uncles," Alex said to Guarneri out of the blue.

He met her inquiry with surprise; then he eased back. "Ah," he said, "you've been doing some checking. FBI files?"

"They were sent to me," she said. "It's not so much that I requested them as they were thrust upon me."

"What about CIA files?" he asked. "I'd like to see those. Have you?"

"What? Seen them?"

"Yes."

"There isn't much," Alex said. "Nothing on you at all. At least not that I've seen. Only minor information on your father. He's a footnote in several anti-Castro operations."

"A footnote to everyone else," Paul said. "Significant in my life. I don't suppose ...?" he began.

"That I could slip you a look?"

"Yes."

"Not allowed," she said.

"Understood."

"Now," she said. "My question. About your uncles ..."

"What do you want to know, Alex?"

"The file says that one is dead. There's no date of death on the other. What can you tell me about that?"

"Why are you asking?" he asked.

"You alluded to your mission being heavily related to family," she said. "Family here and family in Cuba. So what better place to start than with your father's brothers?"

Paul was quiet for several seconds. In the marina in front of them, a massive Chris-Craft flying a Bermudian flag navigated a thin channel and exited toward Biscayne Bay.

Then he began. "One uncle is holding the money for the other," Paul said.

"I thought you said the money was buried."

"It is."

"So now you know better where it is?" she asked. "Better than you knew when we first met a year ago?"

"Much better," he admitted. "I have a source in Cuba, a very authoritative one. Someone in the government, with some influence. I didn't have that source a year ago when Yuri Federov first introduced me to you. Back then, going into Cuba was more of a fishing trip if you don't mind the Hemingway analogy. Now it's Moby Dick. I know which whale I want; it's just a matter of getting it."

"Captain Ahab got killed trying," she said.

"Did he? I never got to the end of the book. That's a spoiler, Alex."

She laughed but was equally vexed. "Don't goof around with me, Paul," she said. "You're good at it. You raise evasiveness to an art form sometimes. I don't like it."

"No offence intended, and I'm telling you what I can. For

now. What else do you want to know? My social security number? You probably already have it."

"Tell me a couple of things," she said. "They're both in Cuba? Both uncles?"

"That's correct."

"Is one of your uncles your source?"

"No. But my task is to move the money from one uncle to the other, then get off the island as fast as possible."

"The FBI file suggested that one brother, Salvatore, is dead. And the other became active in Cuban revolutionary politics."

"That's correct, but it's also misleading," Paul said. "Yes, our family was torn apart. The older uncle, Salvatore, was a casino worker. So he was quickly on the outs with the Twenty-sixth of July Movement, which is what Castro's revolutionaries called themselves. The younger brother was a university student. A good number of students were pro-Castro, as was he."

"So who's dead and who's alive?"

"My father's dead, but when we're in Cuba, if all goes well, you'll see both of my uncles."

"Why do you keep saying that — 'If all goes well'?"

"Because frequently things *don't* go as planned. So I'm saying that this is what's going to happen if they *do* go well."

"You're obscuring things, Paul," she said. "You're being cryptic."

"You're right. I am."

"Why can't you tell me? I'm putting a lot on the line for you."

"Alex, listen. What if this trip gets aborted tomorrow? What if we get turned back from the Cuban beaches before we land? And then what if your employer puts you on a witness stand and puts you under oath about what you learned before this trip got zipped. Where would your allegiance be? To me? To the people who sign your check?"

"Under oath, square as it sounds, I'd have to tell the truth."

"That's my point. I know you would. So if the truth is that you don't know, you can't be forced to tell, and we're both protected," he said. "Right?"

"But after we return, then I'll know, correct?"

"If all goes well," he said with a smile. "Correct."

"Then . . . ?"

"If all goes well, it will no longer matter," he said. "Trust me on that."

"I'm already trusting you."

"So you are," he said. "I appreciate that."

"So trust me on something else," she angled. "Tell me something about Paul Guarneri that I don't know."

Paul rubbed his eyes with fatigue and watched another cabin cruiser for several seconds. "All right," he finally said easily, "let's try this. This might slide a few more pieces of the Guarneri puzzle in place for you."

A slight breeze wafted through. Alex dropped some ice in a fresh glass and sipped another Coca-Cola.

Paul looked away, a far-off look, then his gaze came back.

"I'm going to tell you something, Alex," he said. "Something I've never told anyone else. But I guess you should know. I like you, I trust you, I have a hunch you understand me. So I'm going to tell you something more about why I'm here, why we're here. It's not so much a fact, although it is a fact, as a feeling. Can I share this with you?"

"Go for it," she said.

"Cuba . . . ," he said, "Cuba is the life I didn't lead. I told you, I was born there, I was a kid there. Then, after Castro came in, the family was pretty much split. My father had the two brothers and a sister who never left Italy. We lost touch with her half a century ago. Same way most Cuban families got separated. Fidel has a sister who lives in Miami, for example. She hates Fidel and what he's done to the country. She's an anti-Castro Castro. Did you know that?"

"I'd heard something," Alex said.

"Good. Most people don't. But that's beside the point. See, some in my family chose to stay. They believed in Castro and the revolution. That's okay; I understand that. The American Civil War divided families too. Same as the Spanish Civil War. Same as the Bolshevik revolution. Some circles of hell can't be squared. Some things never work out perfectly. But here's the thing," he said. "There was that night I told you about in 1961. I was a kid, asleep. My mother came and got me. No warning, but she knew ahead of time. She knew because, in looking back, she had been packing, making arrangements. My father was flying us to the U.S. I told you that story, right? My father was connected and knew how to work the citizenship thing. By the time I was fourteen I had a U.S. passport. Never used it as a kid, but my father got it for me. He was probably afraid someone would grab me and try to repatriate me to Cuba. But no one ever did. Thing is, and here's what has dogged me for fifty years: *What if I hadn't made that flight?* What if my mother had refused to go or the police had stopped us? I would have grown up in Cuba. My life would have been so different that I wouldn't have even recognized myself. So that's part of what I'm doing. I'm reconnecting with the life I would have led, as well as carrying out the wishes of my father in setting things straight between his brothers. It's not the only reason that I feel a pull back to the island, but it's a big part of it."

"Okay," she said. "I think I get it. Or as much of it as you'll let me get."

"What's that mean?"

"You still haven't painted the whole canvas for me."

"And when I can, I will, Alex. I promise."

She let his words sink in. Some of Cordero's smoke drifted up from the patio. He had shifted locations, Alex figured. She further noticed that it was now dark outside.

"So that's what lies beneath this, Paul?" she asks. "It's about recapturing the past, repairing the past?"

"I prefer to call it 'coming to grips with the past,'" he said. "'Setting the past right.' Think about it. We have few opportunities in life to do that. I'm taking mine before it disappears forever. That's why I'm here. That's why you're here."

A full minute passed in silence, aside from the sounds from

THIRTY-EIGHT

"I'm Anastacio," the fat man said.

He spoke his name as if it were a challenge. He smelled of sweat and wore a massive pistol on his left hip. He was thuggish and scary. He stood in the driveway of a three-story stucco house, with a tall cement fence around it and a huge iron gate. But when he smiled his countenance went from surly to kindly. Alex had no idea whether Anastacio was his first name or last. It could have been either. She didn't ask.

She and Paul Guarneri had arrived there after a short flight to Key West. Special Agents Cordero and Rosen had traveled with them. The flight had been private from a small airfield south of Miami. They arrived at the Key West airport and were met by a small jittery man named Pete, who had a deep voice, a straw hat, a goatee, and bad breath. He said little and led Guarneri, Alex, and their guards to a white van in short-term parking.

Twenty minutes later, on the south shore of the island, the van arrived at its destination. Pete whacked his horn twice. From within the stucco house, someone must have given a signal because the gate gave way and rumbled open. Then the big man, Anastacio, had appeared and loomed in the driveway. He was fortyish and had a Latin face, arms like ham hocks, and was tremendously obese. He was stuffed into a light blue Ralph Lauren polo shirt and wore a pair of shorts the size of a small tent. He opened the van doors from the outside and extended a fleshy hand to Alex.

"Watch your step, Señora," he said protectively. "*Los charcos.* Puddles. Been raining all day."

"Thank you," Alex said, heeding the advice. Guarneri followed her.

The privacy of the interior driveway and courtyard of the Anastacio house had been carefully created. High black walls rose on both sides, as did foliage. There was a surreal effect because the area was brightly lit, sort of like what Alex had seen in her experience with organized crime households, which prevented any gunmen, cops, or a combination of both, from hiding in any shadows. She had no idea if this was a mob-connected place or a CIA house or both. She only knew it was her route out of the country.

The rain had stopped but the mistiness and the humidity had not. The asphalt driveway below her feet was slippery, as she had been warned. Everywhere around her was the incessant ticking of wet leaves dripping on one another. A squadron of bugs flocked around one of the outdoor lamps. A pair of mosquitoes buzzed Alex almost as soon as she drew her first breath of air, right in front of her eyes. She waved them away.

"We'll get a little rest here maybe and something to eat if you like," Guarneri said. "We can unwind for a couple of hours."

"Got it," Alex said. She looked at her watch. It was 5:00 p.m. She wanted to shower because she had no idea when she would be able to again. And the push-off in the morning would be obscenely early. Sneaking into one of the world's few remaining communist countries was, she reasoned, never an easy thing.

Paul gave her a soft pat on the back, showing the way, which was a flagstone path to the house. She walked as directed. Beyond the house she could see a pier and beyond that, water. Well, they were on a small narrow island after all, so why wouldn't there be water? At the end of the pier she saw two vessels. One was a small skiff, lashed to the pier. The other, moored in the water a few dozen yards beyond the pier, was a small Cessna seaplane. She felt a surge within her, anxiety combined with dread, mixed with, she hated to admit it, a rush of adrenalin over what she was about to do. She fingered the small cross at her neck, again without realizing. Anastacio saw her do it and smiled.

"Good idea," he said.

They all went into the house. The inside of the building was modern and nicely air conditioned. A small, stunningly pretty dark-haired woman presided. Anastacio introduced her as his wife, LaReina. She was a foot shorter than he was, maybe two hundred pounds lighter, and ten years younger. She wore denim shorts and a light green Paulina Rubio *Gran City Pop* tank top. She had a floral tattoo a few inches above her right breast. It never ceased to amaze Alex how mismatched couples like this ended up together.

"Welcome," LaReina said in perfect English. "You won't be here long, but our home is yours for the next few hours. Come with me." Alex took her to be a Cuban-American who had probably never been to Cuba.

LaReina was like a dormitory housemother, officious, generous, and proprietary. She led Alex to the kitchen, where she displayed a spread of food for sandwiches on the counter. She indicated an array of drinks — beer, water, sodas — in the refrigerator. Then she led Alex up a short series of back stairs. They passed a votive to the Virgin of Guadalupe on the steps. A small flame burned.

"The Virgin Mary once visited this house," LaReina said matter-of-factly. "It was in 1976 when the previous owners were here. So we keep the votive going."

"Nice idea," Alex said.

"I'd love it if *La Virgen* reappeared," LaReina said. "How cool would that be?"

"Very," Alex said.

At the top of the steps, LaReina led Alex into a cozy small bedroom, perfect for a short rest. Equally, Alex observed, it would have been perfect for a short vacation. There was a window that overlooked the pier and the seaplane. Looking out the window, Alex also noticed that two chain-link barriers led far into the water, marking the property, protecting the pier, making access difficult. She also saw that there was a huge Doberman chained behind the house, sleeping comfortably on a small blanketed den on the sand.

LaReina pointed out a bathroom across the hall from Alex's

room and said it was reserved for female guests, in this case Alex. Then LaReina left Alex alone.

Alex showered comfortably and, refreshed from washing, changed into a robe that was left for her use. She rechecked her plastic travel packs, the ones that she would strap to her leg or ankle: the gun, the money, the passport. She would put the gun on the right side and the documents and money on the left, she decided.

She opened her small duffel bag, checked its contents for the umpteenth time, and pulled out the clothes she would wear for the flight and the boat entry into Cuba: a heavy T-shirt, a pair of dark hiking slacks that could unzip into shorts, and some canvas hiking shoes. She repacked that day's clothes and closed the duffel. She dressed in the next day's clothes and went back downstairs to the kitchen. She found the men in conversation at a large kitchen table.

Paul Guarneri was talking American football to Anastacio, who changed the subject when Alex came into the room. He informed her that the plane was fueled up and ready to go. "It's down at the end of the dock," Anastacio said. "Did you see it?"

"I did," Alex said. "Cessna of some sort, right?"

"Cessna Caravan," he said. "1986. Fine plane."

Alex nodded. "I think Jimmy Buffett used to fly one of those," she said. "He tipped one over on Nantucket Sound in Massachusetts several years ago."

"Did it sink?" Anastacio asked.

"Not that I remember."

"That's what I mean. Fine plane."

She laughed. The tension eased a little.

"Sit down, Alex," Paul said. "Relax and join us."

He gave her hand a squeeze, let it go, and pulled out a chair for her. She sat and slid into the place at the table next to Paul. There were sandwiches. Alex grabbed half of one and a water.

"You like Jimmy Buffett?" Anastacio asked her.

"Seriously, yes. He's great. I've seen him in concert twice."

"He plays Miami a lot," Anastacio said. "My daughters love him. Me?" he made a equivocating gesture with his heavy palm. "I guess he sings better than he flies. That reminds me. Your pilot will arrive here at 3:00 a.m. His name's Pierre. He's a Dominican-Haitian. Black as the ace of spades, and he's got a heart of gold. Pierre is a good man, *un hombre bueno.*"

He went on to explain that Pierre, who had a lot of experience, had already filed a flight plane from Key West to the Bahamas, without mentioning any stop along the way. "You'll like flying with him," Anastacio said.

"I'm sure," said Alex, although she wasn't. "This doesn't strike anyone at Key West airport as suspicious?" Alex asked.

"Why would it?" Guarneri asked.

"Pierre runs an overnight air courier service. Completely legit," Anastacio said. "He flies from here to Grand Bahama and Andros Bahamas five times a week. That's why we use him for special drops."

"But anyone looking at the flight records is going to see a disparity in the flying times," Alex said. "What's the normal time to Grand Bahama from Key West? Maybe ninety minutes?"

"About that. Give or take," Anastacio said.

"So Pierre's going to need an extra hour at least to divert to the north shore of Cuba," she said, sipping water. "Anyone checking the flying time later is going to spot that. It's probably not a problem, but I'm just saying . . ."

Anastacio smiled. "Your girl here is smart," he said, looking to Guarneri. "That part gets taken care of," Anastacio he answered, looking back to Alex.

"Friendly folks at Key West?" she asked.

"Better," Anastacio said. "We have two radios. Pierre takes off low, stays under two hundred feet until he's six miles out into the Straits of Florida, stays under the radar most of the way. After he makes his drop off the north shore of Cuba, he radios back here, and we coordinate a call to coincide with that take-off. That way he arrives in Grand Bahama right on time."

"But he's in air space he shouldn't be in," she said.

"Yeah, and in a few hours you're going to be on a beach you shouldn't be on. Around here, this part of the ocean, people know better than to ask too many questions. So who's going to know? Who's going to do something?"

"No one, hopefully," Alex said. "And hopefully the air space is empty."

Anastacio shrugged. "It usually is," he said with a smirk. "And if somebody else is in it, it'll only happen once."

Guarneri tapped Alex's hand. "Don't worry," he said. "Stuff like this goes down all the time between Miami and Havana. It takes care of itself."

"Let's hope so," she said.

"You're jittery," Paul said.

"I've seen things go off the rails too many times," she said.

"Who hasn't?" Paul answered. He pondered. "Let's add a final fillip to our disaster plan," he said. "If everything goes haywire at any point and we get separated, there's a nice hotel in Havana called Hotel Ambos Mundos."

"Both worlds," she said, translating.

"Obviously, the two worlds are Cuba and everywhere else," he said. "But it's an Old Havana place. Dates back to the 1920s. Big pink place on a corner, half dozen stories or so, I'm told. Cuban owned, popular with European tourists."

"So what's the point?" she asked.

"If there's a major screw up," he said, "go there and sit in the lobby. Let's say from 3:00 to 5:00 p.m., more if you can, and just wait. We'll each try to find our way there."

"I assume it's easy to find if it's a tourist place."

"You can assume that," Paul said. "There's one other thing, ... and take this any way you want."

"Go ahead," she said. She finished her sandwich as well as her water.

"There are some nasty people in Havana who consider me a friend, some nasty people who hate my guts. It's a family thing going back a generation. There's some messy stuff to be done, but *I'm* doing it; you're not. Okay?"

"Want to tell me what it is?"

"I already did. Grabbing the money and moving it."

"And there's nothing else?"

A long pause, then, "Nope," he said.

"You remember about how I warned you about lying to me," she said.

"What's that supposed to mean?"

"It doesn't 'mean' anything. It's a reminder."

"Point taken," he said.

"I hope so," she said.

"Wake me up when it's time to leave," she said. "Good night."

"Good night," he said.

She went back upstairs and crashed onto the bed. It took several minutes just to unwind, to gather her senses. For some reason — nerves, stress, the weight of baggage, the emotional outburst, the slap, cramped passage in the small aircraft and van — her shoulder was killing her. Or maybe it was just subconsciously reminding her of her own mortality. She lay down in her clothes. Then she pleasantly surprised herself, despite the fact that Cuba, about a hundred miles away, was beckoning. She was, when she finally calmed, able to sleep.

PART ★ TWO

THIRTY-NINE

On the bed in Anastacio's house, in the middle of a muggy Florida night, Alex blinked awake on the morning of June tenth. The door to the room was open. Paul Guarneri was sitting on the edge of her bed, gently shaking her.

"Come on, Alex," he said. "The pilot's here. LaReina made coffee. We can take it with us with some rolls. Got to move."

She sat up and blinked. The new day was unwelcome. Beyond the window the sky was still dark. It was the middle of the night. Then part of her indignation from the previous night started to simmer. "Okay," she grumbled. "I'll be down in a minute."

"Let's just get this done, Paul," she said. "For both our sakes."

"I agree."

He got up and left the room, leaving the door partly open. A harsh light flooded in from the hallway. She waited a moment, then another, then threw off the sheet and blanket. She was on her feet, stepping into her shoes.

Five minutes later, she was downstairs, her waterproof emergency kit strapped to her thigh where otherwise one might carry a gun or a knife. Her gun was on her ankle, also in waterproof packing. Her duffel was in her hand.

True to his word, Anastacio was awake, as was LaReina, who had packed a bag with breakfast rolls and thermoses of coffee, as promised. She was barefoot and wore a thin T-shirt and a pair of men's boxers, her legs tan and supple with a cat tattoo on the back of her left calf. She handed each of the voyagers a stash of granola bars wrapped in waterproof foil. Alex jammed two into her pockets. She went to her purse to pack a pen also. She looked for her silver Tiffany pen, the one her boss had once given her, and couldn't find it. Nor, in her tiredness, could she recall when she had last seen it.

Anastacio glanced at his watch. He held the back door open and led Guarneri and Alex toward the pier. The plane's engine was not yet running.

A huge black man, Pierre, sat in the pilot's seat of the Cessna. He gave his two passengers a big toothy grin, then opened the passenger door. He extended a hand to help Alex aboard, then pulled Guarneri up.

"¡Bienandanza!" Anastacio said. "Godspeed, both of you!"

"¡Vayan con dios!" LaReina added.

In the dark, they held up their hands and waved. Pierre pulled the door closed. The only light was from the house and, an instant later, the airplane's interior. Anastacio gave the fuselage a push with his two hands, and the plane eased back from the pier. Pierre settled into the pilot's chair and cranked the engine. The plane came to life. The engine revved louder, and the aircraft turned quickly on the water to face southward over the straits. Alex and Guarneri settled into their seats next to each other, immediately behind the pilot, and buckled in.

"¿Listos, mis amigos?" Pierre yelled.

"Ready!" Alex called back.

Paul gave a thumbs-up.

"¡Vamos!" Pierre yelled.

A second later, Pierre slammed the throttle forward and they were hurtling across the choppy water. They skimmed the surface for a moment and lifted off; they went upward in a low flat ascent, and then they were on their way. Pierre was flying by the stars and by radar. He had illuminated no exterior lights.

Alex peered over his shoulder. The altimeter leveled out at four hundred feet and stayed there. Alex heaved a nervous sigh and said a short prayer. There were some air pockets and downdrafts, and the plane shook, dipped, and bounced back up for more. She loved this kind of excitement — and hated it at the same time. She felt like a gambler who kept going to a casino with the rent money; deep down, the gambler knows she's eventually going to lose, but the excitement is worth the risk. She wondered why she did it. She couldn't answer her question.

She had another thought. *All the crazy flights I've taken, and all the disreputable men I've flown with, and all the places I've gone — why hasn't common sense stopped me?*

Then the flight smoothed. Hardly a bump.

Pierre reached for a makeshift ashtray by his controls, which was nothing more than a crushed Pabst Beer can. He opened his side window in deference to a lady being present and relit a cigar that had been sitting there half-smoked. He worked it hard in his white teeth and soon had a good cloud of smoke going, most of which he blew out the window. To Alex the cigar stench was awful, and to make matters worse, Pierre seemed to be chewing it as much as smoking it.

"You can't tell me the Cuban navy doesn't have radar or border security," Alex said to Guarneri. "Don't they ever spot planes coming in?"

"Not usually," Guarneri said. "Not if you fly low enough." There was a long pause, and the sound of the Cessna's engine droned smoothly in the darkness. Outside the port wing of the aircraft, the lights of the distant sleeping islands twinkled peaceably on the horizon. "There's always exceptions, but not usually. It's like anything else. Set the plane down, get back in the air quickly, move fast, and beat anyone who's after you." He paused. "Let's face it. This whole area of the Caribbean is notoriously corrupt. Money changes hands; authorities look the other way. Works that way in Florida, works that way in Cuba, and it's the *only* way it works in the Bahamas. The U.S. Coast Guard intercepts a couple of thousand homemade rafts every year. Know how many planes they pick off? Less than a hundred. I looked into it. What does that tell you?"

"There are more rafts than planes," said Alex. "What if they *do* intercept us?"

"They won't," Guarneri said. "First, we're not doing anything illegal. The flight manifest shows us leaving from Key West to go to the Bahamas. That's where Pierre continues to. The plane itself doesn't do anything illegal. It just sets us down, and we do what we have to. You told me yourself that your employers know where you are and where you're going. So I have a hunch this plan has a bit of a look-the-other-way from the U.S. Coast Guard anyway. No one's going to examine whether the flying time was two hours from the Keys or one."

"Or whether two passengers get off or none."

Guarneri laughed. "What passengers?" he asked. "We're invisible, you and me, aren't we? We don't exist." He grabbed the manifest from under Pierre's Dominican passport. He showed it to Alex. There was a big fat zero where the list of passengers was stated.

"How'd you fix that?" Alex asked.

"Pierre filled it out. No one checked," said Guarneri.

"And no one chose to look either," she said.

"Describe it that way if you want. Look, everything's copacetic. We'll be back home in six days, and you'll have wonderful stories to tell."

"Right," she said. "Meanwhile I'm keeping my gun strapped tight to my ankle."

"Yeah, good idea."

The sound of the engine adjusted, and the plane made a dip. Up ahead, distant and emerging through the haze straight in front of the pilot, Alex could see the shoreline of Cuba and the lights of Havana, knotted together on the horizon like little stars. To the left, eastward, she could see a smaller clump of lights that she assumed was Manzanas, which was nearer their destination than Havana. She looked out the window and could see the surface of the water, reflecting the sky and the lights from shore and the occasional fishing boat — or what she hoped were fishing boats — anchored, their dim red and green lights winking on the surface of the water.

Pierre beckoned Guarneri forward and indicated something.

The pilot flew with night goggles and kept consulting a homing device. Alex assumed that he had spotted their rendezvous craft. Alex knew this was one of the trickier parts of the operation, dropping human cargo, particularly nonexistent cargo, with a rendezvous at sea.

Guarneri ended the conversation with a nod and settled beside her. "He's got our contact vessel lined up," Guarneri said. "We should be on the water in five minutes."

They were. Pierre brought the plane in with a hard bump, three bounces, and a long easy skid. The aircraft glided through the water like a dark swan. The propeller decelerated and spun to a stop. Pierre cut the engines to a low idle. Off the port side, in the darkness, a small sailboat turned toward them. Its sails were not hoisted. It had nets for fish. The plane bobbed up and down with the waves. Alex guessed they were about a mile and a half offshore.

As the boat approached, Pierre watched it carefully. His hand went to his sidearm. So did Guarneri's. There was a tense moment as the boat pulled alongside. Alex could hear the hum of the boat's small electric motor.

Pierre slid open the port-side window of the cockpit. Alex overheard a curt conversation in Spanish, presumably containing word codes. Whatever it was, it passed without a problem because Pierre turned and gave a nod to Guarneri.

Guarneri opened the rear door and signaled to Alex. "We're good," he said. "Be sure you have everything. Let's move."

Guarneri went first. He stepped down onto the pontoon of the plane. It was unsteady as waves rippled all around. She remained in the plane and watched. The boat pulled tightly alongside. A man with a carbine stood at the bow. He was burley and dark skinned and wore a University of Miami baseball cap and smoked. A second man approached, brandishing a pistol. Then a third man appeared, a jittery figure at the tiller, dark skinned also, bareheaded, with a black T-shirt and cut-off jeans. He watched everyone's movements like a terrier.

Guarneri jumped onto the deck of the boat as the first man steadied him. Guarneri seemed to know him since they embraced briefly. Then the gunman stepped back, and Alex slid down, balanced on the pontoon, and in the same motion took a big step forward onto the boat. The deck was wet. She nearly slipped, but both men grabbed her, the gunman's hand firmly on her arm, and Guarneri holding her with a two-handed embrace.

The smaller gunman pushed the boat away from the plane as the plane's door closed from inside. Pierre cranked his engine and turned the seaplane for takeoff. The drop had taken less than three minutes.

"We're cool; we're doing good," Guarneri said. He glanced at his watch. "Five after five. Perfect." He motioned to the first gunman. "This is Pedro our bodyguard, and Felix, our other bodyguard. Back there is Leo, our captain," he said in English. "We'll be ashore in twenty minutes. Settle onto the rear deck; it'll be best."

Pedro, Felix, and Leo barely acknowledged Alex. Pedro took up a crouch position at the bow of the boat. Leo kept one hand on the tiller and the other on the quiet electric outboard engine. Felix, with a rifle, sat to the side and looked as jittery as a dozen spooked cats.

Now that she was aboard, Alex assessed the sailboat. It was about twenty-five feet in length, old, maybe thirty years, but neat and nimble. She assumed Leo's livelihood was in an underground economy that was comprised of more things than she cared to consider.

"Like our bodyguards?" Guarneri asked her in a low voice. "Not as professional as your FBI and CIA people, but they have more charisma."

"Charming," she said. "What do they do besides smuggle?"

"Sometimes kill people," Guarneri said.

"That's a joke, right?"

"No."

"Nice," she said. She sat down in the stern and tried to organize her thoughts. So far, things had gone smoothly. Guarneri seemed in control. The sound of the boat's engine dropped down a notch, and she knew Leo had cut the speed yet again, trying to come to shore as quietly as possible.

Alex's mind shifted to Spanish. The rifleman and the captain were engaged in a dirty story about the wife of a mutual friend. Felix sat by quietly, fidgeting, his rifle across his chest. Alex suspected that they knew she was American and therefore didn't understand Spanish. She resented the assumption, if there was one, but played it to her advantage. Her nerves were on tenterhooks, and if they didn't think she understood, she didn't have to talk.

Paul came back, sat, and patted down his jacket until he found a pack of cigarettes. He pulled one out and lit it.

"Nervous?" she asked. "Now that we're almost there?"

The question took him by surprise. "Nah," he said. Then he realized that she was looking at his cigarette. "Oh, I get it," he said. "If I'm lighting one of these, I must be nervous, right?"

"Pretty much."

He lit it and inhaled, then blew out a long thin cone of smoke.

"Well, yeah, a little," he admitted.

He turned and looked toward shore, which was a thin line of lights in the distance, then looked back to her. "Well, whatever. It's Cuba, you know. We're about to arrive in Cuba. You know what that means to me. You'd be nervous if you were me— "

"I'm not—and I'm nervous anyway," she said.

"Yeah, yeah, well. We're mortal, right?" he asked.

"Too much so," Alex answered. "And too easily mortal."

"You got a good head on you, don't you, Alex?" he asked. "You're a smart lady. Just smart enough to be scared because you understand what you're doing."

"Not for the first time," she said. She settled back and watched the coastline draw closer as the early morning hours slid by. Her prevailing sentiment was that she wished this operation were over, and it had barely started.

FORTY

Alex sipped from the water bottle she had attached to her belt. When it was empty, she picked up a new one, hitched it to her belt, and watched Paul smoke. Parallels with Yuri Federov tumbled into her mind, although Paul only indulged in the occasional cigarette while Yuri, ever the Russian, had smoked like a furnace. Then, too, Paul was old enough to be her father, a quarter century older than she. She wondered how many secrets that extra quarter century held, things she didn't know about him, things she sensed, things she liked and disliked.

Many times since Federov's death she had wondered whether she had had an attraction *to* him — for all the wrong reasons — or a fascination *with* him — again, for all the wrong reasons. She was feeling a tiny something here, a subtle pull toward Paul Guarneri, and wondered if her passions, her instincts, her longings, were just completely out of whack following the death of Robert, her fiancé.

She had fallen in love with the right man once, the one she could have shared a lifetime with, had a family with, and grown old with, and he had been taken from her. So now what? Was it really getting even with God to have a meaningless fling with the *wrong* man?

She looked away from Paul and into the water where the boat left its wake. A great blanket of seaweed swung and heaved in the water like a giant brownish yellow blanket. Then a couple of splashes and plops about ten meters off the bow of the boat startled her. She realized they were small creatures leaping from the water.

"Flying fish," Guarneri said. *"Pezes voladores."*

His simple explanation settled her. Not only was he watching her, but he had been reading her thoughts. He was starting to know her too well.

"I remember them from when I was a kid," he said. "We'd sail out just far enough and they'd leap all around us, day or night. They don't really fly, you know. They just jump out of the water, usually to avoid predators. They glide, not fly. But no one wants to call them 'gliding fish.' Is my cigarette bothering you?"

There was a light breeze from the east. It took most of the smoke in the opposite direction from Alex. "Just finish it," Alex said. "You're okay." Then, circling the conversation back a beat, "Are there predators?" she asked. "Larger fish?"

He laughed. "You could say that," he glanced around. "They're around here somewhere. Got to be if the *pezes voladores* are jumping at this hour."

"What sort?"

Squinting into the darkness, she saw an extra ripple. Then she saw a small triangular fin coming up out of the water, followed by a second one about ten feet behind the first. Then, as her eyes adjusted, she recognized the dark silhouettes by the sweeping languid movement of the tail just below the surface of the sea and the seaweed.

"Brown sharks," he said evenly, looking at them swishing through the water. "Four-footers, looks like. They won't hurt you—more scared of us than we are of them. But don't drag your arm in the water either." He watched them for a moment. They both did. Alex couldn't tell if there were three of them or four, but she could follow the little dance of death that the flying fish did with the hungry sharks.

"Brown sharks rarely come within a hundred yards of the beach," Guarneri said. "But the fishermen throw extra chum to them. So they investigate boats." He looked into the swirl off the starboard bow. Then he took a final long drag on his cigarette and flicked the butt at one of the sharks. "Here, buddy, have a smoke," he said.

Soon the flying fish were gone and so were the sharks. Leo

cut the engine and let the boat drift. The small outboard motor died with a wheeze. The dim lights on the boat faded to nothing. There was only nighttime and the sound of the surf and the wind rustling across the water. Alex could feel the breeze. It was soft and warm, fluid against her arms and face. Starlight and moonlight poured down. So far, arrival was gentle.

Leo hoisted a small sail, which clanked upward, waffled for a moment, then filled out. The skiff tacked toward shore.

"Good, good," Guarneri said. "Almost there. We can go in on wind to keep the noise down. Leo's an expert at this."

Paul disappeared for a moment and spoke quietly to the captain. Alex couldn't hear them clearly, but she caught enough to know that Guarneri was indicating a small cove that the boat was to head for, and at the cove would be a green light. The light would flash three times when it spotted the craft; then it would remain on long enough to guide them in.

The sailing was smoother than cruising with the inboard. At the bow, Pedro leaned back, his University of Miami cap tipped back and the carbine across his chest. He looked like the calmest person on board because he had the least to do.

Alex glanced at her watch. It was 5:19 a.m., slightly before dawn. They were exactly within the window of time that would allow them to hit the beach in near darkness, undetected by any Cuban shore patrols or nosy civilians or other traffickers who might be around at that creepy early hour. She looked forward to arrival. Nervous energy was pushing her forward, but fatigue and lack of sleep was starting to set in also. A low mist rolled from shore and sat on top of the water's surface.

Alex took a final inventory. She reached beneath her pant leg to where her gun was encased in heavy plastic and strapped tightly to her ankle. She fingered the case on her thigh that held her money, her maps, her bank cards, and her Mexican passport. Her small duffel was a few feet away, water resistant but not water tight.

Then Leo spotted the green light.

The boat came into a small bay, maybe a hundred yards

across, and Leo, as some sort of precaution, turned his boat and sailed parallel. He wasn't going to land, he said, until he saw the lights flash. Guarneri went to him and spoke, and the two men seemed to be in a small argument. She could just barely make out that Guarneri wanted to press ahead, while Leo, paranoid soul that he was, sensed something was amiss. Not that they had much in the way of options at this point. Sailing back to the Florida Keys was hardly a possibility.

"What's going on?" Alex asked.

"They should be flashing us," Guarneri said. "That's supposed to be the final all-clear signal. They're supposed to flash us. They're not doing it."

Leo dropped his sail and the boat eased to a near stop. Obviously, he didn't like this. Alex started to sweat. Impetuously, Leo took a signal lantern from the helm and aimed it at the shore. He gave three quick yellow flashes across the water's misty surface. Several long seconds passed. Then Leo spotted the response that he solicited. The green light extinguished for a moment, then flashed three times, then went back on.

"There!" Guarneri said. "That's it! We're home free."

Leo muttered something profane about Cubans and turned the tiller sharply. The boat rocked and turned toward the shore. The boom came around fast, and Alex had to duck to keep her head from being taken off. Leo set a sharp final course. They were still out about fifty yards when Alex could discern that the light was on a small dock.

Suddenly, the entire landing area was floodlit. Men in dark blue pants and light blue shirts dashed across the beach, as if rising up from prone positions on the sand. More emerged from behind the dunes and foliage, while others came from within a house farther up the beach and others from behind clumps of palm trees. They held rifles across their chest, and their uniforms suggested local police.

Alex straightened up and stared ahead through the haze, as if in disbelief. "What's this?" she asked.

Guarneri turned sharply and looked also. "Uh-oh," he said, followed by a violent obscenity. "Local militia!"

The squad of men on the beach spread out and went into crouching positions. In the center of the squad stood a small wiry man in a similar blue uniform but with a red beret. He was obviously the commander. He had no rifle, but he wore a sidearm and carried a megaphone. He let the boat ease closer; then he raised the megaphone and started to bark orders in angry Spanish.

"Paul, what is it?" Alex pressed.

"I don't know. I'll handle it!" he said. "Everyone stay calm."

Guarneri moved to the bow of the boat, arms aloft, waving as if in friendship. Leo, at the tiller, looked petrified, as did Pedro. Felix's face seethed with rage.

Alex was about to put a hand to Felix to calm him. Instead, impetuously, Felix broke toward the front of the boat, slid into a low crouching position, and pointed his weapon toward the shore.

Meanwhile, the small man in the red beret continued to bark at them through his bullhorn. He announced that he was Major Ivar Mejias of some police brigade, but that was all Alex could hear.

Paul saw clearly what Felix was about to do, but he couldn't stop it. Neither could Alex.

"¡Felix! ¡Cálmese!" Paul yelled. Stay calm! But it was too late. Felix opened fire on the men on the beach, firing half a dozen shots. "Felix! No! No! No!" Paul screamed.

The commander dropped his bullhorn midsentence and ran for cover. The other men scattered, and Alex saw at least one of them go down, clutching a shoulder, hit by one of Felix's bullets.

Paul tackled Felix and knocked his gun away. But this was followed instantly by a barrage of gunfire thrown back at Leo's boat. Then Pedro, almost as impetuous as Felix, raised his pistol and fired wildly at the shore. Meanwhile, Paul and Felix hit the deck, wrestling.

The first barrage of return fire hit the boat with a series of powerful, heavy whacks. Pedro was the first to go down. He was hit badly, and more than once. He made a horrible guttural sound, and his pistol flew from his hands. Then he got hit again. He staggered as another volley found him, and suddenly he was picked up and hurled overboard, as if by an invisible hand. At the same time, Felix broke free of Paul's grip, grabbed his rifle, and tried to stand, but a bullet found him as well. He hurtled backward, the rifle flying from his hands. It rattled onto the rail and tumbled overboard.

Alex had hit the deck as soon as she could. The boat veered wildly in the water, its tiller not guided by any hand and the boom now swinging freely. As the floodlights illuminated their boat, Alex knew that somewhere along the line — either in the intelligence community, in the underworld, or in some cabal she did not yet know or understand — something had gone horribly wrong.

"Paul!" she screamed. "Paul!"

She could see Guarneri, lying flat on the deck but moving, apparently untouched by the gunfire. The same could not be said for Felix. He was lying across the foredeck, blood pouring from the wounds in his neck and upper chest. Alex had no idea if the man was dead. Not far away, Leo was also on the deck, bleeding badly.

Paul wriggled forward toward Pedro's pistol. Shots continued to hit the small skiff. They hit the hull of the boat, ripped through the sail, and ripped into the wood of the mast. Guarneri put the nose of Pedro's pistol over the bow and began to spray bullets toward the beach. Alex watched for a second, which seemed to last a lifetime. The men had all successfully scattered except for one who was trying to crawl to shelter. No one was helping him. Then Guarneri turned toward her, while keeping his head low.

"It's me they want! They're going to kill me! *You!* Get out of here!"

She made a helpless gesture. *Get out? How?* She was frozen in place. But to delay obviously meant death.

"Get out!" Guarneri demanded. "Jump and swim!"

"No!" she said. She reached toward her own weapon. Her instinct told her to stay and fight. But her hands were soaking, and she couldn't quickly access her pistol.

"Alex!" Guarneri demanded again. She looked up. Bullets continued to hit the boat. "Get out or I'll shoot you myself!" he screamed. And to break her out of her trance, he turned his revolver to her and fired a shot near her. It ripped away a chunk of wood on the hull. It was all the impetus she needed.

She crawled madly a few feet toward the stern and with a quick motion pulled herself over the side. She hit the water with a dull splash, sinking instantly. She never touched the bottom but knew immediately that she was well over her head. A moment later she reached the surface again. The water was warmer than she expected, which was good. That meant hypothermia wouldn't be a problem. Still, if she got hit with a bullet, hypothermia would be the least of her problems.

She stayed behind the boat, with her head above water only at nose level. Even through the mist, the scene was surreal. The boat was still only about fifty yards offshore, but she could hear the angry shouts and curses from the reception party. She moved several feet behind the boat. Stray bullets hit the waters around her with sharp zipping little splashes. Paul threw the occasional pistol shot toward shore to slow the pursuers. He was the only one returning fire, and he was trying to work the tiller, throw the sail back up, and turn the boat at the same time.

She assessed where the floodlights were and whether they would follow her. There seemed to be three of them, two high ones on the top of the building and a smaller one that seemed to be mounted on a truck. At the same time, she counted the men on the beach. There were eight, maybe ten, not counting the little runt in the red beret.

She treaded water for a moment, then knew it was best to get away from the boat as quickly as possible. Yet part of her heart and conscience was in the boat. Guarneri kept firing at the shore party, and they were returning his fire.

Despite her terror and her tears, her instinct for self-preservation took over. She moved a dozen yards from the boat. Then two dozen.

She could feel a strong current, and wisely, she allowed herself to go with it. To fight it would be to spend all her energy and end up where she began. To ride it would allow her to get farther away than swimming alone could take her.

The gunfire continued but was more sporadic. She kept her head low, exposed just enough to breath. She was sure someone, somewhere, was scanning the area with binoculars, maybe even a sharpshooter looking for anyone who had escaped. She kept her arms under water and moved rhythmically with the current, gaining greater distance. The floodlights still blinded her, and she could still hear the crackle of gunfire, and now and then the sound of the bullhorn, as the opposing force presumably closed in on Paul.

Oh, Paul. Oh, Paul. Oh, Paul, she felt herself thinking. But she kept drifting. Then she was confident enough to use her arms to start a slow crawling swim. She guessed she was a hundred feet from the boat. She kept going. When she was maybe another fifty yards away, the shooting stopped. She kept moving, pulling herself along on her back now and allowing herself the dark luxury of watching events unfold. The sailboat's mast had crumbled from the gunfire, and lay nearly motionless in the water, like a great wounded gull. The boat was bathed in floodlight, and now a pair of small craft, filled with pale figures in dark blue uniforms, cautiously approached it.

Then there was another volley of bullets from Leo's boat. The engine started again, and the crippled craft wobbled back out toward the sea. A few moments later the two police boats started in pursuit.

There was no more return fire from the boat.

Alex reasoned that Paul had been wounded or killed. In any case, the battle seemed to be over. Then the heavy floodlight from the top of the old house started to sweep the water around the boat, and Alex knew it was looking to see if anyone had escaped. If they'd been specifically betrayed, she knew, then the police would soon be looking for her.

Once, when the floodlight swept in her direction, she ducked under the surface for several seconds, waiting for it to pass. She was already breathless and could only hold her breath for about twenty seconds before coming up for air. But by then the light was gone.

She looked back. In the middle of the cove, the defenders of the Cuban shore were boarding the battered sailboat. No sign of Paul. Could he too have gotten overboard and evaded them?

She doubted it.

Then they sprayed the water with automatic weapon fire, including a few shots which landed not far from her. But obviously they'd lost sight of her in the low mist, if they'd ever seen her at all. So she kept going. Her emergency pack. The gun, the money, the passport, was still strapped to her body. She could feel everything.

Then she realized. The sky was brightening. Daylight would be her enemy.

Alex pulled herself through the water.

A jetty blocked her view of the landing area, but she noticed another cove about a hundred yards beyond it. Slowly she moved through the water. Getting to land now was her only priority.

By this time the sky was lighter, but the shore remained dark. She continued to pull herself toward the cove, but could not make out the topography. She didn't know if it was an area of sand, rocks, or even jagged coral, which could slice her shoes and feet. She pulled herself along for several more minutes until, finally, her feet touched the bottom.

It felt like soft dirt, mixed with sand and the occasional rock. That was good. She proceeded slowly. She knew a foot or ankle injury now would be disastrous. Next thing she knew, she was wading. First shoulder deep, then waist deep, then ankle. Then, alone and nearly at the point of collapse, she was on a strip of sand that formed a small pleasant beach. She staggered to a small stand of palm trees that would give her cover. Then she collapsed.

Bienvenidos a Cuba. Welcome to Cuba.

FORTY-ONE

The sun was one hour higher in the morning sky when Major Ivar Mejias of the *Policía Nacional Revolucionaria* stood on the beach, his arms folded angrily in front of him. He spat on the ground. He was filled with frustration and rage. On the surface, this should have been a routine operation, picking off some *contrabandistas* as they hit the Cuban sand, grabbing them as they came off the boats or dropped their cargo. He had done this dozens of times in the past, whenever he had received a tip.

But today the bullets had flown for no reason and everything had turned ugly. Now he would have some higher-ups taking a close look at the way this had been handled, poking their long noses into his butt, to use the expression that was common in his bureau, and that was exactly what he didn't want. Worse, the affair might now get turned over to the Ministry of the Interior, whose security division dealt with espionage and sabotage. A little of that — and this whole affair would be beyond his control.

He cursed again.

Two of Major Mejias's men needed first aid and were waiting for ambulances. Both had flesh wounds. Thank God, Mejias muttered to himself, none had been killed or seriously injured. His "men" were little more than boys, if the truth were told. They were conscripts. All young Cuban men owed service to the state and were assigned to either the army or the police. Lately, he was getting a real snootful of these country *chicos* working out of his headquarters in Havana.

Defense of the socialist motherland is every Cuban's greatest honor and highest duty, went the slogan. But a few brains would have been useful under the conditions Major Mejias had encountered today.

He sighed as he looked at his troops, who were just now realizing the severity of the firefight they'd been in. They were a mixed blessing, these kids. They respected authority and were affable. But they were rubes, most of them straight out of the sugar or tobacco fields. Well, so much the better for some of the things Mejias was trying to accomplish in some of Havana's darker corners. They weren't in any position to look over his shoulder and cause trouble and they could stop a bullet here or there to make his unit look good.

He walked the beach. He looked at the impressions in the sand where bullets had struck. For these smugglers, the living ones and dead one, whose bodies were laid out on the beach, he didn't have much sympathy. But he would have to process them in a humane way, which was a nuisance.

The hothead who had started the shooting was dead. But the others were bandaged and being held by his young officers, who stood over the prisoners and held them at gunpoint. The surviving invaders were in shock and not inclined to run anywhere.

The major looked out at the water. A Cuban Navy patrol boat, which had arrived in the last few minutes, had seized the skiff and brought it to within fifty feet of shore. It bobbed gently in the waves now, looking innocent.

Mejias glared at it with anger. All the prisoners spoke Spanish, but Mejias had no doubt where they'd come from. Where do the invaders *always* come from? The north. Well, thanks to the heads-up ahead of time, he knew exactly where these men would land. That's what had made the gunfire so unnecessary. Inside, his fury only deepened. He had rounded up his officers and had come all the way out from Havana to deal with this. And now it was royally loused up.

One of his sergeants walked over to him. Mejias had the reputation for a nastiness that is particular to small angry men in military hierarchies. They're like steers that aspire to be bulls but lack the necessary equipment. Hence they feel they had to make up for it with attitude, and incidents like this one didn't increase Mejias' charm quotient.

The sergeant stood there, waiting to speak.

Mejias turned to him. "What is it, sergeant?" he asked.

"One of the prisoners says there was a female passenger, sir."

Mejias looked surprised. *"What?"* he asked.

"A woman, sir."

"One of their girlfriends?"

"No, sir. A passenger."

"¿Cubana? ¿Norteamericana?" he asked.

"The skiff captain said she was probably American," the young policeman said, "but she spoke good Spanish."

Mejias looked away in disgust, then looked back.

"Well, then," he said. "American. So we'll have to find her, won't we? Before anyone else does. Before she can cause trouble." He motioned rudely to the water. "Or, if we're very lucky, we'll find the corpse."

FORTY-TWO

From the stand of palm trees where she hid, Alex looked toward the area where Leo's boat had come under attack. She could see the reflection of yellow and red lights flashing on the water, so she knew some activity was continuing. She thought back to the botched landing, the gunfire, the three-man crew, presumably now dead, and then to having no alternative but to dive into the water.

What stayed in her mind most, however, was the shot that Guarneri had sent in her direction. She knew he had not meant to harm her. It had been tough love in its most primitive form. He knew that if there was any specific target on the boat he was probably it. But if they were all to be riddled by bullets, he wanted to allow Alex the chance to survive. Hence, his shot had been meant to get her out of the boat.

It had worked. And it had probably saved her life. Yet there was still something about the man that didn't add up.

She continued to lurk under the trees, surveying, catching her breath. Not a human was in sight, but she knew that would change quickly if anyone knew that a woman had bailed out of the boat. She needed to get as far away as she could, and as quickly as possible.

She walked up the beach, away from the water. There were not many footprints in the sand, but she carefully stepped in the prints that were there, lessening the chances of being followed. She came to a narrow road that followed the coast. She began to walk. She knew Havana was to the west, so she headed in that direction. Across the street was what appeared to be a small farm. No house in sight, just some scraggly fields and, beyond that, what appeared to be an orchard. She reached for her water bottle. It was sealed. Right now it was her lifeline. Her mouth was parched, so she drank only a third of it, nursing the water.

Then she heard the sound of motors approaching.

On the beach was a small boat, overturned and lying flat, a skiff maybe a dozen feet long. She hurried to it and got down low behind it. She listened to the rumble of approaching motors.

They grew louder. They were traveling slowly from the direction of the botched landing. As the rumbling grew, she could tell it was a small convoy. Then Alex saw headlights on the road and lay as low as she could. Then they were within a hundred feet of her. Peering out from behind the overturned skiff, she could see a large truck, no doubt a police or army vehicle, and three smaller units behind it. The first two were vans. They looked official. Then a private car. A big stretch thing. It looked as if it might be a Volvo.

Alex stayed low and prayed. The convoy slowed to a crawl, and she knew that if they stopped and searched the beach, she would be captured. There was nowhere to run, nowhere else to hide, and no way she could escape so large a force.

But the convoy kept going. She stayed down till she could no longer hear it. Then she raised her head, looked around, and, seeing no one, rose to her feet. She brushed the sand from her wet clothes and walked away. She crossed the road. A small fence of stones and tree limbs separated the farmland from the road. She climbed over it. The sky was bright now. She moved across the field as quickly as possible and toward the stand of trees, which seemed to be a fruit orchard. After two long minutes she was within the trees, knowing she would have to stay there for safety.

From the position of the sun, she knew which direction was west. Havana represented her only means to rendezvous with her contact and get off the island in six days — or was it five now? Her mind threatened to shut down. But for lack of a better idea, she decided to continue toward Havana. At least there she would find Violette and Figaro and, most importantly, her failsafe contact, Elke, at the American-interests section of the Swiss

Embassy. Seeing herself as a soldier, she had nowhere to march but forward.

She walked for an hour, staying close to the trees, then passing across another open field. She consulted her map and knew that the road that ran along the shore finally merged with a larger one, which continued into Havana. As long as she stayed within sight of the road, she would be going in the right direction.

From a distance, she saw cars and people and trucks in a tiny town, nothing that suggested that a major search was in progress on the beach. That was a good sign, but she couldn't be sure. Nor did she see anything that indicated anyone was looking for her. She took that as a good omen too.

Her spirits rallied. She was alive, after all. What did God have in store for her? she wondered. She passed by a small stream and investigated. Mercifully, it was fresh water, running, not still. Girl Scouts 101. She finished her bottled water first, then refilled the container.

She continued onward as the sun rose higher. Eventually it found a midpoint in the sky. Gradually, she noticed the things that spoke more of the past than the present: rusted old gates, decrepit buildings, faded plaster. An occasional car passed, usually an old one. She resisted the impulse to hitchhike. The day became much hotter, her clothes dried, and finally a consuming fatigue was upon her. Plus, the shock of what had happened was setting in. Yes, the prospect of a rendezvous with her contacts and a rescue in Havana now seemed possible if she could just get there, but she was running on empty. She consumed one of her granola bars but knew that she would have to rest soon.

She found herself at the edge of another small village. Her path had taken her uphill. She was following the road that ran on a small cliff above the shore. Each time she heard a heavy engine approach, she hid. She sat for a moment. She unzipped the bottom of her pant legs and converted her trousers to shorts to combat the heat. So what if her outfit stood out? She would die of the heat if she didn't dress for it.

She checked her watch. It was just past noon now. She knew

she had to rest and eventually find more food. She also knew the worst part of the afternoon heat was soon to follow. She wondered if it might be best to stop somewhere. She checked everything that had been in her waterproof case. Everything was intact. She had money and a gun. But if captured by the police or the army, she also knew she would have a lifetime of trouble.

She asked herself what the date was. The tenth of June, she recalled. The airlift to get her off the island would be in five days. If Paul was dead or had been captured, his mission was blown. So she would have to focus on hers. She tried to think rationally but knew that without sleep, she wouldn't be able to. A battered road sign said she was nearing the village of Santa Clara del Sur. She made a decision. She started to walk.

She walked for hours. Once, she came by a roadside stand that sold fruit. She bought some oranges and bananas and three more bottles of water. And she continued, ducking under cover whenever she heard vehicles approaching. The area was amazingly desolate, and she felt lost, worse than defeated. In her mind, a prayer turned over and over, but she kept moving forward. There were some wooded areas, and she stopped three times for rest, fighting off fatigue and sleep.

She was afraid to hitchhike. She was afraid to look for an inn and didn't see one anyway. She was afraid to go to a farmhouse or any cottage for help. Eventually, as the day died, she saw a small shack in the corner of a small field, and she went to it. She pushed a door and the clasp that held a lock came open easily. Inside, there was a small collection of farming equipment, bags of fertilizer, rakes, shovels, and hoes.

The interior looked as if it had been undisturbed for a while. There was one window, six-over-six panes, but three panes had been broken and replaced by plastic. She entered and pushed the door shut. She sat down and consumed her second granola bar. Her eyelids were so heavy that she could hardly keep her eyes open. She drank more water and had only about a pint and a half left.

Rest. Sleep. That was all she could think about now. She had been awake for eighteen hours following a night in which she had slept for only four hours. She had to recharge her batteries. There was a canvas on a shelf in the shed. It was neatly folded. She opened it and spread it on the sacks of fertilizer. The canvas was surprisingly clean. She pulled her pant legs back on and wrapped herself in the canvas to protect herself from insect bites, forming it into a makeshift sleeping bag.

She bunched up some other cloths and formed a pillow. She closed her eyes and hoped that she could settle in for the night and then continue onward toward dawn.

That was the last thought she would remember as she drifted off to sleep.

FORTY-THREE

"Tombs," thought the old man who passed through *El Cementerio de Cristóbal Colón* in Havana, Cuba. "Tombs, tombs, tombs. It's all about tombs."

He walked with a shuffling gate, the result of a minor stroke that had gone undiagnosed months earlier. His right hand worked with an old hickory cane, carved years ago by a forgotten craftsman, a cane with a handle carved into the shape of a parrot's head.

The old man's eyes were tight and brooding. The flesh under his chin sagged, but not his face. The sun had long since crossed the midpoint of the sky and was now nearing the horizon. Sweat popped from his brow, then from the rest of his body. It was one of those deceptive days in late spring in Havana. He had always loved his literature, so the line from Andrew Marvel occurred to him: "Time's wingèd chariot," he thought, was racing across the sky. He had no idea where thoughts like this came from other than that he had been overeducated in his college years. But who cared about the classics anymore? Who cared about religion, morality, or even wealth? Who knew anything when you were seventy-two years old on a hilltop in a communist country with the sun playing tricks with your brain?

"Who knows, who knows, who knows?" he thought. Then, "Who cares?"

As he walked, he imagined his future beckoning to him from the stones and tombs. He took solace from the dates and names of people who had passed peacefully from this world, leaving little to be remembered except for some numbers and maybe a simple epitaph. "The grave's a fine and private place," he quoted Marvel to himself again. As he wandered, he sought tranquility and consolation, taking comfort from the bittersweet architecture of the sepulchers and the certainty that all mortal beings come to a place such as this. In his way, he sought a tangible link to the past, a window into it, a remembrance of it.

The Christopher Columbus Cemetery was on a hilltop in the old Vedado neighborhood of Havana, Cuba, just south of the Plaza de la Revolución.

El necrópolis. The City of the Dead. Almost a hundred fifty years ago it had been built on top of the old Espada Cemetery. The Spanish architect Calixto de Loira had designed it. The cemetery had been built when Havana had run out of catacombs.

The old man walked by the grandiose monuments and tombs that the tourists came to see, the ones that made Colón Cemetery famous. There was a seventy-five-foot-high column to *los bomberos*, the firefighters who had lost their lives in the great Havana fire of May 1890. The monument was a remembrance of the victims of the blaze. On top of the monument was a statue representing the fallen men. The statue remained the highest point in the cemetery and could be seen for miles, even from the sea. Nearby, a contemporary memorial of shiny metal Cuban flags honored the students killed during their attack on Fulgencio Batista's Presidential Palace in 1957. Martyrs of the Revolution.

There were two monuments to players from the Cuban baseball league, the first erected in 1942 and the second in 1951 for members of the Cuban Baseball Hall of Fame. "A celebration of life or of death?" the old man wondered. There were as many different architectural styles here as there were in Havana. But this was a universe of marble saints and granite angels, stone griffins on tombstones and carved saints watching over small temples, Egyptian pyramids, and mausoleums. Majestic lions sat next to stone-cut effigies of long-deceased dogs and cats. Iron bats flew around family vaults.

In February 1898, the recovered bodies of sailors who died on the U.S. Navy's battleship *Maine* were buried here. A year later, the bodies were disinterred and brought back to the U.S. for burial, some in Key West and some at Arlington National Cemetery. The same thing was going on today, the old man noted with bitterness. The dead couldn't be allowed to stay dead — at least, not in one place. With nearly a million humans buried here, new space was now nearly nonexistent. There was a new policy in the workers' paradise: after three years all old remains were removed from their burial plots, boxed, and sent to a modern storage building.

The old man took stock of the famous as he walked: Ibrahim Ferrer, the musician who became famous with the Buena Vista Social Club; Alberto "Korda" Gutierrez, the photographer who took the iconic photo of Che Guevara; Manuel Arteaga y Betancourt, Archbishop of Havana from the 1940s until his death in 1963, who opposed both Batista and Castro and still managed to live until his eighty-fourth year.

Then the old man found the tomb he wanted. He knelt down beside it. He didn't pray so much as he closed his eyes and attempted to communicate, to seek solace, maybe even some forgiveness. He was sure that a spirit inhabited this place, the spirit of someone he had known and loved at a time that now seemed long ago. So much had happened. So much should have been forgiven, but wasn't.

His shoulders were bent as the sun continued to pound down on him. He said a prayer. He wondered if God was listening. He wondered if God was even there.

In the distance dogs barked, one of the groups of strays that slip into the cemetery through gaps in the old creaking walls. Then the old man climbed to his feet, using the stone itself to steady himself. It was all wrapped up together in this place, the past, the present, and the future. It came together here just as he knew that it would come together soon again in the future.

He turned and retraced his path down the hill, struggling with a gnarled hand on his cane, knowing that a bitter day was coming, and that it would arrive soon.

Very well, he thought to himself. He had said his final good-byes and seen a final Havana sunset from this solemn but enchanting place. Most of the good-byes, anyway. His hand went to the other pocket of his pants where he kept a small pistol, twenty-two caliber, American made. He hadn't fired it in years, but, like himself, it still had life in it.

Some good-byes were more final than others, and the old man wanted to do them all properly.

For Manuel Perez, the trip to Cuba had been much easier than it had been for Alex, since no reception committee was waiting for him. He was in CIA custody, and his new handlers had brought him by unmarked jet into a vast naval base on the southeast tip of the island, where he was well received and well fed.

He was also well equipped. New armaments were given to him. A pistol and a sniper's rifle. He remained at the base overnight and was then moved to Havana. He wasn't there to enjoy the nightlife, however, as much as to be part of it.

His new handlers, after all, had seen to everything.

FORTY-FOUR

Morning: Alex's eyes opened in a flash. Somewhere at the edge of her consciousness, there was a sound, like a door sharply closing. It jounced her. She looked up, and three figures were standing before her. The one in the center wore a uniform.

The first thing Alex looked for was whether the man in the uniform was carrying a gun. He was not. To his left was a younger male, no more than a teenager, but very tall and muscular, obviously a farm kid used to heavy labor. He had the same face as the older man, a son, Alex presumed.

To the man's other side was a woman. Alex sat up quickly. The three *cubanos* were looking at her as if she had just arrived from outer space. Then her gaze settled briefly back on the well-built teenager. He was holding a machete close to his body.

"Señora," the older man said, speaking Spanish. "This is our cabin."

Alex sputtered an explanation. *"¡Lo siento!"* she said. *"I'm sorry!* I was lost and terribly tired. I will ... I will leave."

The man shook his head sharply and put a hand on her shoulder. "No, no," he said. "The area is filled with police and army. There was *un suceso horrible* — a horrible incident — yesterday on the beach. We cannot let you leave. You must come with us."

Alex drew a deep breath. *"¡Está bien!"* she said. "All right."

The woman went to the door and held it open. Obviously, they meant for Alex to follow. The bright rays of the morning sun slanted down onto the floor.

Alex made no effort to flee. The man in the uniform indicated a path that led from the cabin. The boy with the machete stayed behind and closed the door. When Alex looked back, he was using a small hammer to put the padlock and its clasp back in place.

The path was sandy, with small stones. No one said anything. Alex's heart pounded. Was this the beginning of years of imprisonment? She scrutinized the man's uniform, looking for some clue as to his intention, and suddenly she felt relieved. The words CORREO DE CUBA were stitched on an epaulet on his right shoulder. He was a postal carrier. Now she understood.

They led her through a clump of trees to a small cottage with a dilapidated façade and a rusty roof. The man went ahead and pushed open the door. He looked at Alex. His eyes were dark, curious, but not hostile. *"Por favor,"* he said. *"Entre."*

Alex followed. She wondered if she was being taken here to wait for police. She looked for evidence of a telephone but didn't see any. She came into a small threadbare central room with peeling paint but with a comfortable homey feel to it. There was a dining table near a ramshackle kitchen, which was off to the side. Suddenly she became aware of the pistol on her ankle. The last thing she wanted to do was to reveal it, much less use it. She wondered if the police or army had already been notified. Again she wondered if Paul was dead or alive.

"Please sit," the man said. "My name is Carlos," he said. "This is my wife, Maria, and my son, Guillermo."

Alex sat at the kitchen table. She nodded. *"Mi llamo Anna Maria,"* she said, sticking to the lie on her fake passport. *"Soy mexicana."* They nodded. The boy with the machete took a seat by the door, which he left partly open. Looking for someone? Alex wondered. Waiting? There was a napkin holder and a small bowl of fruit at the table's center, apples and oranges. There was a crucifix above the sink on the wall.

"¿Agua fría?" Carlos asked. Cold water?

"Si, por favor," she answered. Please.

He nodded to his wife. She opened a small old refrigerator and pulled out a pitcher of water. She poured a glass and set it on the table. The man turned on a ceiling fan, which created a nice breeze. The woman managed a faint smile at Alex. The woman looked as if she didn't much believe Alex but didn't care either.

Suddenly Alex had never been so thirsty in her life. She took the water with a trembling hand and drank almost all of it. She stole a glance at a clock. It was 9:15 in the morning. Alex finished the glass and the woman graciously refilled it.

"Who are you?" the man asked. "Why were you in our shed?"

She embarked on her cover story. "I'm *mexicana*," she said again. "I was touring Cuba with my husband. He has business here."

"He's *mexicano* or *cubano*?" the man asked. "Your husband?"

"Venezolano," she said, slipping into a convenient and well rehearsed lie. "We had a horrible fight. He threw me out of the car and left me."

The man snorted as if he sensed a ruse somewhere. "Why would a man abandon a woman as *bella* as you?" he asked, with a faint grin. "Even a stupid *Venezolano*?"

"My husband is not a good man," Alex continued without a beat. "I married him when I was very young. He has other women and wishes to discard me. We argued by the roadside and I jumped out of the car. I ran and hid. I started walking, but decided to hide when I saw my husband's car returning on the road. Then I grew very tired and slept."

"Ah," Carlos said. Alex had no idea whether he believed her or not.

The woman looked at Alex with sympathy, then reached for the bowl of fruit and pushed it to her. Alex, starving, took an apple and thanked her. Then Carlos explained that the shack where Alex had been hiding was where they kept supplies for their garden. His son saw that the lock had been knocked off its hinges that morning and went to reseal the building. Then he had discovered her.

"So no one else knows I'm here?" Alex said.

"Nadie," the man said. "No one. Just us."

"I will travel on shortly," Alex said. "I need to get back to Havana."

"There was a disturbance at the beach toward dawn yesterday morning," the man said. "Smugglers maybe. Or local drunks or criminals. No one knows exactly what happened."

"There are rumors," the wife said. "Yankee spies, maybe."

"Was your husband one of those men?" the man asked.

Alex quickly and adamantly answered, "No."

"A small ship came from somewhere," Carlos said. "It's all anyone has talked about." He said he had gone to his work the day before and heard nothing but rumors. Then, this morning, his son had told him about a woman asleep in their shed.

"People heard gunfire at dawn," the boy interjected from where he sat. "There were gunshots. The police and army have been all over the area." He waited for a moment, then added with too much enthusiasm. "I saw an ambulance too."

"The civil guard has been going door-to-door yesterday and today," Maria said softly. "*CDR*. They must have missed our shed." She was referring to the *Comite de la Defensa de La Revolución*. The CDR was everywhere in Cuba, Alex knew. In a high-minded way, they were the civil defense squad, its activities ranging from mass inoculations to political and civil surveillance. It was also the neighborhood fink squad, tattling on everyone.

Alex cringed. She also wondered if Carlos and his family were giving her information between the lines, warning her. She started to grasp a subtext, that they were not anxious to cooperate with authorities.

"Someone said some men were killed," Carlos said. "Intruders from off the island."

"How many?" Alex asked.

"Tres. Quizás cuatro," Carlos said. Three, maybe four. "But we don't know. Stories are everywhere, but stories are cheap." He paused. "Killed or wounded. *¿Quien sabe?* Who knows? Best to stay out of affairs like this," he said.

"I agree," Alex said, feeling her emotions sink again wondering if Paul had been killed.

"My friend Juanes," the boy interjected quickly, "said he saw soldiers. From the garrison at Matanzas. And bodies. Maybe three, I think. I don't know about a fourth."

His father waved him off. Alex didn't want to act too interested.

"It is not safe for a woman to travel alone under such conditions," Maria said. "Police. Army. Intruders, maybe. There is a bus to Havana, but it leaves at 9:00 a.m. It's too late."

"Maybe there's *una posada* nearby, an inn?" Alex asked.

"You may stay with us," the woman said. "You *should* stay with us. We will show you to the bus station tomorrow morning."

Alex hesitated. The family insisted.

"I would pay you," Alex said.

They shrugged. Maria stood and went to the refrigerator. She took out a plate, reached for one or two other items, and went to the counter. She arranged a small plate of food. She returned to the table with the plate. On it were chicken wings, a few slices of celery, and three small tortillas. She pushed the plate to Alex.

"Please eat," Maria said. "You are hungry. And you do not need to pay us."

"Only if you wish to and can," Carlos corrected.

"Whatever you wish to do," said Maria.

"You're too kind," Alex said.

"Please eat," Maria said again.

Alex ate. Carlos spoke again. "Are you American?" he asked point blank.

Alex looked at him. She reached to her passport and handed it to him. They crowded around and looked at it, their gaze alternating between her picture and Alex. Finally the man smiled and handed it back.

"But are you American?" the man asked again.

Alex looked back at the passport and pointed. *"Mexicana,"* she said again.

Carlos's eyes twinkled very slightly. "Very well," he said. "You are *mexicana*."

Alex finished her food. She indicated her clothing, the dirt, and the tears. "Maybe I could wash later," she said. "And maybe clean my clothing."

"Of course," Maria answered. "Do you have other clothes to wear?"

Alex shook her head. "I fled very quickly," Alex said. "I had extra clothes but I left them behind."

The woman laughed. Carlos, fully amused for the first time, shook his head.

"Maybe there is a shop nearby," Alex suggested. "Perhaps I could buy some extra things. Maybe a skirt, a few blouses."

Maria's face illuminated. "Come with me!" she said. "Clothing, yes!"

Maria sprung to her feet, taking Alex by the hand. She led her out of the house and down a long dirt road until they came to a few windy, dusty streets of a town. Maria greeted a few people she met on the way and was soon in front of another small building with a heavy front door and iron gratings.

The door was open for air circulation, as were most doors on the block. She rapped on a wooden door and called out for someone named Ramona.

A small child came into view, then turned and ran. His mother, Ramona, returned moments later and recognized Maria.

Ramona was Maria's sister. The door opened. Ramona ushered Alex and Maria in. The front room of the home had a few racks of used clothing and an area for a seamstress. The place, a small store and tailoring shop in Ramona's home, was a godsend.

"Please," Ramona said. "Find what you like."

Alex riffled through the racks. She picked out a pale green dress, a pair of skirts, one green one to the knees and one ankle length in pale orange, both in a tropical-weight cotton, two white blouses, a pair of shorts, and a pair of T-shirts. The store also had some fresh underwear. Alex used the family bedroom to change and tried to keep her gun well hidden, though she wasn't sure she had. Ramona had a twelve-year-old daughter who helped.

Ramona used her sewing skills to adjust the waist on one of the skirts. Within minutes all three women were laughing as old friends might.

There were some baseball caps there too, and Alex picked one. She avoided American logos and opted for one from a Mexican professional baseball team. *Los Sultanes de Monterrey.* The cap was perfect. Navy blue. It would help her blend into crowds. Then Alex added a pair of espadrilles for walking.

Ramona wouldn't let Alex leave until she had also repaired the damage to Alex's clothes. She washed out the area that had been spoiled with sand and dirt, then went to work with a needle and thread. Alex added a pair of sneakers that fit and also saw a used tote bag. She offered to buy it. Ramona let it go for the equivalent of five dollars.

In the end, Alex wore new clothing out the door.

"I have Mexican pesos and Cuban pesos," Alex said. "Which do you wish?"

There was a pause. Ramona and Maria exchanged a conspiratorial smile.

"Do you maybe have American dollars?" Ramona asked.

Alex paused. "I might have a few," she said. "You'd prefer those?" Ramona nodded, not surprisingly. "How many do you want?"

Ramona couldn't bring herself to ask for such an extravagant amount as she had in mind. So, with a giggle, she wrote the number on a pad and showed it to Alex.

Thirty-five dollars. She looked as if she were ready to bargain.

But Alex exuded gratitude, not a cheap streak. *"Perfecto,"* Alex said. *"¡Treinta cinco dólares!"* Alex peeled off thirty-five dollars. Ramona was ecstatic. Then they chatted about local news and the rumors about yesterday's incident.

Later that afternoon, Maria and Alex strolled back to the house.

Behind the house was a makeshift shower stall for bathing. There would be no hot water. Maria warned that the warmth of the day would soon be gone and the sea breezes made bathing chilly at night. So it was best to shower before their late dinner, while the sun was still on the back of the house.

The water pump wasn't working, Maria warned further, and the showerhead was out of order. But the bathing area would drain properly. So the family directed Alex to the well, where she drew four buckets of water. Guillermo helped carry the water to the bathing area. There was a single shower curtain, badly torn, behind which Alex could shield herself from two directions only, but the family gave her privacy. Maria handed her a small bar of Camay soap, the type found in downscale American motels.

Alex stashed her new tote bag and clothes by the shower stall, safely away from the water. She pulled the curtain and undressed. Maria gave her a towel, then left. Alex hung the towel on an exposed nail outside the stall and washed quickly. She was out of everyone's view. The cool water, fresh air, and soap on her body refreshed her. She closed her eyes and for a moment savored the notion that she had survived the day and might even survive the journey, though the uncertainty about Paul's fate gnawed at her.

Abruptly, she heard a male voice on the other side of the curtain, so close that it jarred her. *"¿Señora?"* the voice asked.

Alex grabbed the towel and covered herself. But it was only Guillermo, the teenager. *"¿Otra toala?"* he asked. He had another towel for her, in case the first one was too small.

"Si, Gracias." Alex answered.

Guillermo flipped the second towel up to where it hung over the bar of the shower curtain. Peeking through one of the rips in the curtain, Alex could see that the boy, bashful, was looking the other way. Alex suppressed a smile. She finished her shower and dressed in her new clothes.

She came back inside, still functioning in an information void of what had transpired the previous morning. She knew the rumors that the locals were spreading, but questions haunted her: Was Paul dead? What was the larger picture? Did Washington yet know what had happened? Who was looking for her? Cuban police, Cuban security? Violette? Figaro? Anyone?

As for Roland Violette, Alex had carefully memorized the contact procedures. She had little choice but to persist in her initial assignment until it blew up completely. But ugly scenarios further presented themselves. What if, by contacting Violette, she was walking further into a trap? What if the CIA wasn't leveling on their intentions with him. There were plenty of questions and some fly-by-night morality. But no answers emerged.

That evening, as the sun was setting, the family took Alex to a small café in town. Alex went warily, not wishing to be spotted by police, but the hour passed uneventfully, during which she watched the street from a corner table. Working men knocked back slugs of rum in the bar lit by fluorescent light. She listened as dominos banged on tables. She tried to tune in on the bawdy passionate conversations among lovers and strangers. The everpresent whiff of *puros* permeated the night air, and she heard the beat of drums and maracas through bad speakers.

Later, Alex sat in the small living room with her new friends and they chatted. Maria seemed to be preoccupied with correspondence that she was writing by hand. They had no extra bedroom for her, so when they retired to their single bedroom at about 11:00 p.m., Alex slept on the sofa.

FORTY-FIVE

At a side-street café in Old Havana, shortly before midnight, business was finally slacking off. Gradually the café El Rincon Cubano emptied out. Two couples still sat at separate tables, as well as a single man in a suit, reading a newspaper. At a table in the rear sat an old revolutionary named Garcia, drinking by himself. One of the couples rose and left, followed by the man who'd been reading the newspaper. Then the other couple started smooching, but soon they got up and left as well. Watching all this was yet another man at the bar, alone, nursing a *mojito*.

José, the bartender, spoke to the barfly. "I'm going to close," he said. "Time for everyone to go home."

The final drinker nodded. "May I finish?" he asked politely.

"You may finish," José answered.

The drinker turned to the window and spotted a man lurking outside. He checked to see if Garcia was still at the rear table. A figure appeared at the door and entered. The man at the bar looked at the new arrival and gave a decisive nod.

José was about to speak when the man at the bar drew a pistol, held it low across the bar, and aimed it at José. He raised a finger to his lips to indicate silence. Everything would be okay if José remained silent.

Meanwhile, the lone man in the suit got up, yawned, and stretched. Manuel Perez closed the door behind him. He went straight for Garcia, who was straightening his jacket.

"¿Qué quiere usted, Señor?" Garcia asked. What do you want?

What he wanted was not conversation. Perez reached a hand into his jacket and quickly pulled it out again. It now held a small powerful pistol, one of those Italian ones that are just perfect for killing in tight areas.

Garcia yelled in terror when he saw the weapon. He tried to bolt but Perez fired. The first bullet caught the old revolutionary in the stomach and hurled him backward over a table. Then Perez pounced on his fallen prey and pushed the nose of the pistol to Garcia's head. He fired point blank.

Two loud pops got the job done.

Perez turned and was quickly out the door. His accomplice gave José a curt nod and packed away his own pistol. He was out the door as quickly as Perez, disappearing into the shadows of a pleasant summer night in Havana.

Alex tried to sleep, but a violent fight between two feral cats just beyond the open screened window woke her up at 2:00 a.m. The animals screamed like banshees and the brawl recurred around 3:40. The next morning at 5:00 a.m., sunlight flowed in brilliant yellow into the living room through the same window, followed by the incessant crowing of several roosters.

The Cuban family gave her breakfast. At 8:00 a.m., Guillermo walked her to the bus stop on the road that led out of the village and westward into the town of San Ferrer. He explained that she should go to San Ferrer first, then take a connecting bus in San Herlito, two stops down the road, which would connect to Havana.

Guillermo stayed with her. A dozen people assembled to wait for the 9:00 bus. Then a blue vehicle appeared at a bend down the road, and Guillermo explained that this was the bus Alex wanted.

"Thank you for everything," Alex said. "And thank your family again for me."

Guillermo nodded. But Alex could tell that the boy had something more to say.

He made sure no one else could hear. "At Doña Ramona's dress shop yesterday," he said, "my mother saw your gun. She told my father."

Alex tried to take it without missing a beat.

"That will be our secret won't it, I hope?" she said.

"Yes, it will," the teenager nodded. "My parents won't tell anyone."

He then reached into his pocket. He pulled out two envelopes. They were letters, sealed, unstamped, and addressed.

"My mother has a brother who lives in Florida," he said. "And she has a grandfather who lives in New York. Maybe you can mail these letters to them when you get back to America."

Alex took the two envelopes. "One way or another, Guillermo," Alex said, "I'll see that these get to the proper destination."

Guillermo nodded. He smiled. "Good-bye," he said in English.

"Adios, Guillermo," she answered in Spanish. *"Vaya con dios."*

"Con dios," he nodded. She carefully put the envelopes at the bottom of her tote bag, near her gun, and zipped the bag shut again. She gave the boy a hug and released him.

The bus was a Toyota, made in Japan, battered but not as old as some of the automobiles on the street. Alex mounted, found a seat, and waved to her host. Guillermo raised a hand and waved back, seeming sorry to see her go. Then he turned and walked away. Moments later the bus accelerated and was gone. Alex settled in for the three-hour journey to Havana. She leaned back in her seat with a smile. She knew that at about that moment, back at the Valdez home, Maria, straightening the kitchen, would find the hundred-dollar bill that Alex had left beneath her breakfast plate.

FORTY-SIX

When Alex arrived in Havana late that morning, it was obvious that early summer had arrived. She stepped off of the bus at the Plaza de Armas, the administrative center of the capital. The Plaza de Armas was also the city's oldest square, a beautifully landscaped park where booksellers bartered with tourists and residents. The trees had flowered and the old square was open and alive with people. She drew a breath and took in the new part of the world that was before her, a city that was vibrant but had the feel of being frozen in another era.

In her new cotton dress and with her tote bag slung over her shoulder, she blended in. On her head, she wore her blue Monterrey Sultans baseball cap. She moved along a street that was populated by people and bicycles and a few moving cars. Many of those that moved were pre-1959 American models.

Alex sighed. More than anything, she felt as if she wanted to call a time-out, to step outside of herself and her assignment for a few weeks, a few days, or even a few hours. The horror of what had happened on the bay two mornings before was still with her.

She crossed the square and walked down two streets before finding a bar that was open. It was on another square, filled with pedestrians and small stores that catered to tourists. Postcards, camera equipment, and snacks to go. Alex sat down at a small wooden table outside on the sidewalk. She ordered a coffee with some pastries. Her morning was slowly transformed into something modestly more pleasant than it had been. She watched the street. Out of nervous habit, her hand checked in her tote bag for her gun.

Now. What to do?

She formed a plan. She would not go to the hotel that had

been her and Paul's designated meeting place — but rather to one nearby. She would register. Mexican passport, Mexican credit card, but no one would be the wiser as to who she was as long as her IDs hadn't been blown. She thought back again to Paul's "catastrophe plan" involving the Hotel Ambos Mundos, and Fajardie's "disaster" advice involving Elke at the Swiss Consulate. She hoped that Paul was still alive and she would attempt to make that rendezvous later in the afternoon. Between 3:00 and 5:00 he had said.

As for Violette and Figaro — they were who she was here for. She would still try to snag Violette, coax him onto the airplane leaving the country. And she would stay alert to any attempt by the phantom-like Figaro to contact her and accompany her to the U.S. as well.

But a further thought occurred to her. What if Paul had escaped but had been wounded? What if he were in a hospital somewhere? She thought this over carefully. To attempt to find him might result in her giving herself away. Yet Paul would need her help to get out of the country. Then again, if he had been captured as well as injured, then there would be no way she could be expected to bring him back to the U.S. And he wasn't even alive as far as she knew. Well, she would wait and play her hand cautiously, she decided, keeping her eyes wide open.

Patience, she reminded herself. Patience could save her life in such a situation. Today, she calculated, was June 12. She had been on the island for two and a half days. Now she would rendezvous at the Ambos Mundos today and tomorrow. Then she would have to play it by ear.

She knew from the smell of the salty air that she was not far from the harbor. She paid her bill at the café and departed.

A sign pointed her to the seafront. She followed the path out to the rocky shore, where she felt the warmth of the sun on her arms and face, combined with the salty spray of the surf crashing on the stones at water level beneath a promenade. Across the water, on the other side of the canal, was the ancient fort of

San Carlos, built as a defense by the Spaniards at the end of the eighteenth century and later used as a prison by the dictators Machedo and Batista — and then by Che after the Revolution. The area reeked with history. With the exception of a few modern boats, the scene before her probably hadn't changed much in a century and a half.

She turned. She recalled from memory the address of the Hotel Ambos Mundos. Trying to look as much like a tourist as possible, she consulted her map and began the short walk through Old Havana. Her path led her through a warren of narrow cobblestone avenues lined with baroque buildings that had changed little since the seventeenth and eighteenth centuries. The street life was vibrant, the surroundings impressive.

Then, eventually, she stood across the street from the hotel. A pink façade fronted a rambling old building. Ambos Mundos: both worlds, appropriately named. Alex walked toward it and entered.

The lobby was a scramble of architectures, faded yellow with appealing dark woodwork. A rickety old Otis elevator cranked and creaked at the far end. Once again, Alex felt as if she had stepped into a time warp.

The lobby was cooler than the outdoors. She looked each way and saw what had to be the piano bar to her left. Purposefully, she walked toward it. It was only moderately busy. Several large plants softened the look of the room. Large chairs were scattered around, comfortable big old leather and wicker chairs. A pair of ceiling fans turned slowly. The carpet was reddish and threadbare, and a piano player softly weaved a muted samba into the air.

As she entered, several men, seated alone at the bar, turned their eyes toward her. She scanned them quickly. No Paul Guarneri.

Who were the men? Tourists? Undercover police keeping an eye on the place? There were a couple of dozen people in the room and she tried to take them all in.

She had hoped to see Paul there. She masked her disappointment. *Please, God, next time, let him be there, alive and well. Please.* She sent prayers off into the void. No answer, no acknowledgement. If only it could be that simple.

Well, wrong time, she reminded herself. Not wrong time for prayer but wrong time for Paul. She turned and left the hotel.

Then, working from memory and with only one glance at the map, she found her way down a maze of side streets to the old Iglesia de San Lázaro, a faded edifice in blue stucco. It was her primary drop site, but she wasn't sure what she would find. The front door was ajar. There was a lovely pair of antique stained-glass windows on each side of the front portal, but one had been cracked. A plywood board protected it.

She entered and, in keeping with her plan, slid into the back row on the left side. She reflected for a few moments, as if in prayer, and stared at the ornate rococo cross above the altar. She took stock. No one else present. God, she mused, had provided her the perfect time and opportunity for her visit.

She looked around. Any spies? Any observers whom she hadn't seen at first glance? Her nerves were suddenly on edge again. Who needed post-traumatic stress when she could have her traumatic stress while the events were taking place?

Her thin cotton dress stuck to her skin. She felt sweat pouring from her. Inside, it felt like a dozen hummingbirds were zipping around her stomach.

Then, convinced that no one was looking, she kneeled forward to pray. She closed her eyes and slid her right hand under the pew in front and groped along for several feet in each direction. She prayed it would be there.

Finally her fingertips hit something—pieces of heavy plastic tape, such as Maurice Fajardie back in Langley had suggested. She followed these along until she found metal, a little square of it. Her heart surged. She could tell before she even retrieved it: a cell phone, complete with a power cord for recharging. She pulled it out of the tape and held it in her hand. She turned it on.

It powered up. She checked it for messages. There were none. She examined it to see if it had been tinkered with in any way. She found nothing that alarmed her. As a precaution, she shut it down, removed the battery and the SIM card, then reassembled it. Then she slid it into her tote. She made sure it was turned off to minimize the chances that it could serve as a GPS for an enemy.

Then she heard a loud bang behind her. In an instant her hand, still in her tote bag, jumped from the cell phone to her gun, and she was convinced she had waltzed into a trap. Her wet palm closed upon the weapon and clutched it.

She turned. A priest. He was a small elfin figure, much like the little men in black cassocks she had seen in remote Italian towns when she was a college student. Her eyes swept the space. No one else. She was safe, or so it looked. She looked back at the priest. His hands were clear and clean. Not a fake priest who was actually a gunman or a cop, she deduced. She released her own gun.

The priest crossed himself, then reacted in surprise to see a pretty young woman sitting in a rear pew. He nodded to her, smiled, and mumbled a blessing in Spanish.

Alex returned the greeting. Then he walked down the center aisle and went about his business of tending to something behind the altar. She watched him all the way, making sure he was okay. Then she bowed to the cross and quickly exited the church.

She returned to the small square near the Hotel Ambos Mundos, where she caught her breath and let her heart settle. She searched her soul. With all that money sitting in a bank account in her favor in New York, did she really need this? Is this truly what she was supposed to do with her life?

Alex sat down at a table at a café on the square. A waiter—handsome with an easy smile—approached her. He spoke in Spanish and she answered easily.

"I'm hot and very thirsty," she said. "What would be good?"

His smile widened. "Orange juice, just squeezed," he said. "Or lemonade."

"From a bottle or fresh?" she asked.

"Both are bottled," he answered.

"Lemonade would be excellent," she said.

He nodded and disappeared. She turned her attention to the plaza. She watched the city live and breathe. She was relieved that no one paid her any special attention. She was used to catching the eyes of men, and she was used to being able to ignore it. The linen dress she wore was reasonably demure. The hem was at her knee. She felt highly vulnerable.

She finished the lemonade and was hungry again. She ordered a small plate of shredded pork with rice and beans. She noticed from people at other tables that Coca-Cola had slipped past the embargo. So she ordered one. Then a second, both with ice. A slight breeze kicked up. She felt better and began, for the first time, to relax.

For a moment, she scanned the city street. There was not a brand, nor a neon sign, nor an advertisement of any sort. Rather, there was just a view of time slowly drifting from the far past into the present, with no particular hurry. The square was baked in Caribbean sunshine. Cuban socialism had created a strange mid-twentieth-century aesthetic, a city freed from agitation, caught in a strange state of decay and quietude.

She saw vast spaces, away from the assault of every form of commercial message and, for that matter, far from Twitter and email as well. The global mall was nowhere to be seen in this city, and, in a way, she cherished it. It was so different from New York. Even when she took a taxi in New York, a television would come on with its infomercials. Here she could watch the square, watch the modest traffic, watch the sunlight on the walls of the old city, watch lovers passing, watch businessmen expounding, watch cab drivers negotiating, watch children smiling. Here was the idle sensuality of the pre-Blackberry age.

Beyond street-level doors were courtyards, some shabby, some fine. Her eyes, rising one flight up, saw that Havana had also preserved its antique wrought-iron balconies and its old baroque Castilian flourishes. Even if the city was crumbling, even if it could be interpreted as a monument to the failure of communism, it had its charm.

She left the café and wandered across the square to the hotel once again. She took stock. She decided to walk to a nearby hotel called La Posada Cubana, a faded plaster building, just off the main square, with a tattered blue awning. She registered without a problem. The *posada* was close enough to the Ambos Mundos to be convenient, but far enough away to help her keep a low profile. She didn't want to register at the Ambos in case it was a trap.

She went to her room. The window looked out onto a backstreet. She examined the ledge and the nearby rooftop and quickly assessed that the window could make an escape route if necessary. She was pleased.

She drew the curtain and took out the cell phone. She opened it and turned it on. The connection remained. What was that number again? Who were those two presidents? Bush Johnson. Eight eight six four. Better pick the correct Bush and the correct Johnson, she mused. It was the first funny thought she had had since the bullets had hit the boat.

Again she was aware of the sweat on her back. It told her that even if she felt calm, her insides were set to explode. On the other end of the phone was the click of a pickup. No voice, no human hand, just an electronic response.

"I'm here," she said and then disconnected. Then she dialed another random number and clicked off before it answered. That way she cancelled out any record of the last number she dialed. Okay, she told herself. At least her better instincts were working.

Good vibe: She felt as if she were back in Lagos or Kiev or Paris or Madrid or Cairo. She was back in the game, liking it against her better judgment.

Bad vibe: Things had blown up in all those places. So much for better judgment.

She glanced at her watch. It was 3:45 p.m. She went back to a café on the square and ordered a cold drink. Then she examined the cell phone. Yes, it had worked. But there was no return message. The waiting game for the scummy Roland Violette, such that it was, had begun.

She finished her meal and paid. The cost was equivalent to five American dollars. She stood, crossed the square, and fell in with the pedestrian traffic. Again she entered the Ambos Mundos. It was still rendezvous time. Or not.

The faded yellow lobby was cool and refreshing again after the hot city streets. The old elevator continued to crank and creak, and once again, Alex felt as if she had walked into the past.

Again in the lobby, she looked each way — there was no Paul. She walked to the piano bar where the large fans still whirled on the ceiling and lazily cooled the room. The wicker chairs had been rearranged in the past hour. No surprise there. The carpet was still reddish and threadbare, and the piano player was still playing sambas.

Then, just as she was again scanning the men at the bar, whose eyes had once again turned to her as she entered, she heard a familiar voice behind her. "Alex," said the male voice shyly. It said her name so softly and reassuringly that it seemed to come up out of the ground. English with an American accent. "Well, I'll be darned," the voice said. "Imagine seeing you here!"

She turned sharply and looked behind her. Seated in a small alcove, partially obscured by a large potted plant, positioned where he could watch everyone who came and went, was the man she knew. He was alive — in a fresh suit and seeming to be no worse for their crash landing on Cuba's hostile shores.

"Paul!" she said too loudly. "Holy . . . !"

He held a finger to his lips. For a moment, she stared. Then, his lies and his anguishing casualness notwithstanding, some pent-up emotion in her broke. She was thrilled to see a familiar face, and just as thrilled to know that he was alive.

"Paul!" she repeated. "Thank God!"

His long legs unfolded, he stood, and his arms opened in a broad welcoming gesture. She rushed to him. She didn't know whether to kiss him or throttle him, so instead she let him call the tune. He held her in a long powerful embrace and finally planted a kiss on her cheek. With that one gesture, their joint mission seemed to be back on track. And to Alex, the world seemed much less of a lonely, foreboding, frightening place.

Across the square from the Hotel Ambos Mundos, Major Ivar Mejias stepped from an unmarked police car, which had just cruised to an abrupt halt at the curb. His shirt was crisp and white, he proudly displayed his sidearm as well as his badge, and displeasure and impatience were written all over his face.

Two other police cars jounced to the curb behind him. The drivers stayed with the cars as a small phalanx of uniformed city policemen assembled near their commander. Mejias signaled with a nod of his head toward the hotel's side of the street. Half a dozen other police officers fell in stride behind him.

All of Mejias's officers wore bulky sidearms. Two carried shotguns. It might have been a routine midday patrol, one that made the tourists feel safer and kept the *jineteras*, the street hustlers, on the defensive. Mejias and his small detachment would normally go from bar to bar, shop to shop, eyeballing people and places, running with whatever they saw against anyone for whom they might be on special alert.

The shotguns, however, indicated that something out of the ordinary was afoot. Mejias was a very angry man today, and nothing about this patrol was ordinary. In fact, nothing, he felt, could ever be ordinary again until he located the two people — a man and a woman — who had slipped away from the skiff on the beach.

FORTY-SEVEN

Paul was, Alex was reminded quickly, a big man and a strong one. His arms were tight around her, and he hugged her dearly, as if they were expiating for what had happened at the shoreline. The hug lasted for several long seconds. Then he released her. She looked him in the eye. She had to fight back the wave of anger that was now resurgent.

"What the—?" she began to sputter. She checked herself, then spoke softly but angrily. "What happened on the beach?"

"Well, I'd say we had a calamitous arrival," he said in low tones. His breath was boozy. "How would *you* categorize it?" he asked.

"Sheer hell," she said.

"That would work as a description," he answered. "Hey, look. There's a lot to talk about, but we haven't been knocked out of the game," he said. "Not at all."

He motioned for her to sit down. There was a wicker seat, very welcoming, close by an overhead fan and a huge plant. She settled into the seat. There was a tall *mojito* on the table, half finished.

"Can we talk here?" she asked.

"There are better places, but I think we're okay. What the Cuban government can put forth in venality, they surrender in incompetence. I don't think we're being recorded, if that's what you mean."

"That's what I mean," she said, looking around. The piano player, fortunately, covered their conversation, which is probably why Guarneri had chosen the place. With the music and the din of conversation, motor noise, voices from outside, and the activity in the lobby, it would be impossible to eavesdrop. Then, turning back to Guarneri, she said, "Tell me about our reception committee."

"I don't know much more than you do," he said, "other than we both got away."

"And the three men on the boat?"

"Didn't make it, apparently," Paul said. "I'm sorry about that."

"They got hit badly," she said.

"Yes, they did," said Guarneri, working a sprig of mint from the *mojito*. "Dead, I'm afraid. There's going to be some nasty feedback in Miami when word gets back."

"Who was shooting at us?" she asked again. "Militia? Army? I thought I saw uniforms."

"You did see uniforms," Guarneri said, "but I didn't recognize them. I was trying to keep my head down too. I got to the controls of the boat and reversed the engines, while I got in a few last shots. I hit the water not long after you did and went in the opposite direction. That way at least one of us would have a better chance of making it to shore ... or that's what I hoped."

"I'm surprised they didn't see us," she said.

"Remember that mist on the water," he said, "like a low cloud? It must have been just enough to hide us. You're religious — say a prayer of thanks sometime." He looked for a waiter and signaled. "What are you drinking?" he asked.

"I just had a Coca-Cola," she said.

"That's what you just had, but what are you having now?" he asked.

"Paul, I'm not looking to get smashed in the middle of the afternoon."

"Why? You got something better to do?"

"As a matter of fact, I do. I have a certain Mr. Violette to locate."

"He's waited twenty-six years," Paul said. "He'll wait twenty-four hours more."

She reached into her tote bag and pulled out the cell phone.

"Ah. You've been to the dead drop already," he said.

"Yes."

"And that's the phone?"

"That's it."

A waiter arrived, a nice-looking young man in a short white service jacket and black pants. He looked like he could have fit into Perez Prado's band in 1957. Alex covered the phone. They were still uncommon in Havana, cell phones, though not illegal, which they had been till recently.

"The *mojitos* are excellent," Guarneri said. "If I had ten bucks for every mojito that Hemingway knocked back in this place, I could retire. Try one."

"I don't like to mix."

"Don't be a killjoy," he said. "We're not doing anything else for a while. Let some air in your sails. *Somos de vacaciones. Mia querida. ¡Viva la vida!*" he added facetiously. "We're on vacation. Have some booze. Live a little."

The waiter smiled patiently.

"Un mojito, por favor," she said, acquiescing.

"¿Un grande, como Señor?" the waiter asked. *"¿Doublé?"* A double?

"No, no," she said.

"¡Si, si!" Paul insisted, ordering a double for her. He shooed the waiter away.

"I'm glad you're alive," she said. "Despite everything."

"And I'm glad you are, Alex," he said. "I was worried. I really was."

He placed a hand on her leg and gave it a squeeze. Then he released it.

The bartender, watching them, made a show of assembling the drink. Mint leaves crushed on ice, lime wedges, rum, rum, and more rum, then a dash, and just a dash, of club soda. He proudly moved his concoction to a serving tray.

"By the way, that's the law over there," Guarneri continued in a very low voice. "Cops. Undercover. *Clandestino.*" He didn't move his head. He signaled by pointing his eyes toward the far end of the bar.

Alex scanned fast and found two men in a conversation.

They wore plantation shirts, long and not tucked in. She saw just enough of a bulge on their hips to conceal side arms. Both men were right-hand draws, so she knew what to watch for. Everyone could see the weapons, but then again they couldn't. That's how it worked here, she concluded. Police, but don't ask and don't tell. Stay away from them and hope they stay away from you. The men were keeping an eye on the crowd. She began to sweat again. She wondered if they were after her. Not these cops, particularly, but whatever cops dealt with shore intrusions.

"I should find another line of work. I didn't see them," she said. "What if they come over?"

"We speak Spanish to them and make nice. And we remain very, very polite. You have your Mexican passport?" he asked.

"Of course. You have your Canadian one?"

"Wouldn't travel in a commie country without it," he said.

"And what if they ask how we know each other and what we're doing in Cuba?"

"Our original cover story stands. Husband and wife. Tourists." He eyed her. "What's the matter? Nervous?"

"You bet I'm nervous," she said in a low voice. "We just entered this country illegally. Or have you already forgotten?"

"Just chill and go with the flow," he said. "We'll be fine."

The waiter arrived with the drinks. He set the frosted glass in front of Alex. She reached for her purse, but Guarneri stayed her hand. "When I order drinks, the woman never pays," he said. "You have your religion and I have mine. That's mine." He handed a carefully folded ten dollar bill to the waiter. *"Quédese con el vuelto,"* he said. Keep the change.

"Gracias, Señor," the waiter answered. He gave a respectful nod and took off.

"The almighty dollar is welcome here, I see," she mused.

"Why wouldn't it be? It's preferred. Americans are welcome too. Cubans like Americans. It's just the American government they hate, even more than they hate their own. But a lot of Americans don't like their own government either," Paul said. "So right there Americans and Cubans have a bond. That's something that can be built on."

"Sure," she said. Nervously, she gave a sidelong glance at the two cops.

"Don't worry," he said. "They're not after you. They're just goofing off."

"Good thing," she sighed.

"I've got your back," he said. "You should know that."

"You've got my back? Like on the boat?"

He shrugged easily. "You're alive, aren't you? You got away, didn't you?"

"Barely!"

"Well, 'barely' counts," he said. "And don't worry about the police. They walked in about five minutes before you did, so they're not trailing you. They came in through the back exit to the bar, which leads through the kitchen. That way they wouldn't have to cross the lobby. They do it all the time. They know the ways in and ways out, they move around close to the walls, particularly at night. Like rats. Which is what they are."

He watched them without looking directly at them. So did Alex. She took another sip. The barman here knew how to make these things. The Cuban rum was bold and sugary, almost chewy. As she listened to Paul, Alex kept an eye on the two cops, who had their backs to the bar now, reclining slightly, cold bottles of Bucanero, the Cuban beer, in their hands as they surveyed the patrons.

One of the cops glanced in Alex's direction.

She hid behind her drink, not actually drinking it—one of them needed to stay sharp—but pretending to enjoy a leisurely moment with her husband.

"What if the cops had seen you paying in U.S. currency?" she asked.

Guarneri scoffed. "They probably would have asked for some for themselves," Guarneri said. "Who wants a lousy Cuban peso? No one. The money is less than useless. There are two official currencies here: the tourist peso and the worthless local peso. You don't think the Cubans buy consumer goods from Europe and Japan with pesos, do you? That brings us to the unofficial currency. Euros and dollars, mostly dollars. Fifty years of Cuban Marxism and the currency is worthless. What does that tell you about far-left economics?"

"Several things," she said.

"Name one."

"Marxism doesn't work," she said.

"Good. Name another."

"The American embargo made sure that Marxism didn't work."

"I'll allow that. Name a third."

"I want to get the job done and get out of here as soon as possible," she said. "Havana is vibrant, charming, fascinating — and it gives me the creeps. So why don't we get down to business and get a move on?"

"What do you want to know?" he asked.

"Why was there an official reception for our boat?" Alex pressed. "That tells me that something has gone terribly wrong with at least one end of this operation."

"You're right, of course," Guarneri said. "But there were all sorts of reasons the boat could have been making that run and that the Cubans wanted to intercept it. They could have thought it was smuggling black market goods into Cuba, or picking up Cubans who wanted to buy their way *off* the island. It's more unusual for people to try to sneak onto the island than off it." He paused. "Pierre, the pilot that dropped us off. He's a smuggler. That won't shock you, will it? It was his boat and those were three of his men. They're Miami underworld, all of them. Bad guys, but you don't get many good guys in that line of work. They take their chances, and they know that someday the odds will go against them."

"Human life is human life," she said. "I don't like the taking of it."

"You think *I* do? Well, you're wrong if you do," he said. "I don't. So light a candle for them if you want, but you'd be wise to go about your business. The world is what it is. Pierre, Leo, and their cronies had a lot of enemies. The most likely explanation for what happened was that the reception committee was for Leo and his boatmen, not us."

"But you don't *know* that."

"But we go on that assumption," he insisted. "I know there are people here who have me in the crosshairs. Probably more than I know. I'm in enemy territory. The walls have ears and people talk." A beat and he added. "I have relatives here. You knew that, didn't you?"

"Of course. You mentioned an uncle and my best friends at the FBI filled in a few blanks, also."

"That was nice of them," Guarneri said."What about a CIA check?" he asked. "Surely you got a briefing there too."

"You asked me that already and the answer hasn't changed. I talked to several CIA people," she said. "The subject was Roland Violette more than you. If they had anything on you, they weren't willing to share it with me," she said.

"I'm flattered. Or insulted," he said. "Eventually I'll know which. Can't ever trust them, you know," Paul added with a smile.

"*Who*? Trust *who*?" she asked.

"CIA," he said. "Bunch of rats if there ever were some. Goes way back. Batista. Kennedy assassination. Bay of Pigs. Five hundred plots against Fidel. Jimmy Rosseli. Sam Giancana. Lucky Luciano. I don't think those button-down buttheads in Langley have told the truth one percent of the time when it comes to this island. They've told the same lies so many times they actually believe them."

"I know," she said. "But there are some people at the Agency I know personally. Them I trust. Most of the time, not all of the time."

"We're on the same page, then," Guarneri said. And he drained his glass. "You haven't heard from 'the Violet,' right?"

She snuck a glance at her phone again, just in case there was a message waiting. There wasn't. "No," she said.

"Then I suggest we proceed with my mission here," he said. "If you hear from your pigeon, we'll recalculate the time."

"Fair enough," Alex said.

"How much do you know about this place?" Guarneri asked. "I mean, *really* know?"

"What place? The hotel? Havana?"

"Cuba."

"I'm learning fast," she said. "And I'm getting the idea that an hour of hanging with you is worth two weeks of study back in New York."

"That's probably true. Look, bribery is a way of life here, just like anywhere else in Central America," he said, rambling. "There's no legal way to get ahead so everyone jockeys for an illegal way, or at least those who are still trying to get ahead. Most of the population here has been beaten into the ground. The clever people have left, the wealthy people have left. The only people of any import who are still here are the people who can't beat the system. Most work for the government. You know how that operates. The people pretend to work and the government pretends to pay them. You know what would work best?" he asked. "You know what would get this place moving again? If the Castro Brothers drop dead at the same time, the embargo gets lifted, American companies pour in, and the economy gets jump-started ..."

While Paul talked, Alex sipped her drink. Then she watched as the two undercover policemen ditched their beers onto the bar. They snapped to attention. They were more in her line of vision than Paul's. A wiry little man had come into the room, white shorts, badge, and a hefty sidearm. He seemed to be a commander of some sort. The cops at the bar were afraid of him, and a team of uniformed people followed. Everyone in the area gave way.

Horribly, the realization was upon her. Her heart kicked in her chest. "Paul, put down your drink and shut up," she said.

He stopped in midsentence. "What?" he asked.

Alex nodded toward the bar as a tense scene unfolded. The wiry little man was vehemently chewing out his undercover guys, who looked scared to death. Other drinkers moved away. The other uniformed officers lurked behind their commander who was making the guys in the plantation shirts sweat.

"What's going on?" she asked.

He looked, took a second to focus, then looked away.

"Uh-oh. We've overstayed our welcome," he said with rising urgency. "That's a political division of the police department. That sawed-off little stump with the 'stache is a commander. He's ticked because his guys were goofing off. He's only going to be on the street checking if something big is afoot. The shotguns tell us they're ready for serious trouble."

"It's worse than that, Paul," she said.

"Why's that?"

"Take a *good* look," she said. "And try to get the booze out of your system. Don't you recognize him? That's the commander from the beach."

He looked again and turned away fast when he recognized the man. Paul cursed long and low. "Okay. We need to get out of here," he said. From a mood of boozy reverie, he was suddenly sharp as a tack again.

"Fast. But not together," Paul said, leaning back and turning away. One of the men with a shotgun was scanning the room.

"They're blocking the door," Alex said. "We have to walk right past them to get out."

"Yup," Paul said. "That's exactly what *you're* going to do."

"*Me?* Alone?"

"In thirty seconds," he said, "before they start giving this room a thorough toss."

"What are *you* going to do?"

"Leave through the men's room window," he said. "It's got a grate that lifts off."

"How do you know?"

"I checked it earlier," he said.

"What if they have that exit covered?"

"Then I'm sunk," he said.

"How about *I* go through the window and *you* try to waltz past them?" she suggested.

He shook his head. "Won't work, Alex. They're more likely to recognize me than you. I get the window, you get to flirt past the *toros* like a good Latin *chica*."

"You're a pig."

"I know. We'll discuss that later."

He reached into his pocket and drew out a set of keys. He opened the ring and separated one key from the rest.

"Listen carefully. Five blocks from here, south on the Calle 43, there's an old Toyota Land Cruiser. Dark green, beat up, looks like a Jeep, and a license plate ending in four-three-one. It's a family jalopy. So I'd appreciate being able to return it without bullet holes."

"You're cautioning me about bullet holes after the landing we had?" she demanded.

"Yes, I am," he went on. "I want to return the Jeep without a problem at the end of our visit. Anyway, it's just past the La Sultanado intersection. This is an extra ignition key in case I don't get there."

"What about the door key?"

"There are no doors. This is Cuba."

He handed her the key. "Are you checked into a hotel?" he asked, as the cops were starting to wander through the crowded room.

"Posada Cubana. Across the block down a side street."

"Good. I'll find it and meet you there tomorrow between noon and three if we get separated," he said. "If I don't turn up, assume I was arrested. Now. Go to the car. Right now. I'll try to meet you there. If I don't show up, leave in ten minutes."

"Where should I go?"

"Anywhere for a couple of hours. Just lie low. Got it?"

"Got it."

"What if you don't show up tomorrow?"

"My problem, not yours, so have a nice life. Now you get out of here first," Paul said. "And do it now. Flash a smile, a leg, whatever you have to do. Anything to get past these guys. You won't have a second chance."

"Okay," Alex said. She knew the drill.

He gripped her hand quickly to give her courage, then released.

She hooked her bag over her shoulder, brushed back her hair, and turned. She moved quickly through the crowd without looking back. She passed one uniformed man, then another. She smiled and winked. They pretended not to notice her but obviously did.

Success so far. Then, twenty feet from the door, she felt a rough hand on her arm. She turned and gazed into the censorious brown eyes of a uniformed policemen.

"¿Cubana? Turista, Señora?" he asked. Tourist?

She stopped but didn't answer. She only glared.

"¿Habla español?" he asked. Do you speak Spanish?

"Si, hablo español. Pero soy turista," she answered. Yes, but I'm a tourist.

It occurred to her in a heartbeat that Cuban women weren't supposed to be in places like this, and if they were, they were probably catering to the sex travelers. They might have thought she was a hooker. Here was an incident that could get out of control.

"¿Tiene pasaporte?" he demanded again. Passport?

Another uniformed man sidled over. The captain started to turn away from the undercover men he was berating and took an interest in Alex as well.

"¿Nacionalidad?" the second one asked. What country?

They were good at bullying women. She could tell. *"Mexicana,"* she answered.

"¿Pasaporte?" the first man said again.

With evident annoyance, she reached into her bag and pulled

out her Mexican passport. No better way to test a CIA product than to run it past foreign police. This was, however, not an anxiety that she needed at the moment. By the time she held the passport out, she was surrounded. She had drawn all four of them. Was this Paul's plan? she wondered. Let her create the diversion while he worked his way through the window?

She handed over the passport.

She stood quietly and watched as the Cuban officers studied her passport. She waited. Her dress stuck to her ribs.

From beyond the four men, came one strong arm. The commander's. His name tag said MAJOR MEJIAS. He took the passport. He stared at it, looking down, looking up, looking down again, and then looking back up.

"Yours?" he asked.

"Who else would it belong to?" she asked.

"Good question," he answered. "Let's find out. *Espera*." She was to wait.

He stepped away for a moment, still holding her document and pulled a cell phone from his pocket. One of the cops with a shotgun went to the door and stood. One cop remained with her as the others continued to wander through the room. Alex wondered whether Paul was gone by now. She threw a glance in his direction via a wall mirror. Their table was empty. The drink glasses remained.

She looked back at the man who stood next to her. He was looking at his commander and had removed a set of handcuffs from his belt. She wondered if she should just run. She glanced at the door. The officer with the shotgun was staring at her. No chance.

Major Mejias was on the phone. He looked serious and seemed to dwell on something in her passport, some detail. Then he had a sneaky smile. He laughed to whoever was on the other end. He looked at Alex, then looked away, then back to her. He rang off, came back to her, and still in Spanish asked, "So. You are Anna Tavares?"

A beat. "I am Anna Tavares."

"And that is your actual birthday?"

"Of course."

He closed her passport and stared into her eyes, as if he were trying to burrow into her to find a hidden truth.

"What work do you do back home in Mexico?" he asked. *"¿Trabajo?"*

"I work for a newspaper."

"Which one?"

She had rehearsed the lie. *"El Universal,"* she answered quickly.

"You're a writer?" he asked.

"I work in the financial department."

He held her passport. "If I phoned there, your paper, they would know you, Anna Tavares?" he asked.

"Of course they would," she lied boldly. "Once you got past the switchboard. You know what Mexico is like."

His eyes narrowed. "I know quite a bit about the world beyond Cuba," he said.

"What are you suggesting, Major?"

"Nada," he said. Nothing.

"Then what's the problem? Have I done something wrong?" She was ready to bolt to the door, as hopeless an act as that might be.

"You've done nothing wrong," Mejias said. "You have the same birthday as my daughter. Same day, same year. *Extraordinario.* I just called her to tease her." He handed back the passport.

"You called your daughter just to tell her you had a woman in front of you the same age as she?" Alex asked.

"I did."

Alex knew better than to say anything else, though much ran across her mind.

"You are very pretty," Major Mejias said. "Same as my daughter. I like to talk to pretty women. Maybe you would like to stay and have a drink with me. We can talk about the world. How would that be?"

"Am I free to go?" she asked indignantly.

"Why wouldn't you be?"

"Your men are blocking the door."

"They won't be as soon as I tell them not to," he said.

"And when might that be?"

"I don't know," he said. After a pause, he asked, "Does the name Roland Violette mean anything to you? What if I told you Roland Violette was dead?"

She felt a surge within her. She kept a lid on it. She had been in these situations before and knew the tactic. He was looking for any reaction, any weakness. She shrugged. "I'd say send my condolences to his family," she answered boldly. "But I have no idea what you're talking about."

Mejias stared deeply into her eyes, then broke a grudging smile. "See that the Violette name *remains* unfamiliar to you," he said. "You'll live a longer, happier life."

He handed back her passport and signaled to his officer at the door. The officer stepped aside.

"*Adios*," she said.

"Hasta la vista," he said. He tipped his cap.

She was out the door in a flash. As soon as she was around the corner, she weaved in and out of shops and pedestrian traffic till she was convinced she was alone.

FORTY-EIGHT

Five minutes later, sweating and breathing hard, Alex was walking down a quiet side street. She spotted Paul, arms folded, leaning against the fifteen-year-old Toyota version of a Jeep. The vehicle was a clunky old beast with a canvas top and open sides.

"Good to see you," he said.

"Are you always so blasé?" she snapped.

"Not always, no."

"You had an easier time than I did," she said.

"But your passport worked," he said, "or you wouldn't be here."

"They stopped me. They examined my passport and quizzed me about Violette," she said sharply. "I was able to BS my way past them, but not by much. And if Violette is in play, that means Cuban intelligence knows what's going on. That means they have at least a vague idea of who they're looking for. You might be clean but I'm not."

He blew out a long breath. "I hear you. Anyone follow you?"

"I don't think so." She settled slightly. "I did my best to lose anyone following."

"We need to get moving," he said.

He held out a hand to help her up into the Toyota. She accepted it. There were no seat belts, and the car had a strange smell, as if fish had been stored there at one point and forgotten. As she settled into the shotgun seat, Guarneri came around the vehicle and climbed into the driver's seat.

"How was the squeeze through the window?" she asked.

"Fine if you don't mind a few nicks and scrapes." He showed where his arm had been scratched and his shirt torn. "And if you don't mind a couple of Cubans laughing at you as you go up over the sink and out the window," he said. "But it's better than a bullet, so I'm not complaining."

"Do me a favor," she said. "Just get us out of here."

"That's what I'd planned." He turned the key and the Toyota clanked to life. "Okay, look," he said, "before we get moving, let me bring you up to speed, and you bring me up to speed. I have an uncle on the island. Uncle Johnny — Giovanni. You know about him if you've read the FBI file."

"He's the one who went in the other direction," she said. "Right?"

"If you mean pro-Castro, Marxist, and worked for the government, yes," he said. "He was a young Commie, and now he's an old Commie. And his health is failing. He and my dad were estranged for years. That's where I was."

"Where?"

"Visiting. My uncle lives about eighty miles from here. Along the shore beyond Matanzas."

"You've seen him?"

"Yesterday. I went straight out there the day we landed," he said.

"Instead of looking for me?" she asked.

"I looked, but I had to keep my head down too. You and I had our backup plan, and it worked."

"Sure — and I forgot to thank you for leaving me on the beach," she snapped.

"You left me on the boat!"

"You ordered me out!"

"And I saved your life doing it," he said.

"My life wouldn't have been at risk if it weren't for you!"

"So we're even," he said. "And you said yourself that your head would have a hole in it if I hadn't phoned you at just the right time in New York. You owe me." His tone was midway between playful and deadly serious.

In the same spirit, she punched him in the shoulder. "How's that?" she said.

"That's great. Makes me feel like I'm back in Brooklyn."

She shook her head, exasperated.

"Look. Are we on vacation here?" he asked.

"No, we're *not* on vacation!"

"Then you can't blame me for doing what I came here to do, same as you're doing what you came here to do. Now, I got an aging red uncle. I hate his politics, but he's also flesh and blood. Flesh and blood of a generation that's in short supply for me, so we got to do what we got to do. Okay?"

"Okay." She paused. "You said you had *two* uncles here."

"That's right. Salvatore's the other one."

"Where's he?"

"Here in Havana. Been here for years."

"How old is he?"

"You read the FBI report. Born in 1931. You do the math. Why are you asking if you know the answer?"

"Am I going to see him?" she asked.

"If things go smoothly."

"There's that phrase again."

"There're those questions again."

"Do I get to talk to Uncle Salvatore?"

"If you want."

"Will he answer me?"

"If he feels like talking."

"You're full of charm and evasion, aren't you, Paul?"

"Consider it intentional and call it 'a sense of purpose.' Can we let it go at that? We pick up the money, I do with it as I need to, you babysit and evacuate your CIA stooge, and we all get out of here in one piece in four days if we're lucky — or in forty years if we're not."

"You're not answering my question. Why?"

"Because I don't want to. How's that for a game plan? I help you, you help me."

"It'll work," she said.

"The guy *you're* here to help is more disreputable than the people *I'm* here to help. So don't give me grief about my family or what I need to do." His voice settled slightly. "Okay?"

"Okay. But you're still a pig. Boorish, crass, self-serving, and self-possessed."

"Sorry you feel that way. You're everything my wife wasn't. I like you. Ready to travel? You and I are going to drive out to my uncle's place. It's on a strip of land past the tourist spots. It's called Playa del Rio. It takes three hours, and we can stay there overnight." He paused. "It's a few miles from where we landed."

"We're going back there?"

"Not much I can do about it. We'll go by different roads part of the way at least. You got something better to do?"

"I need fresh clothes."

"Of course. *No hay problema.* Where exactly is your *posada*?"

"Not far from here. It's on the Calle San Martin," she said. "*Treinta y uno.* One block that way, turn left, then straight three more blocks."

"Let's do it," he said.

Paul pulled the Jeep out onto the narrow street and executed a U-turn. He drove back to the main square and merged into the light traffic. Within five minutes, he had pulled up in front of the hotel. He leaned back in the front seat and cut the engine.

"I'll wait," he said.

"Thanks. I'm not going to check out, I just checked in. I'm just going to grab some things."

"That works," he said.

She jumped out of the Jeep and easily took the two flights of stairs. Having reunited with Paul, and having survived a passport check that afternoon, she felt better about things, about this assignment. Maybe things would work out, though a ton of questions remained.

In an open second floor hallway, out of precaution, she went to a window on the front of the building. She pushed aside the flimsy curtains. She looked down and could see the old Toyota.

Paul was standing outside it now, watching his back also, fingering an unlit cigar, and looking as if he was going to smoke it.

She watched him as he walked away from the car for a moment. Her suspicions were again aroused. Where was he going? He stopped at the pushcart of a street vendor. She watched as he bought a bag of ice, several bottles of chilled water, and a touristy straw hat that he popped onto his head. He put the water and ice in a plastic bag and walked back to the car. He must have felt her eyes on him, because he looked up, saw her, gave her a grin and a wave.

She waved back. She scanned the street too. Paranoia? Maybe. But no one appeared to be trailing them. She went back to her room and then to the closet. She pulled out her second and third dresses. She threw them, undergarments, and her few toiletries into her tote bag, along with her gun.

Glancing at her watch, she realized it was check-in time with the elusive Roland Violette — it was his window to phone. She checked her cell. No calls, no messages. Nothing. She bounded down the stairs.

When she arrived back on the street, Paul gave her a big smile, as an old buddy might, more than a working companion.

"You set?" he asked. "You okay?"

"I'm good," she said.

The cigar was still in his hand, unlit. "You mind if I smoke?" he asked.

"Go for it."

She climbed into the vehicle. He watched her, then came around to the driver's side. He stood outside the vehicle for a moment, clipped the end of the cigar, and lit it. He took an extra moment to make sure the *puro* was drawing, then slid in. Then he flipped the match out of the Jeep, tilted his hat back, and started the engine.

"Ready to roll," he announced.

She settled into her seat, one leg up on the dash, her skirt pulled back slightly. She pulled her new baseball cap tight, let the

FORTY-NINE

Paul guided the Toyota through the back streets of Havana. Alex took it all in with fascination. Like much else in Havana, the poorer neighborhoods were a confrontation with time. Like the better-kept sections, these neighborhoods were sprawling, eclectic, and disorganized. Grand old mansions with majestic high columns had been converted into small apartments, an air of neglect existed immediately adjacent to suggestions of past splendor. All of this splashed up against a vibrancy of the streets, music coming out of small storefronts and homes, men at tables playing dominos, and kids kicking soccer balls or playing impromptu games of *béisbol* in the streets and alleys. Old church towers functioned as landmarks every few blocks, rising above most other buildings. They were ornate and suggestive of the Moorish architecture that had been imported from Spain. Some churches had their doors open and obviously still had congregations.

"Didn't the Marxist government crack down on religion?" Alex asked.

"Yes, but not successfully," Paul answered. "The churches were never officially banned, but always harassed. Like everything else, religion in Cuba is a mass of contradictions. The constitution recognizes religious freedom and diversity, but the government does what it can to keep a lid on it. Meanwhile the old buildings remain because no one would be foolish enough to knock down a sturdy old building when it's so difficult to build a new one."

They approached the entrance to the big highway that traversed the island, *la autopista*. Guarneri made a move to access it westbound, then at the last second gave the wheel a sharp twist.

The Toyota hit a low divider, jumped into the air, and bounded over. Suddenly they were headed ninety degrees in a different direction.

"Paul! What's the problem?" Alex asked, startled.

Guarneri scanned in every direction. Then he calmed. "Just making sure no one's on our tail. The new highway is the faster route, but we're taking the old road. *La Carretera Central.* More scenic. We have time. And the other thing is I can tell better if we're being followed." He poked his head out the window, even checking the sky. His expression darkened.

"What?" she asked.

"A helicopter over the water," he said. "About ten miles behind. Probably just a coincidence. There are shore patrols all the time. But you can never be too careful."

She pulled a hand mirror out of her duffel bag and held it out the window. She found what bothered him, but it was only a speck.

"Should we be worried?" she asked.

"If we keep seeing it, yes," he answered. "I'd rather be paranoid than spend time in a Cuban jail."

"Ditto," she said, pulling the mirror in.

"Okay," he muttered. "I have a few tricks too, just in case."

"Why am I not surprised?"

He looked at her and winked.

They rode in silence for several minutes. The road swept through a few small towns, then a sugar plantation. The surface was narrow and often barely paved. Modern it wasn't. It reminded Alex of some of the back roads and old rural routes she had seen on visits to Louisiana and Mississippi. She had worked for Habitat for Humanity on spring and winter breaks as a teenager and had seen that part of America while helping construct homes.

They took the road that ran east from Havana. The highway snaked its way around the beaches and shoreline. Guarneri worked the stick shift with deft flowing motions, and though the ride was bumpy, it was fascinating. There were few other cars and not many trucks. The highway, like much of the rest of the island, seemed frozen in the 1950s. There was one lane in each direction with no dividing line.

"Highways that I've traveled," Alex thought to herself. She thought of the super-highways of southern California, the swift sleek autobahns of Germany, and the packed expressways of the northeastern corridor of the United States. Then there was the insanity of the highway in Ukraine, scorched into her recent memory, as she raced to the airport, and then, a little more recently, the packed highways of Cairo where cars passed over the lane dividers when traffic was already three abreast. She recalled the highways surrounding Lagos in Nigeria. Those had often been littered with piles of garbage that had been set on fire, or tires ablaze, or even dead bodies.

This was peaceful and gentle, with tranquil vistas of sea and shore on one side and verdant fields and foliage on the other. Keeping the island in the previous century, she mused, had had its upside as well.

There was only one problem. Half an hour later, without asking, she stuck the mirror back out the window and scanned the sky.

"Still there?" he asked. "The chopper?"

"I think I see it," she said.

He slowed and again poked his own head out the window. "Yeah, yeah," he said. "That looks like the same bird. It's probably okay. Probably shore patrol. Bear with me."

"You think you can slip away from it?" she asked.

"I know I can."

The road elevated and there was a stunning view of the Caribbean. They had been driving for twenty minutes more when Paul pointed to a small village that hugged the shore, a cluster of small shacks and low buildings with a small harbor cluttered with modest boats.

"That's Cojimar," said Guarneri. He nodded toward the small village.

"Cojimar is where Hemingway sailed from when he lived in Cuba, right?" Alex asked. "When he wasn't drinking, cheating on his wives, or writing."

"You nailed it," Paul laughed. "Papa Hemingway kept a fishing boat here for years. It was called *La Pilar.* It's now at the museum in Havana, I think." He gave another nod to the hamlet by the water. "It's a popular tourist spot. So I think we should stop. We're tourists. It also gets foggy this late in the day. Get it?"

"Got it."

They left the highway and pulled into the hamlet, which was thick with trees, old buildings, and small shops. Paul parked, carefully choosing a spot that was near other cars that would all look similar from the air. When they stepped out, Paul offered his hand. They walked to the marina, bought drinks, stood and chatted in Spanish with fishermen returning for the afternoon. Their eyes kept to the sky and they watched as the helicopter approached and went past them. They stayed until it was far to the east of them. It had either overshot, abandoned them, lost them, or never cared about them in the first place. At the same time, a small late afternoon fog rolled in as Paul knew it would. They hustled quickly back to their vehicle. Forty minutes after stopping, they were back on the road.

FIFTY

Havana: late afternoon. The old man who had walked in the Cristobol Colón cemetery was again taking his last look at many things. He knew he would soon leave Cuba. For a better place? For a worse place? Only God above knew. That's what he would have said if anyone had asked him. Only God knew. Mortal men make plans. God laughs. The old man was deeply religious, always had been.

"Heaven," he thought to himself. "Heaven, heaven, heaven. I wonder if there is a heaven."

He had a few nervous ticks. He kept fingering the parrot's head on his cane with one hand. With the other, he kept patting his left pocket to see if that little Colt .22 was still there. It was. Reassured, he returned to his thoughts. In his way, he would miss this place where he spent so many years. Despite the poverty, the isolation, the dangerous political games, he loved this place as much as anyone who had been born here. That's why he was taking last looks. When death came, he told himself, he wanted to have that image of Cuba in his eyes.

Today he ambled along the famous boulevard, El Malecon, perched along the stony fortress-style bluff above the ocean on the Havana waterfront. He relied more and more on his hickory cane, the one with the carved parrot's head, as so many old men in Cuba did. The bright sun was still bright in the west on this late afternoon, and he watched couples walk arm in arm along the colorful boulevard. To the old man, Havana made him want to go back to a time when each day seemed slower and less compressed. Life was simpler then and the living was easier. Or at least that's the way he remembered it.

He recalled days when he was one half of one of those happy

couples. It didn't seem so long ago. A lifetime? Recently, he had lost the woman he loved. He still mourned.

He was educated, this old man was. He had gone to university. He had read many languages, but mostly English and Spanish. He loved the great writers, Fitzgerald, Hemingway, Twain, Dickens, Cervantes, Lorca, and the modern Afro-Cuban Nicolás Guillén.

He loved his writers, the novelists, the poets, and the historians in particular. In the waning time of his life, there was a line he couldn't shake from Mark Twain's work, *Eve's Diary.* Twain's story ended with Adam's speaking at Eve's grave, "Wherever she was, there was Eden."

Well, the woman the old man had loved had departed. His Eve was gone and so was Eden. He sat for several hours on a bench along the waterfront as the daylight faded, watching the sea and the horizon. There was a tear in his eye. Even timelessness seemed to have a finite number of hours today. And always, his thoughts faded into the past more than the future. The old man moved to a nearby café where the owners knew him. He took a seat way in the back and slumped down in his wicker chair. He nodded and snoozed as the evening wound down, the cane leaning against him, the .22 caliber pistol in his left pocket.

The whole world left him alone.

FIFTY-ONE

"There was an old Cuban named Gregorio Fuentes who lived in Cojimar for many years," Paul said as the sun began to set over the outskirts of the town. They had just returned to the car and were beginning the final leg of their drive. "He was a fisherman and the first mate on Hemingway's boat. Some people say he was the model for Santiago, the fisherman in *The Old Man and the Sea*. Fuentes *insisted* he was, of course. He gave tours in the latter part of his life, let the tourists have their pictures taken with him. He was his own industry. Lived to a great age. A hundred, I think, till he died a few years ago."

"You ever meet him?" Alex asked.

"About five years ago," Paul said. "No photo though. I just thought that would be a bad idea, a picture of me in Cuba."

"Probably," Alex agreed.

Alex admired the way Paul could be a mass of amiable contradictions. He was disreputable and high-minded at the same time, thuggish, boorish, quick-witted, intellectually omnivorous, mobbed-up, and innocent. He was a devoted family man yet divorced and currently unattached, or so he said.

Alex laughed. "Your cultural references are all over the place. How do you know all this stuff?" she said.

"Same as you. I read a lot. I majored in American lit at Cornell and minored in history with a second minor in finance," he said. "I spent five years there and was in an accelerated program that gave me a BA and a master's. I liked college. No one knew the family links, so no one bothered me."

"Cornell's Ivy League. Must have been expensive," she said.

"You got that right. Twenty-five grand a year. My old man had a million-dollar life-insurance policy when he got killed. He must have known what was coming someday, so he sought to provide. And provide, he did. Whatever else you thought of him, gangster, gambler, underworld guy — who knows what else? — he loved his families, both of them. And we loved him. He left us all well-off."

Paul thought for a moment as he drove. Alex was not inclined to interrupt.

"I owe my dad," he said. "To this day, I owe him a lot. He could have ignored us, left us in Cuba, or just walked. I can remember when it happened ... when he was murdered. The last time I saw him was on a summer day in 1973. We'd just bought tickets to see the Mets at Shea Stadium. He had bought tickets from a scalper, some guy he knew from the racetrack. We had some real good seats just behind the Mets dugout. Next thing I knew, he had been shot to death."

The distant light of Cojimar had now disappeared behind them. The road evened out.

"I had a lot of time alone as a kid," Paul said. "I stayed inside a lot, out of places where I'd be vulnerable. Know what I mean? With my old man being connected and all. He was always afraid some enemy would strike the family. So I'd fill an afternoon by picking up a book."

She smiled. "I used to do the same thing."

They came to another town. The architecture ran the gamut, from old Victorian houses by the sea to blocks of sterile Soviet-style apartments from the 1970s. They took a turn and were on a narrow, bumpy, sandy road that led between huts with thatched roofs and huts of concrete and discarded wooden panels. Some of the huts had windows with no glass, entirely open to the elements. Alex looked at them and shuddered; the flies and mosquitoes must be fierce.

They accessed the main road. Traffic was minimal, mostly old cars and slow trucks, an occasional diesel bus spewing smoke. For the next hour the Toyota rambled past small farms and villages. For a long time they rode in silence. Alex glanced at the speedometer and noticed that it barely nudged above forty-five.

Eventually, the road rose onto a plateau. In the distance, to the left and the north, Alex could see the blue sea. The view to the south descended into rolling fields and dark foliage.

From time to time, they scanned the sky. No whirlybird. They were convinced no one was tailing them. Several minutes went by as Alex relaxed and gazed out the window. For a while, she sought to put her assignment and the pressing danger out of her mind and enjoy the view of part of the world she had never seen before.

"Tell me about Robert," he said.

"Robert?" she asked, turning toward him.

"The man you were engaged to," he said. "Is there another Robert?"

"No," she said, looking back to the road. "There was just one. A wonderful man." She gazed at Paul, waiting to see if he would direct his questions to any details. Nothing further came. "He was wonderful and I loved him," she said. "Strong. Supportive. But romantic and capable of great tenderness. Understanding, fair-minded, and kind." A mile of the old highway disappeared beneath the wheels of the Toyota before she spoke again. "Sometimes he and I seemed so close that I didn't even think of him as another person. He was an extension of me, and I was an extension of him. Can you follow that?"

"Easily," Paul answered.

"Part of me died that day in Ukraine ... and remains dead. Like a window that's been sealed shut," she said. "I can see through it, I can admire what's on the other side, but I can't open it. What makes it worse, what makes it so much harder to accept, what keeps it so unsettled, was the suddenness of it. The arbitrariness of it. The jolting reality of how the end happened and how someone I loved was taken so far before his time." She paused. "I know, I'm dwelling a bit. But you asked. And the wound is less than a year and a half old. It's still there and hurting."

"I understand. My father's been gone for thirty-eight years," Paul said. "I still miss him. If he came back and stood in front of me, I have no idea what I'd say to him. But I miss him. See, you know, that's what lurks here between us, Alex. That's what we have in common. Important people were taken away from us. Taken unfairly, taken by murderers, taken suddenly and violently."

"You have a point," she said. She directed the conversation back to Paul. "I don't know how you got me going on this. I've never told anyone what I just told you."

"I asked," he said. "My question was as much about the man you lost as how you're dealing with it. You answered both, which was what I was looking for."

Behind them, the sun had long since fallen below the horizon. Deep evening approached. They stopped once to search the sky again, but saw no choppers. They stepped back into the car with great relief but rode the next half hour in silence, other than the tinny cackle of the radio.

Toward their destination, the highway wound through steep hills and pristine forests, coming down to the side of the sea. Then it continued to the east for a final stretch. There were several rest stops on the side of the road, and in each there were children selling fruit, strings of bananas, guava, and *mamey*, a sweet orange fruit with the shape and consistency of avocado. They passed some crumbling stucco houses where people, mostly old, sat on sagging sofas and sipped drinks on decrepit verandas. Children played in the streets, mostly in ragged shorts, and gave way with excitement as the four-wheel-drive vehicle eased through them.

Then the road turned into a private driveway lined with flowering plants in large industrial drums. Paul pulled the Toyota up to a veranda on the side of a house that was particularly imposing due to its setting. The veranda, and the house it was attached to, did not sag, and Alex could tell it was in good condition. There was a battered Peugeot 404 parked to one side, also. It was a faded maroon with rust and dents.

A screen door opened. A lithe brown woman in a short green dress appeared quietly. She stepped out and looked carefully at the arrivals. Across her chest, held carefully and at the ready, she carried a rifle.

"We're here," Guarneri said. "Be careful. She's a sweetie, but she can be trigger happy. I'll get out first."

FIFTY-TWO

"This is Thea," Paul said to Alex, introducing the woman with the rifle. "She's a cousin of mine. Or maybe she's my sister and no one ever told me. Who knows? I lose track."

Thea laughed.

"You're a beast, Paul," Alex said.

"That I know," he answered.

Thea stepped forward, and smiled. She was tall for a Cuban woman, perhaps five ten, with reddish brown skin and eyes that suggested a hint of an Asian lineage. She was thin and wore a simple green cotton dress that flowed to her mid-thighs. She had a pretty, unaffected face and a wide smile.

Paul introduced Alex by her real name, indicating to Alex that these were people Paul could trust.

"Bienvenida, Alejandra," Thea said to Alex. Thea spoke no English.

"Muchas gracias," Alex said. *"Mucho gusto, Thea."*

Thea had an easy grace as she led her guests to the house and set aside the weapon. The veranda had an awning above it that presumably gave it shade during the hot Cuban afternoons. Several wicker chairs with cushions were scattered around and a large red cat sat quietly, inspecting the new arrivals.

Once inside, Alex could see that there were many rooms, joined together railroad style. The colors on the walls were bold and contrasting. Decorating the walls were an array of seashells, bottles, and driftwood, cleverly designed to look like animals, marine life, and human faces. The furniture ranged from the modern to the threadbare. Thea led her guests to another screen door, which led to an outside sitting area, one that was enclosed by a screen but which faced a vast, empty stretch of beach.

"I'll get my uncle," Thea said when Alex and Paul were seated. "He's sleeping now. May I get you refreshment? Tea? Wine?"

"Either would be fine," Alex answered. "Something cold would be good."

"Of course," she said. "We have a refrigerator ... and electricity so the refrigerator is running. Does that surprise you?" She laughed and smiled broadly. "Please make yourselves comfortable. I'll get Señor Johnny. Please, Uncle Paul, show our guest around."

Thea disappeared. Alex looked around.

"Señor Johnny?" Alex asked.

"It's what my uncle likes to be called. Go with it," he said.

"Absolutely," she answered.

She noted a garden in a different direction and what appeared to be a small farming area with chickens. Paul saw her looking.

"Step outside if you want," he said.

"May we?"

"Of course. This is family."

"But you've been here, what? Once in fifty years?" she asked.

"It's still family."

Paul led her through the screen door. The air outside was salty and fresh. "Who do they think I am, by the way?" Alex asked.

"You agreed to come to Cuba and pose as my wife," Guarneri answered. "So here you are, and that's what you're doing. It's really mostly for Señor Johnny's purposes. He has very traditional values. He'd be heartbroken if he knew I'm divorced."

"So we're lying to your family?"

"It's in their best interests right now. I'll set them straight eventually."

She shook her head. "I don't know what to say sometimes."

"That's usually a good time to say nothing."

There was no sound except the waves rolling onto the shore, gentle white surf upon the dark water. Alex caught a whiff of a fire, smoke from a grill, followed quickly by the aroma of food cooking. Nearby, an array of fishing rods leaned against the screen from the outside. The rods looked worn, but also as if they'd been freshly used.

"Everyone here fishes," Paul said in English, reading Alex's thoughts. "They catch grouper, turbot, snappers. Also crabs and eels. It's a simple life, unspoiled, for better or worse."

"Your family seems to have done better than most," Alex said.

"They're smarter and better educated," Guarneri said. There was a pause and he added, "Better connected too."

"In what sense?" Alex asked.

Guarneri glanced back to make sure they were alone. "As I said, my uncle was a *héroe de la revolución*."

"A hero how?"

"An early supporter of the winning side," Guarneri said. "He left the university in 1957 and joined the revolutionary Twenty-sixth of July Movement, which Castro had formed in Mexico. In March of 1957, Johnny was one of the students from the Revolutionary Directorate who attacked Batista's presidential palace. The attack was a miserable failure. Thirty-five students were killed, and then scores of others were tortured or murdered in the days that followed. Johnny went underground after that and eventually found his way into the rebel army." He paused. "Somewhere in the house there are photographs. If you want to see them, he'll show you. With pride."

Alex felt her fascination battling with her own convictions. She was in the belly of the beast, the home of the enemy. As an American, and a practicing Christian, as someone who believed in democracy, the man she was about to meet had spent his life on the other side of history's battles. Yet she was in no state of mind now to refight old wars.

"You seem to celebrate this sometimes, Paul," she said. "Your family was torn apart by the Castro revolution, many of you lost property, and the island has been isolated for years thanks to the revolution. You can't be in favor of it, can you?"

They walked to an area where the sand was wet. Alex removed her shoes and continued to walk by Paul's side. Paul's eyes found the horizon on the distance, then came back. "No," he said, answering her question after many seconds. "Of course not. I'm not a Marxist or a socialist or a closet apologist for Castro. But sometimes one can see heroism in those whose views differ from one's own. Can't you? Look at what a horrible regime preceded Castro's. Who can blame people for rising up against it? In the generations before Castro, much of North America treated Cuba as its gambling den and brothel. My own father was part of that. I'm not here to be judgmental. I'm here to get some answers and do a job. Same as you, right?"

"Right," Alex said, "but if you really believed all that, then what's the big deal with the money?" she asked. "Why not let it lie where it's lain for all these years?"

"Why did you use that expression?" he asked. " 'Lie where it's lain'?"

"Just a figure of speech," Alex said.

"Alex," he said, "I can poke gaping holes in my uncle's Marxist-socialist values the same way he can poke holes in my Western capitalist ones. So what? At some point a man gets tired of looking for the weaknesses in everyone else's system. I know I do. What did I say a moment ago?" he said amiably. "In the end, it's just people. It's family."

"Did your father stay in touch with his uncles in Cuba over the years?" she asked.

"No. They hated each other for what they believed in. Never spoke again. Never in their lives."

"So what this trip is about, for you, is reconciliation, of sorts," she said. "Setting things right. History. Family."

"You could say that."

"And no hard feelings?"

"On *my* part? To whom? No, of course not, none."

Thea's voice, calling from the main building, interrupted them. They turned. She walked to them. "Everything okay?"

"Just fine," Alex said. She liked Thea.

"Señor Johnny's awake. My boys are helping him. I have two sons — Manolo, who's ten, and Willie, who's eight."

"Wonderful," Alex said. She made no mention of a husband or father, and Alex knew better than to ask.

"Dinner will be ready in fifteen minutes," Thea said. "Alex, let me show you something first." She took Alex by the hand and led her to a small farm that they kept at a low plateau that ran down toward the beach. They continued to speak Spanish. "We keep chickens and rabbits back here." She indicated chickens in a fenced-in yard and the rabbits in various hutches. "We trade with the people in the town. It all works out very well. Over there in that field, we raise potatoes, carrots, and onions."

"No cash?" asked Alex, intrigued.

"Do we raise cash?" she laughed.

"No. You don't use cash for your transactions?"

Thea shook her head. "Money is scarce. *Troquamos*," she said. *Barter.* She indicated a small inlet that ran up against their land. The water seemed shallow, forming a small tidal basin that was alternately blue and reddish in the light from the setting sun.

"In the evening, crabs and eels come into that little cove to feed on minnows," she said. "I go out to where the water comes in and we catch them. Do you like eel?"

"I'm not sure I've ever had it," Alex answered. "Maybe once. Pickled."

"You liked?"

"I don't think so."

"You should try fresh," she said.

"Algún día."

"Yes, someday," Thea agreed. "Tomorrow is made up entirely of somedays. I wish you could stay longer. I'd catch and cook eel tomorrow."

"Someday," Alex said again.

A screen door slammed up at the cottage. "Ah. Here's my father," Thea said.

A trim, tanned Cuban stepped out. Alex looked at him. His appearance was so similar to an elderly version of Paul Guarneri that it was frightening. For a split second she thought she was seeing his father back from the dead. But this was Señor Johnny.

A smile creased his lined face. He lifted his left hand and waved to them. He walked forward a few paces with a shuffling gate, the result of the minor stroke he had suffered a few months earlier.

He waited till his guests had walked up the path to his home. Then he greeted Alex warmly, placed a hand on her shoulder, and welcomed her into his home. It was in that instant that Alex completely understood how Paul had been so easily made to feel like family by people who had lived in a different world than his own.

FIFTY-THREE

They sat in a small dining room, Johnny, Paul, and Alex seated at a table for six. Thea moved in and out of the cottage, completing her dinner preparations. Her boys helped, briskly going in and out of the house with slams of the screen door. Paul and his uncle sat and talked quietly in Spanish over a shot apiece of *calambuco*, a local moonshine rum. The drink was dark and thick. When they offered her some, Alex declined.

Thea cooked a dinner of chicken and rice, plain but delicious. The chicken was freshly killed and grilled over driftwood on an open-air grill on the north side the house. The rice had been cooked in a pot that boiled on the same grill. Thea added greens from her garden and served. Paul's uncle chatted and rambled, his cane leaning against the table near where he sat. He told a story about an abandoned building that had recently collapsed in Santiago. The fall of the building had killed three men and two women who lived on the first floor. Like much else in Cuba, he remarked, the building was a paradox. If the building were abandoned, why were there people in it when it collapsed?

"The reason they were there was because they were stealing bricks from the support pillars of the building," Johnny explained to Alex. "But it wouldn't have collapsed if it had been completely abandoned. That's Cuba today." For some reason, Uncle Johnny thought this was funny, or at least ironic. He tossed back his head and laughed. The old Marxist retained a twinkle in his eye. He treated Alex and Paul as a couple.

"You two, who do not live on this island," he said toward the end of dinner. "Perhaps you do not know things politically. Can you tell me the difference between a Cuban socialist, a Cuban Marxist, and a fascist?"

Paul shrugged.

"Dígame," Alex answered. Tell me.

"A Cuban socialist has two cows. The government takes one and gives it to his neighbor. A Cuban Marxist has two cows. The government seizes both and provides you with milk. A counter-revolutionary fascist has two cows. The government seizes both and sells you the milk. You join the underground and start a campaign of sabotage." He turned to Paul. "How does it work in America?" he asked.

"We have two political parties," Paul said, "who do things differently."

"¿Cómo?" Johnny asked.

"An American Republican has two pigs. His neighbor has none. 'So what?' the Republican says. An American Democrat has two pigs. His neighbor has none. So he feels guilty. He votes people into office who tax the pigs, forcing him to sell one to raise money to pay the tax. The people he votes for take the tax money, buy a pig, and give it to his neighbor. He feels righteous."

Paul's uncle laughed and so did Thea. Then conversation drifted.

Afterward, they wandered into a sitting room next to the screened porch on the back of the house. The sound of the surf punctuated the night. As promised, there were pictures on the walls, old black-and-whites in frames that didn't appear to have changed from the 1960s or '70s. In each, in varying poses and places, Alex spotted Johnny as a young man, often in his military uniform in the revolutionary army.

Johnny lagged behind. Paul gave Alex a walk-through of the photographs.

"My Uncle Johnny left university in 1957 and served in Castro's regiment in the Sierra Maestra mountains," Paul said. "He rose in the ranks. Then Castro's rebel army split in half and a second division was formed. Uncle Johnny was a major under General Guevara. Johnny knew Che personally. Very well, in fact."

They arrived at a wall photo that evidenced what Paul was

saying. Several revolutionaries huddled together under tree branches, a setting that appeared to be jungle. Paul indicated his uncle with an arm around a thirtyish Guevara.

"As the war continued in 1958," Paul continued, "Guevara led his divisions west for the push into Havana. They traveled by foot for seven weeks, entirely at night to avoid ambush. Sometimes they didn't eat for several days. In the final days of 1958, my uncle was promoted again to take the place of revolutionary officers who had fallen. He became part of the high command with Guevara. The rebels cut the island in half with an attack on Santa Clara, the capital of the La Villas province. Santa Clara was the final military victory of the revolution. Johnny was wounded there. Fractured kneecap. But he stayed with his men. A few weeks later, he rolled into Havana on a captured government tank. Guevara's regiment came into the capital six days before Castro's and two days after Batista had fled to the Dominican Republic."

And there, on the walls, the way some men post diplomas or family pictures, were half a dozen photographs of Havana in January of 1959. In each, Johnny Guarneri was somewhere present: assembled with army riflemen, crouching along the *Plaza Vieja* with comrades, smashing slot machines that had been ripped out of the Tropicana and hauled out into the street, and in the living room of Batista's former mansion, feet up on the sofa.

Alex and Paul heard footsteps and turned away from the pictures. Johnny entered, glanced at them, and grinned. "Half a century ago," he said, following their thoughts. "Sometimes you look back and you think, 'How did I get from there to here?' " He laughed. The old warrior exuded a strange charm.

Paul crossed the room and offered an arm to his uncle and guided him to the sofa. Johnny seemed older than his years by a decade. He had a lined face, a battered body, and knobby hands.

"The things you do when you're young," Johnny said. "God help us. No do-overs, though. You get one chance, one go 'round." He glanced at the wall. "Castro, Batista. Meyer Lansky, Che Guevara. What you don't know when you're a young man," he said, "is that they're all corrupt, every one of them. And if they aren't before they get power, they are after they've tasted it."

He paused again. Thea arrived and gave Johnny a glass of water, with ice in it. The ice cubes clicked against each other. With the hand that held the glass, Johnny pointed to the photographs. "Interesting, aren't they?" he asked.

"Very," she said.

"I showed your husband night before last. He had never seen them."

"So I'm told," Alex said.

"Well, I saw it all close up," Johnny said, recalling. "I remember New Year's Eve when the government fell. The evening started out calm, a little tense maybe because everyone knew the rebels were close to the city. But no one expected Batista to use the cover of the midnight party to catch a plane to Miami. I was still with Guevara's army, and we were about five miles southwest of Havana. But once the word got out that Batista was gone, people started to come out of their homes to celebrate. The local militias that were stationed in the working neighborhoods came out and stormed the casinos and the police station. Guevara woke us up and told us it was time to move into Havana. It was 4:00 a.m. We started to move to the capital. We didn't get there till daybreak, and by then there was chaos. Happy chaos. Our army of happy *campensinos* overran the casino lobbies. If doors were locked, we broke them down. If they weren't locked, our people surged in. After six years of fighting, the end was swift and efficient." Johnny laughed. "One group of farmer soldiers drove a truck full of pigs into Havana and set them loose in the lobby of the Riviera. They defecated and urinated all over everything. They destroyed the place as much as the rebel soldiers smashing the roulette wheels."

"The Riviera was Meyer Lansky's pride," Paul said, explaining the significance. "It was a special insult and years in the making. The gangsters had been a huge part of the Batista regime, and they'd kept the regime in power. So the casinos were targets."

"So were the homes of the gangsters," Johnny continued. "In the streets, there were fires blazing. All the mobster's possessions—curtains and furniture—were pulled out of the casinos, soaked with kerosene, and ignited. Parts of the interiors of the casinos were torched too, as they deserved to be. Then when the sun rose on January second, mobs stormed out to Miramar where most of the gangsters had mansions. They overran the mansions and looted the place. All the mafia guys were gone though. They knew what was coming. They'd filled suitcases with money and took off for Miami in private planes and boats while Castro's army moved toward the city. It was terrifying but it was beautiful," the old man remembered. "Like a hurricane hitting the island. *Valiente. Audaz. Podoroso.* The criminals were swept away by revolutionaries in green khaki who motored through the streets with automatic weapons, waving the black and red flag of the Twenty-sixth of July Movement. One night the casinos are filled with mobsters and their whores in suits, diamonds, and furs—and the next night illiterate warriors from the provinces, bearded and with bare feet, are destroying everything linked to Batista."

Johnny reached for his water and took a long sip. Alex and Paul remained quiet.

"Within another day or two, the airport was shut down. Castro went to the army bases and the soldiers flipped their loyalties on the spot. The navy had already flipped sides, and it became harder to escape the island. Revolutionary bands started arresting anyone who'd been associated with Batista or the gangsters. People went into hiding. There were great amounts of cash flying around. Meyer Lansky finally left with several million dollars in a suitcase. Batista had left with so much that he had abandoned three million in cash in his home and probably never missed it. Then *El Commandante*, Fidel Castro, came into Havana on January 6 after a victory march from Las Villas. Already there were scores of gangsters in the custody of the *fuerzas revolucionarias*. They wanted to be deported to America, but Castro was having none of it. He made the pronouncement. 'We are not disposed to deport gangsters,' he announced. 'We are inclined to shoot them.' "

Not for the first time this evening, Alex thought back to Sam Deal's spiel in New York on the subject of Guevara. *Guevara was Castro's chief executioner. Under Che, Havana's La Cabaña fortress was converted into Cuba's Lubianka.*

"Summary executions began immediately," Johnny continued. "No trials. Batista's death squads and the *yanqui* gangsters were put up against walls at La Cabaña fortress and finished by firing squads. *That* was justice! Someone asked about whether the U.S. would intervene, and Fidel made his famous remark, 'If America intervenes,' he said, 'there will be two hundred thousand dead gringos in the streets of Havana.' "

"That remark didn't go over well in the American press," Paul put in. "Fidel later saw fit to retract it and apologize." His eyes shifted and sharpened.

"This is where the story catches up to Paul's other uncle and his father," Johnny said. His gaze found Alex, eye to eye. "Paul's father, Joseph, he was one of the lucky ones. He had a suitcase full of money. Maybe, what, half a million dollars in cash, was it?"

"That's what my father always said," Paul answered.

"Salvatore, my other brother, who worked at the casinos and racetracks for Lansky, had a higher profile. The rebels came after him and arrested him. Took him to the prison fortress. He was held for fifteen days; then Guevara passed sentence and signed the execution papers. But he had a suitcase of money too. It was known that he was my brother. I was allowed to go to his home and get a few things for him and to clean out his belongings. That's when I found that he had a hidden supply of money too. The day of the execution came quickly. I did not witness it; I did not care to. At fortress La Cabaña, they executed their prisoners, then sent the bodies to the undertaker, who was very busy in those days. I was allowed in the prison when the execution took place. I had the rank of a lieutenant colonel in the revolutionary army. So I was also allowed to accompany his body to the mortuary. I took my brother's suitcase and removed all the money. It didn't belong to him, but it didn't belong to the rebels either. I was thinking only, where can I put it so that no one will find it? How can I hide it from everyone? I could think of only one thing to do. I sealed the money tightly in a canvas bag. It was all stacked together and tightly tied, so it handled easily. I knew people would be looking for it, but no one would be looking for it at the mortuary. When my brother was placed in his coffin, I took the bag and reshaped it. It was the size and shape of a pillow. Family was allowed to witness the closing of the casket. So while I said a private good-bye, I removed the pillow that my slain brother's head was on and exchanged it for the parcel of money. I put two pillow cases from the undertaker's supplies, which were right in that room, and I placed the new pillow under his head. Then I called the mortician. Before my eyes, as I stepped back, the casket was closed and locked. The burial was the next day."

"In Havana?" Alex asked.

"In the big cemetery," Johnny said. *"El Cemeterio de Cristóbal Colón."*

Alex reacted in shock. "The money's been sitting in a grave for half a century? *Your brother's grave?*"

Paul's uncle nodded. "Until now," he said. "Or more accurately — "

" — until tomorrow night," Paul finished the sentence.

Old Johnny grinned like a gargoyle. Alex took the smile to mean that some of the money was going to be coming his way. Then he rose with surprising agility and looked at his watch.

"The undertaker was further bribed," Johnny said. "We felt that if my brother was buried under his own name, the revolutionaries would come and desecrate the grave. So he had this favorite ball player of the era named Chico Fernandez. Cuban. Used to come here with the Brooklyn Dodgers in the spring. So we changed the name on the death certificate and sent the body to a different mortician. It's under the name C. Fernandez. That's what I didn't tell your husband till yesterday." His eyes searched them back and forth. "C. Fernandez. Plot 234, Section SW4. Life is strange. So is death." He eased back, as if a burden had been lifted. "Come along. It's late," he said. "You should go to the bedroom you will share tonight. Have you made love yet in Cuba?"

"No," Alex said after a moment of mild astonishment at the old man's candor. To her side, she could almost feel Paul suppressing a smirk.

"The moon will be upon your window, and the ocean will be in your ears and your soul," the old fellow said. "You will have a wonderful night. If you make a baby, you must give the child a Cuban name."

FIFTY-FOUR

In the late evening the old man woke up in the back of the café and ambled into *Habana Vieja*, the old section of Havana, for a final look. Live music was everywhere for the *touristas*, and hundreds of *Habaneros* were performing in bands, in shows, and at the restaurants in order to earn their daily convertible pesos, so that they could buy what they needed at the dollar stores. An armada of foreigners swept through the streets. He strolled quietly, keeping to himself and watching with amusement as the tourists were hustled by *jineteras*, the friendly, charming scam artists who specialized in swindling tourists.

Sometimes it was hard to love this country and its isolation. On occasion, back in the 1990s, the old man, significantly younger then, used to go out to the José Martí International airport on Sundays. It was moving to see the hundreds of people standing there in the morning waiting for their visiting families arriving from the U.S. Even though the man and his wife at the time were never expecting family to come, it was still emotional.

But he knew friends who had family.

They would all talk about the feeling they had when the plane was descending toward Cuba. The visitors could see the mountains and the rolling hills and everywhere the royal palm trees. They couldn't believe how pretty the land was from the air, how fresh and unpolluted it seemed. It was a different world from the Cuban part of Miami that they were so used to, even though a less-glamorous reality waited on the ground.

Eventually, the old man found a table in another café. It was night now. He savored the smell of Cuban tobacco, which remained different from all other tobaccos in the world, and to his tastes finer. He bought a Bolivar cigar and began to smoke.

He ordered dinner. To him, it was still so wonderful how well a good cigar went with a Cuban evening, much like the Cuban coffee went with the local milk.

He looked around the square. The most amazing thing remained how old and untouched many of the modern things were. The cars. The colonial architecture, much of it crumbling, much of it still magnificent, even in ruin. He would have liked to have written a Valentine or a love poem to his adopted city. He had an idea where he might start such a letter.

Havana he might have described as an old diva who'd been forgotten by all her suitors but was still trying to look her best. Havana was frequently compared to her sister city, San Juan, Puerto Rico, which was modern, prosperous, and flourishing. Havana had been allowed to fall and deteriorate — physically but not spiritually.

The old man stayed in the café on the square till the music faded well after 11:00 p.m. He looked at his watch. He glanced down the block where his old acquaintance, Jean Antoine, the Frenchman, had his restaurant. He knew the Frenchman's schedule, having observed it for years. The Frenchman would be in the back of his place, cleaning, setting up for the next day, and counting his receipts.

The old man stood. He took a stroll. He cut through a side street and an alley and came to the back door of Jean Antoine's place. Sure enough, the place was closed and the staff had gone home. But there at a table, counting his money and credit card slips, was the Frenchman. The door was basically an iron grate.

"Perfecto," muttered the old man. *"Perfecto, perfecto, perfecto."*

The old man knocked. The sound startled Jean Antoine, who reached for a pistol, then stopped when he recognized the visitor.

They spoke Spanish. "Oh," the Frenchman said. "It's you."

"Me," said the old man. "Me, me, me."

"What do you want?"

"Some company."

"I'm busy."

"I'm hungry."

"You're a pest."

Jean Antoine finished with his cash and stashed it all in a strong box.

"I'm hungry," the old man said again.

"You know how the lock works," said the Frenchman.

"Ah. Yes. I do."

The old man slipped his hand through the grate and undid a latch, which was obscured from the outside. But the old man had visited many times over the years. There had been friction between the two men, serious grievances going each way, but all had apparently been forgiven over the last few years.

The old man entered. He walked with difficulty.

"There's food in the kitchen," he said. "On the counter. Take what you want."

"Thank you."

Jean Antoine was busy with the credit card slips, working the calculator, trying to finish for the day.

"¿Somos amigos, si?" the old man asked. "We're friends, yes?"

Hardly paying attention, Jean Antoine answered. "We're friends," he said. "All is forgiven."

"That's good of you," said the old man.

He passed behind the Frenchman and stopped. He reached into his left pants pocket and pulled out the pistol. Then he thought better about what he had come here to do. Gunshots were so noisy. He slipped the pistol back into his pocket. He went to the kitchen. There was some leftover bread on the counter and some containers of soup. Not far away from them was a cotton dish towel and a large carving knife.

The old man picked up the knife and hid it in the towel. He tucked the two into his belt behind his back. He stayed and enjoyed some soup, watching the Frenchman close out his accounts for the day. He finished his soup.

Without speaking, the old man walked to the back room and passed behind Jean Antoine again. He stopped. The Frenchman ignored him. The old man reached behind him and gripped the knife. He drew it out. With the towel around the handle of the knife, he lifted it high over his head and brought it down into the neck of the restaurant owner.

Jean Antoine screamed and tried to protect himself. But the attack was relentless and he fought back too late. The old man brought the knife down into the victim's body five times, then a sixth. He left the weapon imbedded in the victim's back and was on his way.

FIFTY-FIVE

The bedroom that Thea guided them to was a long chamber with a low ceiling. It had two old wooden dressers, one queen-sized bed, a couple of chairs, a mirror, and an overstuffed old sofa that stood against the north wall below a long window. The window opened onto the beach. A sea breeze blew through the thin gauzy curtain that hung by the window but was not drawn. And as the old man had promised, there was a moon, a three quarters one, bright yellow and brilliant, and it sat above the Caribbean as if a gifted artist had painted it there.

Alex and Paul entered together and closed the door.

"We can speak freely in English," Paul said. "The old man doesn't speak it, and Thea knows only a few words. The kids, *nada*."

"Okay," Alex said. It was the first English they'd spoken for hours.

"We share a bedroom?" Alex said.

"We're married, remember?"

"How could I possibly forget?" she said with an edge. She tossed her overnight bag to the side of the bed.

"If you did, I'd remind you," he said.

Tired, she eased into one of the chairs and settled back. "I need some sleep soon."

"I know. I get it," he said.

"I think it's monstrous," she said. "A blasphemy."

"What? Sharing a room?" he asked.

"Digging up a grave," she said. "That's what you have in mind, isn't it? That's what you came here to do, right?"

Paul flopped down on the room's only bed. He quaffed from

a bottle of water that was on a night table and looked back to her. "Yes," he said.

"And you knew that ahead of time?"

"Yes."

"But you didn't tell me."

"Would you have come if you knew that we were going to disturb a grave?"

After a moment, she answered. "Maybe not ... probably not."

"Well, that's why I didn't tell you," he said. "Look, Thea's going to drive us back to Havana tomorrow. We need to rest a bit during the day. Tomorrow night we're to meet behind the south wall of the old cemetery at 10:00 p.m. There'll be a truck and some men with digging equipment. The guards have been bribed. We'll either go through a gate that's been left unlocked or we go over the wall. We dig, we get what we want, we put everything back in place, say a short prayer if you want, and get out as quickly as possible."

"And you knew about this all along," she said.

"No. I knew the money was buried with my uncle, but I didn't know where the grave was until two days ago. Uncle Johnny has lived with the knowledge for a lifetime. He's old now. He wishes to travel to get medical care."

"I thought the medical care was supposed to be good here."

"It is. But it's better elsewhere — if you have money."

"How can he leave?" she asked.

"He doesn't have to. There are clinics. Doctors come here. It's a black market of sorts." Paul paused. "Johnny also wants his family to be taken care of. So he told me what happened, where the cemetery plot is, and what's down there."

"So you're going to be the facilitator of that?" she asked. "Grave robbery. Would that be too strong a term for it?"

Guarneri thought about it. "Let's call it archaeology," he suggested. "Recovery of historical artifacts."

"From a grave?"

"The museums of the Western world are filled with such stuff," he said, dismissing it. "Ever see the King Tut exhibit?"

"Yes, and I've been to Egypt too."

"Then you've seen the artifacts from the Pyramids. And the mummies."

"I know where you're going with this," she said.

"Of course you do. Excavating those tombs is no worse than what we're going to do. Did you object when you looked at the mummies and the relics from their graves?"

She looked at him and sighed. "You have a silver tongue, Paul."

"I think of it as a rather cozy idea, myself," he said. "One brother guarding the other's fortune for half a century. The dead guarding the money and reaching out from the grave to enrich the lives of the living. I like it."

Paul triggered thoughts in Alex's head about the money Federov had left her. She wondered if he knew and was flirting with the topic. Part of her wanted to pursue it, but the wiser voice inside her suggested that she let it go. For now, at least.

A thought hit her. She opened her cell phone and looked to see if there was a message from Roland Violette. There was none. She began to wonder if her mission was doomed to fail. Well, if he didn't show up, that wasn't her fault. But why, she wondered, would he have dropped off the cell phone if he wasn't planning to defect?

She closed the phone and looked up.

Paul was reclining comfortably on a pillow, watching her. "Anything from your spook?" he asked.

"No," she said.

"Who knows, with someone as unstable as that?" he said. Paul continued to gaze at her. "So?" he finally asked.

"So *what*?" she answered.

"So this trip to the cemetery tomorrow night. You'll go with me?"

"I'm not comfortable with it, for more reasons than I can count."

"Compared to our hard landing in Cuba," he said, "it should be a cakewalk."

"I've heard that one before," she said.

"Hang around long enough," he promised, "and you'll probably hear it again."

Another thought hit her. "Tell me again," she said. "How did you get away from the boat when we landed? There were police everywhere."

"The same way that you did. I jumped in the water and swam."

"But as I was swimming the gunfight was still going on," Alex said.

"You can thank *me* for that," he said. "I provided cover for you."

"Which way did you swim?" she asked. "I never saw you."

"The opposite as you," he said. "Intentionally. I explained all that."

"But I still don't understand how you eluded them."

He went to the closet. He unbuttoned his shirt, slid it off, and pulled on a T-shirt for sleeping. Alex watched him in fascination, wondering if he was going to change completely in front of her.

"Like I said before, there was a low mist on the water. When I guided the boat out farther, I realized the mist was getting thicker. Almost a fog. That's when I hung over the far side of the boat. But I turned the outboard motor back on so the boat would continue to move — out to sea. By the time the Cubans got to it, they had no idea where I was. Nor could they see me."

"So you hit a beach farther up toward Matanzas?"

"Yes. I hid out during the day and let the sun dry my clothes. There were a lot of police and militia around. In the late afternoon I found a farmer with a truck. I hired him for a hundred U.S. dollars to drive me out here to Johnny's and keep his mouth shut."

"So what did you and Johnny do your first night here?" Alex asked.

"You know." He shrugged. "We just sat around and shot the breeze," he said. "Lot of catching up to do."

"And what about yesterday?" she asked. "Something seems off. Did you stay here last night as well?"

"Why are you asking?"

"Because I want to know. What did you do during the day yesterday?"

"Same as you," he said. "Laying low. Trying to avoid the police and the shore patrols."

"But did you try to make it into Havana to find me at the hotel?" she asked.

Paul said, "It's not easy to travel in Cuba, so my intent was to get somewhere and stay off the streets. So no, I didn't get to Havana until last night."

"Then where did you stay last night?"

He paused. "At the Ambos Mundos," he said. "Two floors above where you found me today," Guarneri said. "It's pretty run down, as you noticed, but perfectly acceptable for Cuba. Hemingway lived there for a while. I don't think they've changed the plumbing or the TVs since Papa put the gun to his head."

"Don't change the subject. Apparently they haven't changed the window grates in the men's room either," she chided. "So did you check in under your real name?"

"You think I'm crazy? I used my Canuck passport. Why are you always asking so many questions?"

"Because I'm trained to."

"Okay, that's healthy enough. So are you finished asking me questions so that I can ask my 'wife' one?"

"Sure," Alex said. "Go for it."

"There's only one bed in this room. Will I have the pleasure of my wife's company in it?"

She laughed. "We can share the bed, but we're not having sex," she said. "Is that where you were going with that?"

"I thought I'd try to steer it in that direction."

"I thought you would too. You actually steered it off the road."

He laughed. "Well, you can't blame a man for trying. Anyway, I'm going to go down the hall to take a shower. Unless you want to go first. The water is warm, not hot. There are towels and soap in the bath area. It's rustic but it works. It has a certain primitive charm. You might like it. So? Who first, me or you?"

"I'll go," she said.

"Want me to show you where?"

"If I can find my way from the beach outside Matanzas to Havana I can find my way down the hall to the shower," Alex answered.

"I'm sure you can," he said.

From her bag, she took a pair of thin shorts and a cotton T-shirt to change into for sleeping, plus her toiletries. The shower room had a 1950s feel to it, one pipe coming out of the wall, above a tile floor with a drain. She undressed and blasted her body and hair with the tepid water. There was a plastic container of a Mexican shower soap hanging on a metal hook. She unhooked it, washed thoroughly, and felt refreshed.

She dressed in the shorts and the T-shirt. She toweled her hair and combed it out. It was still wet when she returned to the room. Paul had left the door half-open to maintain a breeze.

While he was in the shower, she could hear the water running. She eyed his belongings, one bag and some clothes, where he had left them across a chair and dresser. She went to the door and glanced down the hall. She walked quietly down the hall to make sure he was in the shower. He was.

She returned to the room. She listened for any approaching footsteps, heard none, and couldn't resist. She prowled through his things, looking at everything from his passport, his backup pieces of identification, his clothes, his Browning automatic, and the bullets with it. The weapon, upon close examination, gave an indication of having been fired recently, and it still smelled faintly of gunpowder. Of course, he had fired several shots on the morning they arrived. But were they fired from his own gun or from one that he had picked up on the boat? Memory failed her. She couldn't recall.

She looked at his passport again. A fine piece of work. And so were the supporting documents: an Ontario driver's license and an American Express card. They were just fine, she thought to herself, except they were completely fake: same as her own.

Her hand did a quick pat down of the rest of his suitcase. She came across an envelope, legal size, standard 4 ⅛ by 9 ½. She squeezed it. Cash. She opened it. Franklin and Grant. Large denomination American currency. Fifties and hundreds. A quick calculation told her that he must have had twenty grand in cash. Well, there was another reason to pack a pistol.

She heard him turn the water off. She put everything away again, eased back, and settled into her chair, shaking out her hair, enjoying the feel of the sea breeze on her arms and legs.

Paul returned. He closed the door but not all the way.

"Time for some sleep," he said. "Which half of the bed do you want?"

"Whichever half you're not on."

"Good answer," he said.

"Take the left; I'll take the right."

"Deal," he said. He climbed in. There were light blankets and a sheet.

She came to the bed and sidled into it on the opposite side. The room's final light was on her side. She extinguished it. The sheets were cool and soft, the bed more comfortable than it had any right to be. She exhaled a long breath and tried to think of sleep as they lay side by side. Then he moved his arm. His hand found hers and held it.

"Well?" he asked after half a minute. "Yes or no?"

"Yes or no *what*?" she asked.

"The *big* question for tonight," he said, turning toward her in the dim light. "The issue I've been wondering about since we walked into this room and closed the door."

She turned toward him. "I already answered you," she said. "I'm not going to let you make love to me."

"No, I already shelved that idea," he said. "It was the other thing I was wondering about, the one you didn't answer."

"And what would that be?" she asked.

"Are you going to the cemetery tomorrow? You still haven't answered."

She watched the thin curtains flutter against the breeze and looked at the shadows that the moonlight threw into the room. The room was deeply quiet, except for the rumble of the surf on the beach.

Tomorrow. The cemetery.

The notion raced through her head that, in spite of everything, this location was comfortable and the people around her were good — even Paul, in his rough and strangely ironic way, even though he alternately irritated her and amused her. Then, of course, there was the danger and the fascination with everything that was going on, an equation that added a shot of adrenaline to everything. She almost disliked herself by getting so turned on by the excitement, the risks, and the challenges.

She turned back toward him. She spoke to his silhouette against the feeble light from the hallway. "I'll go," she said. "I don't like what we're going to do. But I'll go."

"Excellent," he said.

He rolled over, away from her. She rolled over away from him.

A few minutes later, she was at the edge of sleep when her cell phone came sharply alive. It jolted her. She sprang from the bed and went to her clothes. She stood in the reflected moonlight from outside, snapped the phone open, and answered. "Hello?"

Paul lifted himself up on one elbow and watched. For a moment it bothered her that she was so well on view to him, shorts and T-shirt in a moonlit bedroom. Then it stopped bothering her, and her mind bounced back to business.

"Hello," an emotionless voice said. "You know who I am, yes?"

"I know who you are," she said quietly.

"Then who are *you*?" he asked. "Tell me who."

"I'm Anna."

"Anna who?"

"Anna Marie Tavares," she said.

"You know why I'm calling?"

"I know," Alex said.

There was a painfully long silence. Then, "Hotel Plaza Habana. Tomorrow, 3:00 p.m.," the voice said. "Remember ... 3:00 p.m.," he repeated. "The lobby. Can you do that?"

"I can do that," Alex answered.

Then the line clicked dead. Alex folded the phone away, heaved a sigh of exhaustion, and turned back toward the bed. Paul was still sitting up, smiling slightly. With courtesy, he lifted the sheet and blanket on her side to welcome her back into bed, as a husband might.

"Violette," she said. "He's ready to play ball."

FIFTY-SIX

The next morning Paul took the Toyota Jeep again. He and Alex drove back to Havana. By early afternoon, Paul had parked in the garage of a man whom he said was a family friend. Then they found their way to the Hotel Plaza Habana, on foot. It was about a fifteen minute walk. Alex tried to memorize the route but wasn't able.

The Plaza Habana was one of the oldest hotels in the city, built in 1909. Unlike much of the rest of Havana, it was charming and beautifully restored. It stood proudly on Calle Agramonte in Old Havana, where Agramonte intersected with Zuluete, not far from the Ambos Mundos where she had rendezvoused with Paul the day before.

Alex entered the hotel with Paul fifty feet behind her. The lobby was vibrant with sunlight, tourists, and bright mosaics. A floor of off-white tile gleamed. There was a surprisingly festive air, supported by groups of laughing Italian travelers. An upbeat salsa melody pulsed from the sound system.

Alex, nervous, scanned the lobby and proceeded directly to the first-floor bar. She carried her small tote that she had bought on her first day in Cuba. Her gun was in it, beneath her traveling clothes.

The bar was bright like the lobby. It jutted out from the main hotel building, a separate one-story annex with a high ceiling. There were tables for four, topped with white Formica and light wood. A skylight lit the room and a fountain bubbled unobtrusively at the center. More music was piped in from somewhere, but a different track than in the lobby.

Alex picked a table where she could watch both doors. Paul, following her a minute later, disappeared to a table in the corner.

A waiter found Alex, and she ordered a Coca-Cola. She waited. From the corner of her eye, she watched Guarneri order a drink and start a small cigar. From a nearby table, he picked up a newspaper. *Trabajadores*. The Cuban workers' newspaper. Well, that would raise Paul's consciousness a little, Alex mused.

She scanned the bar again. Like the lobby, it was filled with tourists, mostly Europeans, and some wealthy South Americans. A group of eight young backpackers had pushed two tables together, four girls, four boys, college kids probably, their backpacks bedecked with Canadian flag appliqués. They sat around bottles of Cuban beer, in no hurry to go anywhere. There were no cops that Alex could spot, nor anyone she could ID as Cuban security. For that, she was thankful.

According to the legends that Paul had told her about on their drive that morning, Babe Ruth had once made the hotel's Suite 216 his personal den of iniquity during his barnstorming tours through Cuba in the 1920s and '30s. Also, several of the top dancers from the clubs in the 1950s had had suites there, and more than a few American GIs spent debauched R&R weeks there during World War II. Albert Einstein once attended a banquet there. Somehow, the Plaza had navigated both the Batista and Castro eras with comparative ease. Somewhere, Alex concluded, someone knew whom to pay.

Her soda arrived.

A quarter hour passed. Alex's anxiety level spiked. The afternoon heat continued to build outside and started to overpower the air conditioning. Alex looked up and her heart jumped. She spotted a figure at the entrance to the bar. Roland Violette. She recognized him instantly from the surveillance photos she had seen in Langley.

He looked much older in person. In his khaki pants and rumpled shirt, he looked thin, almost frail, and stooped. He would have been about six feet as a younger man. He moved with difficulty, as if he had arthritis in his hips. His hair was thin and flecked with white, and his dark glasses wrapped around his narrow mocha face. He carried a cardboard box, about the size of a double ream of copy paper.

He was jittery and moved cautiously, as if at any time he might spot a gun aimed at him. He carried a pack of cigarettes in his right hand — Winstons — which seemed to be his security system, keeping him calm. Alex watched for several seconds and didn't miss the irony of the cigarettes. She had seen it before. Even those who vilified America most often clung passionately to American products and culture. Ho Chi Minh smoked Kools. Castro loved baseball. Khrushchev had loved Fred Astaire movies. Kim Jung Il loves Elvis. Go figure, she mused.

Violette spotted Alex almost as quickly. His gaze settled on her. She gave him a subtle nod and a smile. She held him in her gaze, eye contact all the way, almost like radar to bring him to her table. He stopped and scanned the room. He didn't seem to sense that Paul was an accomplice, though he took a long look at him. Or maybe he just didn't care.

Violette came to Alex's table and sat down.

"Anna from America," he said in English. "Anna. Anna. Anna. Anna and the King of Siam. Anna from America come to take me home? Right?"

"Good guess. Right," she said.

"Wasn't much of a guess," he said. "I used to be a spook. But you knew. You knew that."

"I did," she said. "That's why I'm here, right?"

"Guess it is," he said. "Guess it is."

Her instinct was to extend a hand. In a flash everything Roland Violette had done went through her mind — the slaughtered agents behind the Iron Curtain in the final days of the cold war, the flight from Spain, the profligacy with his amoral Costa Rican missus — and she withheld her hand. Then another part of her was in rebellion against her moral instincts. She reminded herself that she was on assignment and not supposed to pass judgment. So she offered her hand.

He assessed her up and down. He gave her a dead-fish

handshake and moved his left hand toward his left pocket. Her eyes shot down and spotted the contours of a small pistol. Her nerves simmered. He withdrew his hand. She pulled her own bag closer, just in case.

"I'm surprised they sent a woman," he said.

"They?" she asked.

"The CIA people," he said. "The Careless Intelligence Analysts. We all know who we're talking about. So don't flirt. Don't flirt. Never used to do that, never used to do that. Send women, I mean. If I'd known women who looked like you I might never have left."

"What's done is done," she said.

"Yes. It is. It is done."

She wondered if he was acting or if his screws really were as loose as they seemed. "You had a wife for many years," Alex said.

"Yes," he said. "So I did."

"I heard she passed away. I'm sorry."

"I am too," he said. "She's in heaven. Waiting for me."

Alex wasn't sure if it were another place where his wife was, one even hotter than Cuba in the summer.

Violette stared at her. "Do they ever ask you to be a hooker?" he asked.

"What?"

He repeated. "You know. For spy stuff. Honey traps and all. Be a whore for Uncle Sam."

"I once posed as one, but I never became one. In Cairo last year," she answered.

"Nice," he said.

"Does that excite you?"

"Not today. I'm too sick."

Violette rubbed his face, then his chin. He had more nervous ticks and twitches than there were peanuts in a bag. A nervous eye flickered. A tick at the left side of the lips wouldn't quit. Two fingers on his right hand wouldn't stay still, and the other hand still was playing hide and seek with the pistol. She wondered if he had some neurological damage somewhere. Drugs, maybe, or a thrashing he had sustained somewhere. Or were his nerves just badly shot? The guy was one unhinged piece of work, Alex decided quickly. No act was this good. That made him even more dangerous. He might not respond to logic in a pinch, and that was exactly how she was supposed to make her pitch to him — with logic.

Violette sighed, long and loud. "So about time and all. You're going to get me out of here, right?" he said.

"That's my assignment. Assuming you want to leave."

"Yeah, yeah, yeah. Roger. I do," he said. "I want to go."

The waiter reappeared. Violette ordered a Pepsi with ice in a separate glass. Embargo or not, the waiter nodded and disappeared.

"That's good, that's good," he said. "Getting out of Cuba. Been here too long, you know. Time to go home."

"You're lucky they'll take you back," she said.

He shrugged. "Jail time," he said. "Going to have to pay some dues. I have prostate cancer, you know. I'm sick."

"I'm sorry," she said.

"Got a prostate the size of a grapefruit," he said. "That's part of the deal. Well, you know what the deal is," he said. "I come back, do some prison time, get an operation in federal slammer. Maybe I die there. Who knows? It's all part of the package. If I die in America, they bury me in America. If I survive jail, I live my last years in America. Win-win. Get it?"

She nodded. So that was the angle. The waiter returned with two glasses, one empty and one filled with ice and a bottle of Pepsi, or at least something the color of cola in a Pepsi bottle. The waiter started to pour. Violette shooed him away, indicating he would administer to his own beverage.

"Just asking," she said, "how do you know the CIA is going to keep any deal they make with you?"

"Why? You think they won't?" he asked sharply.

"No. Just wondering. Seems they might still be plenty mad at you."

"I'm sure they are," he said. "Because I beat them at their own dirty games. I have a lawyer in New York," said Violette. "A smart little Hebrew with a big nose and a shiny bald head. He negotiated a deal for me."

"Uh-huh."

"It's all money, you know. Who you can buy, what you can buy. That's the only thing that counts, money, money, money. Capitalist system. Just business. Screw everyone before they screw you. Nothing personal."

She couldn't help herself. "Is that why you sold out to so many other people?" she asked. "Just business?" She had expected that he might at least be troubled by the morality of what he had done, even two and a half decades ago, then realized she had been naive to entertain such a thought. If Violette was troubled, he didn't show it. Instead, he held up the glass with the ice in it, examining the cubes carefully in the light from the ceiling window.

"Never know what's in the ice in Havana," he said. "I've found ticks as big as my toenail and toenails as big as ticks. Sometimes glass ... sometimes I find glass. And fleas. Lots of fleas. World wouldn't starve if everyone ate fleas." Then he turned to her. "What?" he asked.

"Just business?" she repeated. "The money you took from the Soviets to give up spies? It was just business?"

"It was a long time ago."

"But it happened. People got killed."

"So what? They would have sold me out just as easily," he said. "They were selling out people themselves. They were Russians, the people I sold out, mostly Russians, and they were squealing on their own people. Dog-eat-dog. Bow wow wow. I needed money."

"If your Communist system works better," she asked, "why are you coming back?"

He laughed. "System here doesn't work," he said. "System

here stinks. Castro sold out his own revolution. I've had a snootful for twenty-six years. I can tell you all about it."

He poured his soft drink and spent several seconds examining the bubbles, as if to find a deeper truth in them. "Everyone thinks I'm some sort of latter-day Leninist," he said. "Not true. You know what? I love America. I just wish America would be true to America." He drank half the glass. "American soil, American soil. See, that's the thing. I want to live my final years on American soil and be buried in American earth. That's where I came from, so that's where I go back to. That's my only wish."

"So I hear."

He eyed her. "Why should it bother you?" he said. "What were you, five years old when it all happened? A gleam in your horny father's eye? How old are you, twenty?"

"Thirty," she said.

"Thirty," he scoffed. "You're less than half my age, less than half. Thirty is the new fifteen. When are you getting me out of here?" he asked. "I want to leave." His eyes shot to the door and back.

"If the connections can be arranged, we leave in forty-eight hours," she said. "You ready to travel?"

"I'm ready to travel. Been ready for two years, if you want to know. It's your own Justice Department people who've been dragging their feet."

"What about the twenty-six years before that?" she couldn't help asking.

"What about them?" he stiffened.

"Just asking," she said. "Earlier, you seemed quite content here, from what I saw in your file. Now it's a different story."

"Ah," he scoffed. "Different times. Rica was alive. Life was merrier."

For several seconds, Violette stared at Alex in an unfocused way, as if trying to see through her or discover some inner truth that he hadn't found in the Pepsi bubbles. Then he ducked his eyes and picked up what remained of his thought patterns. "None of us are perfect people," Violette said. "Not me, not you, not Rica. She spent me into oblivion, changed the course of my life, ran off with another man, then came back. But she also brought me more happiness than I've known with any other woman. It's all over now. I know that."

There was a white stubble on his face that, when the light hit it in a certain way, made him look like a very old man. He rubbed the stubble.

"Know what Mark Twain wrote about Eve?" he asked. "Eve in the Bible, I mean. What Adam said when Eve died?"

"Why don't you tell me?" Alex said.

"Adam looked at Eve's grave and said, 'Wherever she was, there was Eden.' " He paused, and for a second Alex thought she caught a hitch in his voice. Then he went on. "I've been waiting for Rica to speak to me since she died. But she doesn't say much, except in my dreams."

Alex nodded. "You're bringing documents with you?" Alex asked.

He nodded. He indicated the box he had with him.

"I need to glance at them," she said.

"So do it," he answered.

He pushed the box toward her. The box made her nervous. If the police came in and swept the place, she would be busted for espionage for sure. But she had the idea that Violette wasn't letting it out of his sight, and she didn't want to let him out of hers.

So Alex opened it. Keeping the contents out of sight of any onlookers, she quickly glanced through it. The documents were all in Spanish. Alex fingered her way through for two minutes. From the corner of her eye, she saw Paul rise and move toward the entrance. He was watching the door for her. Meanwhile, Violette grew increasingly twitchy and jittery.

She tried to comprehend what the papers were all about. Police stuff. Communist party stuff. Army stuff. She ran her eyes across the dates. Some were fresh, some were from the last five years. It wasn't Alex's place to verify the authenticity of the documents, but at first pass they looked good. Not fantastic, but good. Middle-range stuff. Probably worth the trip, probably worth coddling the defector, assuming they got back safely. Who knew how the CIA would inventory the stuff. Again, not her concern. She closed the box and gave it back to him.

"There's more," he said. "I wouldn't be dumb enough to bring it all at once."

"How many more boxes?" she asked.

"Three."

"Where'd you get it?"

He paused. "Friends. Women mostly. Various parts of the government. They work in offices and photocopy stuff for future favors." He smirked.

"What sort of favors?"

"Me helping them get off the island," he said.

"You're barely able to get yourself off," she said. "How do you get anyone else out?"

He shrugged. *"¿Quien sabe?"* he asked. "Who knows? That's what I tell them and they believe me."

"Just business?" she asked.

"Just business," he answered.

"Okay, then. Be here at 7:00 p.m. two days from now," she said. "With whatever you're going to bring with you. One backpack, that's it, and that has to include the papers. All four boxes or there's no deal. I'm supposed to tell you that if you're not here, the deal is dead, and there'll never be another one. Can you handle that?"

"I'll be here. I'll be here."

Violette finished his drink and the meeting too. He took back his box and stood. For an instant, his cuff slid away from his sleeve and Alex caught a glimpse of the Patek Philippe on his wrist, the one that had been his undoing in Spain three decades earlier. She wondered if he had been nuts way back then too.

Then he was out the door.

FIFTY-SEVEN

Alex and Paul met that evening at 10:00 p.m. on the southwest corner of the Plaza Vieja. The square was busy with tourists, which made the pickup all that much less conspicuous. A white Nissan pulled to the curb in front of Alex. The man behind the wheel was a glowering hulk with a Havana underworld look to him, the type that Alex had not seen during the day. Paul obviously knew him, and she didn't ask from where.

Paul approached the car, gave a raised hand to the driver, and guided Alex to it. He let her slide into the backseat ahead of him. The driver checked his passengers and then checked his rear view mirror. *"¿Listo?"* he growled. Ready?

"Listo," Paul answered. The car pulled from the curb and they were off, quickly disappearing from the tourist world into the shady backstreets where darkness reigned, where there were few strollers. A number of people stood in dark doorways, including a woman in more-than-suggestive clothing. The driver watched the doorways, and Paul sat sideways in the backseat watching for followers. There were none.

"We're good," he finally announced, calming.

The drive to the Colón Cemetery took twenty minutes. The cemetery occupied several city blocks and the driver circled it twice. Once they passed a small red Opel truck going the other way. The driver flashed his lights.

"That's our contact," Paul said softly. "We're good so far."

They spent a quarter hour driving around the grounds again and the high brick fence and iron gates that sealed it off. At one point, the thuggish driver stopped short and did a U-turn, obviously to see if they were being followed. They weren't. When they were on the north side again, Alex recognized the Opel truck parked by one of the smaller gates. Alex's driver pulled up on the wrong side and parked nose to nose with the truck. For a moment they sat. Then Paul was the first to jump out.

From the truck emerged six sturdy men with big shoulders and dark expressions. Two of them were obviously the leaders, and they seemed to know Paul well. Their names were Jorgé and Enrique. Alex stood behind them. From the back of the truck, one of the men pulled a canvas sheet away from some equipment. Alex saw shovels, rakes, and hoes. Jorgé walked down to the gate, looked both ways, then pulled a set of keys from his pocket. He reached the gate and unlocked it. He pushed it open.

"Amazing how far money can go in Cuba," Paul said, "particularly if it's a bribe."

"What about the local police?" Alex asked.

"We're good with them. It's the national police we'd have a problem with. Got to work fast. Let's go."

In the shadowy darkness, the men moved like phantoms, each with a shovel. They were inside the gate like a bunch of ghosts. The driver remained outside and tossed Paul a cell phone. Paul caught it.

"Around 3:00 a.m.," the driver said.

"What's that?" Alex asked.

"Our pickup," Paul answered.

Then they began to walk, a spooky trip through the old cemetery, guided only by the dim flashlights they carried. The two Cubans who led the way walked to the top of a steep sandy hill in the southeast quadrant of the cemetery. It was pitch dark and well past midnight by now. They stopped to make sure that everyone was together. There were eight of them, including Paul and Alex. Then they proceeded.

The path wound down a slope, past a jagged audience of markers and monuments that took eerie, shadowy shapes in the dim moonlight.

"Down there, Señores," said one of the Cubans, pointing.

"We're still with you," Guarneri said.

Alex's eyes finally adjusted. She watched the Cubans lead the two Americans down to a flat area at the foot of the long, sandy hillside. They faced north and could see the lights of Havana burning beyond the walls of the cemetery. They continued to walk. The terrain was soft, uneven, and marked with litter and brush. The Cubans knew where to step and where not to. Jorgé carried the best light, a hand lantern in one hand, and a shovel in the other. Alex was aware of her heartbeat. There were moments on every assignment when, if everything blew up, nothing but disaster could follow. This was one of those moments.

"Watch their feet," Paul said to Alex. "Step exactly where they step."

She obeyed, carefully following the leaders' footsteps one by one.

They found a set of steps, boards across sandy soil crossing another incline. They walked on rotting slats. Jorgé clicked his lantern to a higher beam for a few seconds and slashed the pathway with a quick yellow light.

They continued downward. They passed a small sea of wooden crosses, jagged and crooked. The headstones and statuettes made another small army of witnesses in the moonlight and the reflected shadows of the torches. They walked another fifty yards. After a few more moments, Jorgé stopped. He looked at a formation of crosses and monuments. He pointed to a patch of clay and dirt. They went fifteen paces in that direction until they came to a grave within a low fence.

Alex saw the name *C. Fernandez* on a tombstone that bore an ornate cross. Just *C. Fernandez* and the dates 1931 – 1959. She drew a breath. She knew the moment she dreaded was at hand.

"There, Señor," Jorgé said softly.

He indicated the tombstone and a flat stretch of earth.

"Okay," Paul said softly. "Let's get this done."

The Cubans went to work. They pulled up the small fencing. Four of them wobbled the tombstone until it loosened from the earth. It was of heavy granite. Eventually it came free. It took all six Cubans plus Guarneri to lift it and lay it to one side. Once they had done that, the six men went to their shovels and began to dig.

The earth came up easily. The diggers worked efficiently. Paul took Alex by the hand and guided her to a space a dozen feet away.

"This is an abomination," she said. "You know that, right?"

"Of course it is, and of course I know," he said. "But we need to do what we need to do."

Alex settled in on the edge of a large flat stone. A chilly breeze swept across the cemetery from the east. Paul put an arm around her as she shivered. Against her better judgment, she felt comfort from his arm; then her eyes rose and, by chance, saw a small speck of light flashing in the sky toward the horizon.

"Paul?" she asked.

"What?"

She indicated. A helicopter.

"It's over the harbor," he said. "Shore patrol. Cuban navy. I wouldn't worry about that one."

"You sure?"

"No," he said, "but we've made our move. I think we're clean. There's no turning back now."

The crew dug for an hour, little mountains of dirt rising up on both sides of the violated grave. From time to time Paul walked over and looked into the deepening hole. Each time, he would wander back and not say anything. Then, suddenly, they both heard a distinctive crack from the shovel. The Cubans had hit the old bronze coffin.

Jorgé quickly looked at Paul.

"Stay here," Paul said to Alex. He went to the gravesite. Enrique took the lantern from Jorgé. Three Cubans climbed up out of the hole. Alex watched them. Paul gazed down.

"Keep going," he instructed. "Get the soil off the lid." Alex felt another uneasy surge in her stomach. She heard the shovel blades rapping the metal of the casket. The field of death was very still, very quiet. Even the tortured souls and spirits weren't immediately to be heard from. Three diggers remained in the grave. They enlarged it so that the lid could be lifted from the coffin. Their arms flew in a nightmarish ballet. It took another thirty minutes to create the space they needed.

They knelt down to work. From Alex's vantage point, she could see that they were removing the lid from the coffin. She lowered her eyes and tried to suppress her disgust before it turned her physically ill. She stepped farther away and folded her arms in front of her. She wondered why God could have put her in this place unless it was to learn, to think, to reflect.

Nervous, Alex left her seat and paced with short steps, staying out of the way, but watching everything that transpired. Eventually, she heard a loud creak and knew that the lid had come off. She heard a low conversation in Spanish. Paul was leading it. Somehow, they loosened the lid and passed it upward. It clunked onto the ground next to the mounds of dirt. Then Enrique tossed Paul a canvas satchel, and Paul went back down into the grave. The diggers stood by, looking downward.

Paul was in the grave, working. She could only see him from the shoulders up.

Working? Robbing? Stealing? Defiling? Recovering? Whatever one wanted to call it. To Alex, he was down there for a long time, which was actually only about thirty seconds. Against her better judgment, against everything that she considered sacrosanct, Alex rose and walked to the open grave. She looked down into the hole as the torchlight swept its contents. Nothing she had ever experienced prepared her for what she saw.

The body that had rested there for five decades was preserved better than anyone could have imagined. The upper part of the skull was skeletal, but the dried flesh of the forehead was in perfect condition. The rest of the cadaver was well preserved also. Alex could see the contours of the head and face, the skeletal knees that had worn through the fabric of the funeral dress, the bones of the wrists and the hands. The nails on the hands shown as if the body had just had a manicure. Much of the rest of the burial clothing was intact. And Salvatore Guarneri's feet were bare. He had been buried shoeless.

In the midst of this, Guarneri was balanced on the firm side of the casket. His hands were quickly working. He was reaching beneath the head of the corpse and removing the tightly bound stacks of currency. Alex had never seen anything like this in her life and hoped never to again. From the satchel that Enrique had provided, Paul had also pulled a pair of small pillows, sturdy ones, which he would use to replace the money.

Like a spectator transfixed by a traffic accident, Alex continued to stare until she couldn't take any more and turned away. For a moment, she thought she would throw up. She drew two sharp breaths and suppressed the nausea.

The dark ballet in the grave was over within two minutes, with Paul making sure that he had everything that he was there to get. Alex walked back and looked down again, against her better instincts, but wanted to be a reliable witness. Then, with the pillows in place and the money secured in the satchel, Paul did something that surprised Alex even more. From one of his pockets, he pulled what appeared to be a Holy Card, the type of thing that Roman Catholics issue at their funerals. He tucked it into the remains of his late uncle's jacket pocket. Then he turned. Alex and Enrique offered him a hand up. He accepted both.

"Back from the dead," he muttered. "Who says it can't be done?"

Alex turned, walked back to the memorial slab, and sat again.

Paul brushed the soil off his hands, then washed and disinfected them with rubbing alcohol. He held the valise, came back over to Alex, and sat down next to her. The diggers began to fill in the grave.

"You okay?" he said.

"I'm all right," she said. "Stunned. Horrified. Revolted. Repelled. But not for the first time in my life and probably not the last. So I'm all right."

"Quite a night," he said.

"Quite a night," she agreed.

The crew of diggers was efficient with the back end of their assignment. They filled the open grave within thirty minutes, tamped it down, and replanted turf on top so that it would not immediately appear to have been disturbed. They replaced the marker and steadied it. Then they replaced the low fence. To Alex's amazement, Paul huddled everyone together. He tucked his pistol into his belt and led a short prayer for his deceased uncle's soul. She was amazed at his apparent sincerity but wondered if he was doing it more for the conscious of his very Roman Catholic crew. There was no way to know.

They retraced their path to the iron gate that led to the back side of the burial grounds. While walking, Paul telephoned his contact to inform him that pickup time was at hand. When they came out of the cemetery, three vehicles were waiting: the red truck, the white Nissan with Paul's driver inside, and the battered old Peugeot 404 that Alex recognized from the family home by the sea. Alex could see movement inside the French car but not much more.

Paul had an iron grip on the satchel.

"Paul, how much is in there?" she asked softly.

"More than I expected," he said. "I did a vague count as I was packing it. Maybe eight hundred thousand dollars. There were more hundreds and fifties than anyone would have thought. All U.S. currency. Still legal tender."

"Not a bad night's work," she said.

"Nope," he said. "Not bad at all." He motioned. "Come with me." He walked to the Peugeot. There was just enough light for Alex to see. She recognized Thea, Paul's cousin, as the driver. There were two young men in the car with her, one in the front seat, one in the back. They looked expectantly at Paul.

"Yo lo tengo," he said to them.

The driver's-side window was open. Paul handed the satchel to Thea. She pulled it in and set it at the feet of the young man next to her. The young man quickly covered it with a small blanket. He sat close to her, so close that he appeared to be a friend or a fiancé. He gave Alex a nod and a slight smile. Thea had a pistol on her lap and the two young men had rifles.

"Give Uncle Giovanni my love," Paul said. "Alex and I have to leave the island quickly. We'll be back when we can. It may take a few years, but I'll be here again."

Through the window, Paul embraced his cousin.

"Vaya con dios," Thea said.

"Vaya con dios," Paul answered.

Thea offered Alex an embrace as well. Alex accepted.

Then the Peugeot backed up, turned, and drove away.

"They'll be safe with all that money?" Alex asked.

"They're going to a friend's home in Havana," Paul said. "They'll be safely indoors in three minutes."

"So Uncle Johnny gets the money?" Alex asked.

"And his extended family," Paul answered. "It'll be spread around wisely. They deserve it. They spent their lives in this infernal place living under a Marxist regime. To them it's a fortune. Things will thaw in the next few years, probably during an Obama second term, if there is one. The family will have some seed money to start over with. I pray to God that the next regime is kinder than the ones that have preceded it. God knows the Cuban people deserve better."

"Agreed," she said. They walked back to the white Nissan.

"Get in the car if you want," Paul said to Alex. "I need to take care of the men. Then I'll join you."

Alex hesitated, then went back to the Nissan while Paul walked back to his crew. Warily, she opened the rear door but did not enter. She held one hand on her Walther, still wary of trouble. She checked the sky but saw no aircraft. She looked back at Paul. His faithful diggers huddled around him. Paul carefully withdrew an envelope from under his shirt and paid the men for their night's work. It was the same envelope that she had seen in his belongings, she realized, the one with the stack of hundred dollar bills.

Alex watched him count out ten to each of them, and fifteen to the thug who drove the Nissan. It was a fortune in Cuba, a thousand dollars of hard currency. Paul thanked each man with a handshake and a hug. A voice inside Alex suggested that Paul might have been a distant Corleone relative, working the street, building his organization from the ground up, dispensing largesse.

The men looked ecstatic, thanking Paul with effusive smiles, bows, and hugs. Alex realized that Paul was buying loyalty and silence also. *De tal palo, tel astilla*: like father, like son. The apple rarely falls far from the tree.

With payday complete, the men piled into the truck, and the drivers returned to their wheels. Alex slid into the backseat of the Nissan behind the driver. Paul slid in across from her. Both engines started. The truck pulled away.

"Wait! Give him half a minute," Paul said in Spanish to the driver. "Two cars together will look suspicious at this hour. We don't want police."

Paul drew his gun and held it across his lap.

The driver grunted a profanity. He was itching to leave. When the truck turned the corner and was out of view, Paul spoke again.

"Okay," he said. The Nissan moved forward with a small lurch. Paul turned to Alex and spoke in English. "Lock your door and keep your gun ready," he said. He gave her hand a squeeze of appreciation, then released it.

"Expecting trouble?" Alex asked.

"No. Just in case."

She drew her weapon and held it in her left hand.

They drove through the sleeping city, down narrow backstreets where there were no lights from residences and only an occasional street lamp. There was no traffic, only an infrequent stray dog or cat crossing a dimly lit street. At one moment a police car pulled up next to them at a stop sign. A tense moment passed as the cops eyed their car. But Paul, confident, gave the cops a friendly gesture, a wave combined with a thumbs up. The cops were satisfied. They continued on.

"I have a question," Alex asked in English. "Those men who did the digging. I saw a few weapons. Were they all armed?"

"I imagine so," Paul said. "You don't get doctors and school teachers to come out in the middle of the night to do a job like that. I assume they all had pistols and knew how to use them."

"Then what stopped them from turning on you once the money was out of the coffin?" she asked. "They could have shot you and split the money."

Paul laughed slightly and smiled. "Oh, I was keeping an eye on them. They wouldn't have dared," he said.

"Why?" she asked. "Because your name is Guarneri and your family is still known here?"

"You could say that. Cubans respect the past. And they look forward to the future."

"What's the future? A restoration of old property and old influence?"

He laughed again. "If I knew the future, I'd know what horses to play and what stocks to pick," he said. "But I don't. One can only hope."

"You didn't answer my question," she said.

"I thought I did," he said.

"A restoration of old property and old influence?" she said again. "You're looking to a personal future as well as attending to the past. Putting things in order, establishing loyal organization at street level as you filter in and out of Cuba. Those men, they know your name, who your father was, and they know you'll be back. They wouldn't mess with a Guarneri even after all these years. Is that it?"

"If you want to see it that way, I can't stop you," he said. "But as I said, who knows what the future holds?"

She looked out the window and watched as they passed a block with small shops with metal gates drawn across doorways.

She turned back. "You know, against my better judgment, I like you, Paul," she said. "But you're a crown prince of evasiveness. Deep down, you have a dark streak. You can be a bit of a rat. I don't like that part."

"It's late," he said, dismissively. "We can talk in the next couple of days. Eventually everything makes sense ... except when it doesn't."

Their driver returned them to Old Havana. Paul had secured a small apartment for the occasion. They went to Paul's address first. It was only a block from Alex's *posada*. The driver stopped.

"Come on up," Paul said to her. "We can have something to drink and celebrate. Then I'll walk you back to your place."

"Paul, it's past 4:00 a.m."

"You can sleep tomorrow. I need the extra gun right now." He looked her eye to eye. Then he gave her a flirtatious wink. "Come on," he said. "Live on the edge for a couple more hours."

After a moment, maybe due to fatigue, "Okay," she said.

They stepped out of the car. Paul dismissed the driver. They looked both ways, then walked quickly to Paul's door. He kept his hand on his Browning.

They went through an outer door for which Paul had a key. No problem. They entered a dark courtyard, and Paul turned on a timed light. No one else was there. He signaled with his head, and they crossed the courtyard quickly, found a staircase, and climbed. Paul unlocked his door with a second key and entered with his gun drawn.

Alex came in behind him and pushed the door shut. He reached past her and threw the bolt. The apartment was small, two rooms and a primitive kitchen, high ceilings, battered furniture, and fading wallpaper. Guarneri checked both closets and under the bed. Then he allowed himself to relax. They were alone. He put his gun away. He flopped down on an old sofa in the living room and shook his head.

"What do you know?" he said. "We did it."

She flopped down next to him. She leaned back and exhaled

a deep breath. For the first time, she realized how thoroughly exhausted she was. She felt her breath was as heavy as her eyelids. She responded to him with silence.

"I know," he said. "I'm not a complete philistine. That was nasty stuff this evening. Unpleasant and horrible. But we got it done! Let's do some rum; it will help us wind down."

"Sure," she said.

He reached to her, put an arm around her, and gave her an embrace. He kissed her, and out of fatigue and ambivalence and overall relief, she allowed it. Then he rose. "I'll get something to drink," he said.

"Sure," she said again.

He was gone for several minutes. She slid sideways on the old sofa, intending to nap for a few seconds. But she crashed harder than expected and was sleeping soundly before he returned.

FIFTY-EIGHT

On the sofa Alex blinked her eyes open and looked at her watch. It was barely past 7:00 a.m. She shook herself into consciousness for the new day and sat up.

The events of the previous night tumbled back to her mind. She felt another surge of disgust over what she had seen. She blinked again and took stock of where she was.

The small apartment was quiet. So was the street outside. She got to her feet and looked into the bedroom. Paul was sleeping soundly. Then thoughts of Roland Violette came into her head.

All right, she told herself. Paul had accomplished what he had come to Havana to do. Now it was time for her to complete her mission and get all of them back to the U.S. the day after tomorrow.

She went to the front window and pushed back the shade. The street seemed calm. There were a few parked vehicles and a street cleaner. Nothing suspicious. She gathered her things. She tossed her Walther into her bag and quietly let herself out of Paul's apartment. She shouldn't have even fallen asleep there, she reminded herself, but fatigue had won a battle with her common sense. She could go back to her own *posada* and sleep the rest of the day; then she would meet Violette again the following evening. Then the next day they would all rendezvous at the small plane and get off the island. With luck, the worst was over.

She crossed the courtyard. A caretaker was bagging garbage. She gave him a nod. He smiled back. She went to the front door and stepped out.

As soon as the door closed behind her with a loud click, the sidewalk came alive and her morning exploded. Two men jumped from the car parked to her left, and two women in the light brown uniforms of local police emerged from another. Alex knew she was trapped. The men had cell phones, were barking into them, and rushing forward.

From somewhere, another pair of men started running toward her.

"¡Señora!" someone yelled. The men drew guns. The women had batons. There were so many of them that they seemed to be coming up from beneath the pavements and falling out of trees.

She tried to run forward and through them, hoping they wouldn't shoot out of fear of hitting each other. But it was impossible. There was a rough hand on her arm. She straight-armed the Havana cop who was trying to pull her down. She broke free, but he had slowed her long enough so that her other assailants could converge. She threw a sharp elbow at one of them and must have caught him fully in the jaw, because she felt an impressive impact. The man recoiled.

She screamed and shouted. Loud enough to rouse the dead. She flailed. But now there were hands all over her, trying to pull her to the ground. Someone yoked her from behind; Alex thought it was one of the women. She caught one of them with her leg and wobbled a little, and then they were all falling, the whole scrum of them, onto the filthy pavement and then into the gutter.

Alex was face down. Her clothes were wet. The police were tearing at her arms, trying to pin them behind her and handcuff her. She kicked and screamed until someone held a hand to her mouth to muffle her. Then a pair of cuffs clicked onto one wrist behind her and then onto the other. Her arms felt as if they'd been pulled out of their sockets. She continued to fight, but two of the strongest men now had her pinned.

As she struggled, she looked up and caught a brief glimpse of Paul's dimly lit third-floor window. He seemed to be standing at the window, the shade slightly to the side, watching. All she could think of was how she had just left him and that he should flee as fast as possible. Or, she wondered, had he set her up?

The hand at her mouth pulled away. "What are you doing?

Who are you?" she demanded in Spanish of her captors. "I've done nothing wrong. I'm a citizen of Mexico."

But they weren't listening. The insults came back.

"¡Puta!" Whore. Crook. Criminal.

"Fight like a little pig, do you?" taunted one of the men. "Little pigs get stuck and grilled in Cuba."

To take the fight out of her, someone kicked her in the ribs. She saw the kick coming and blocked it with a wrenched arm. She cursed long and hard again. Then someone, it might even have been one of the women, grabbed her by the hair, jerked back her head, and then drove her skull forward into the street. This time she was glad for the garbage since a soaking discarded bag lessened the impact.

Still, the blow stunned her. It took the rest of the fight out of her. The police pulled her to her feet. She felt wobbly and dazed, as if her feet didn't work. More hands were all over her, frisking her, feeling her, taking whatever she had in her pockets, including money. Something was in her left eye, and she realized that her forehead must have been gashed because blood was running into her eye. It continued to flow and dripped onto her blouse. At the same time, one of the uniformed men was going through her bag. He pulled out her gun, made a fuss over it, and showed it to the others.

She wiped her forehead on her shoulder as best she could. She raised her eyes to the window again. Guarneri had vanished. Or maybe she had seen the wrong window. The police forced her into the back of an unmarked car. It was obviously state security of some sort because the interior was fitted as a police cruiser might be, complete with a divider between the front seat and the back.

From the window, she noticed two vans and more people pouring into the building. Then lights flashed on the dashboard. It started to move, but there was no siren.

The car pulled quickly away from the curb, and she was on a fast bumpy ride through the backstreets of Havana and then on some major ones. Alex was terrified. She tried to memorize the route, but the effort was useless and ended in confusion. There was no point of reference, just unfamiliar streets at dawn in a hostile city.

She trembled. She muttered a prayer aloud. Her body began to ache where she had received hits: forehead, ribs, and arms. Her left breast felt bruised as if she had been punched or groped. The blood continued to trickle steadily into her eye, and she kept wiping it away with her shoulder as best she could.

After a wild ride of several minutes, the police van pulled up in front of a gate. A pair of police guards manually raised a barrier and signaled the car through. The car followed a driveway that led to a garage. Then they were within a police installation.

The driver and his assistant opened the rear door and roughly pulled her out. They marched her into the station. A female guard fell into step beside the officers. They stopped at a booking station. The police undid the handcuffs and gave her a small towel to hold to her forehead as the cut was still trickling blood.

"I'm a Mexican citizen," she said to anyone who would listen. "I want to see a lawyer. I've done nothing wrong."

No one paid her any attention, as if they all knew exactly who she was. Meanwhile, some mumbling was exchanged between one of her captors and a superior. Alex took this occasion to protest again, claiming she was a citizen of Mexico and demanding to know why she had been abducted.

One of the arresting officers came back, looked her in the eye with doleful brown eyes, then cracked her across the face with his open palm. She staggered back, and someone else blocked her fall. She thought it was one of the female officers.

"Enemy of the Revolution," he said. "*That's* who you are!"

He made a gesture with his arms that suggested holding a rifle. "*¡Pelotón de fusilamiento para ti!*" he said. Firing squad for you. Then he laughed.

They sat her down and questioned her. They wanted to know who she was and when she had come into the country. She stuck with her Mexican identity and claimed she had arrived by air from Mexico City and that she had had a fight with her husband and he had dumped her.

She knew that if they checked her story about her arrival she was sunk. She prayed that they kept bad records. Then they stood her in front of a camera and took her picture. She was too dazed to resist. When the picture taking ended, another female guard took her arm and shoved her along a hallway to a cell. An iron door with bars swung open. They pushed Alex in among several other female prisoners, all of them much darker skinned than she was. There were no bunks, just fetid mattresses on the floor, a dirty cracked sink, and a single metal toilet. Everyone looked as if they'd been there for days.

She huddled in a corner on the floor, wondering why anyone with two millions dollars in the bank would accept a job that brought her to a place like this.

How could she have been so crazy? This, she decided, was insane! It went without saying that the operation with Violette had probably crashed now. Or had Violette been a setup to create an incident, to lure an American spy into Cuba?

If she ever got out of here, she told herself, she would live differently. Tears weren't far away, but she was afraid to show them. She wondered what had happened to Paul—had he escaped or been killed? Then she wondered how anyone would ever find her here.

She trembled not knowing the answer to that question. She was more frightened than she had ever been in her life. Nor had she ever felt so alone.

On the south shore of Cuba, less than a hundred yards from a small inlet twenty miles southeast of Cienfuegos, Manuel Perez was back in his element. His new employers had set him up in a cheerful little sniper's nest that overlooked the tiny isolated beach. In less than forty-eight hours, his target would appear.

He nursed his provisions and spent many hours examining the new rifle that they had provided for him at Guantanamo. One good shot, one direct hit, was all that stood between him and liberty, as well as freedom for his family, who were still being held by those CIA thugs.

Perez had missed his mark in New York. But he now came to see that as a once-in-a-lifetime event. This time when his target emerged, the range would be shorter, and thanks to the sand on the beach, his target would be moving more slowly.

This one was a setup. As easy as walking into a restaurant and shooting a man in the face. Can't miss and can't lose, as long as one gets out of the area fast enough.

That had been his mistake in New York.

He had hung around too long.

It was like missing a shot: learn by the mistake and don't do it again.

FIFTY-NINE

In jail, Alex lost track of time. Hours passed, hours on end. No one had a watch. The other prisoners mostly stared at her. The cell was obscenely hot, humid, and sticky — and infested with roaches. It smelled of urine, sweat, and disinfectant. A film of white powder covered almost everything, dust from the disintegrating paint and plaster on the walls.

She offered no conversation to any of the other women. Then night came. She barely slept. Breakfast was served: hard bread, a banana, and water. Then, in what must have been midmorning, a male guard arrived, called her name, and grabbed her. The guard pulled her out of the cell and ordered her to walk.

Alex was led to another area, deeper within the prison where the heat was even more relentless. The guard pushed her along when she didn't walk fast enough. She tried to engage the guard in conversation, to find out if she could get a lawyer or a public defender, but she was told to keep quiet, otherwise she would be sent to solitary.

"Solitary sometimes lasts for months," the guard said. "So shut your mouth, *cabrona*!"

Alex's mind was already doing somersaults, but she knew she needed to get a message back to Washington or New York, to tell them where she was, at least to the extent that she knew, and what had happened. She realized, however, that she was unlikely ever to be free again if her captors found out she was American. Her only hope would be a neutral third-party nation.

But she knew that Paul Guarneri was part of this picture as well.

Why had he come to Cuba? What was the *real* reason? The money? And more importantly, had he been arrested as well? She wasn't sure.

And then there was the CIA — wouldn't they simply find it easier to ditch her?

"Follow," the guard said. With trepidation, Alex obeyed.

They went into a small room, where a medical technician waited with a female nurse. A doctor walked in. He was middle-aged, with a big belly and bad breath. He told Alex to undress. She resisted at first by standing perfectly still. Then he shouted the order at her. She undressed down to her undergarments and stopped. This seemed to satisfy him. He told her to sit on an examination table and she did. The nurse stood nearby and observed.

The doctor made a visual inspection. He had Alex open her mouth; then he checked her ears and eyes. His attention settled upon her shoulder and the wound marks left by bullets. "What happened here?" he asked in Spanish.

"I hurt myself," she said.

"How?"

"Playing sports. Archery. An arrow ricocheted," she said.

"Looks like a bullet wound," he said.

"It was an arrow," Alex insisted.

The doctor laughed. "Undress completely," the man insisted.

Having no choice, she did. He then examined her gently but thoroughly. Alex had the impression that he was looking for microchips. He found none. Silently, she prayed an old prayer she had known from childhood, just to take her mind off the indignity of the present.

Meanwhile, the female guard took her clothes out of the room and returned with a tunic and three fresh pairs of underwear. The doctor had finished, a lousy physical exam and a thorough humiliation at the same time. He told her she could get dressed. Alex did, quickly, as the female guard watched. Then the female guard took her to yet another cell, this one having a more permanent feel to it. There were eight bunks in it and seven other women who stared at her when she entered. A single open toilet stood against one wall. Six of the women were dark skinned, one was mocha skinned. Alex stood out like a nightlight. The other women had removed their tunics because the heat was so intense, sleeping only in their undergarments, if that. Alex kept her tunic on because the mosquitoes were worse than the temperature.

One more night passed completely. She had been a prisoner for two full days. She knew she had missed the rendezvous with Violette and the mission now bordered on catastrophe. Her spirits were in freefall. She spent a good deal of time praying quietly to herself, praying as she never prayed before. She assumed the airplane had left that morning without her, and the thought tortured her.

In the middle of the third day, in what Alex thought was the afternoon, almost all of which she spent sitting on her bunk, the mocha-skinned woman came over to her. She started a small halting conversation in Spanish.

The woman was Creole, it turned out. Alex switched to French. The woman said she had come to Cuba with a male friend, and he had abandoned her. The woman's name was Margritte, and she had been arrested a month earlier for stealing food from a market. She had stolen the food, she said, because she was starving. She was hoping to be deported to Barbados, since she had family there, and then she could work her way to her home village in the mountains.

The woman also had a small wooden cross around her neck. For some reason, the guards had not taken it.

"How long do you think they'll hold you here?" Alex asked.

The woman shrugged. "Many years," she said, as if she didn't have anywhere better to go. Then she began to touch Alex with some longing and affection. Alex pulled away.

On the evening of the same day, dispirited and tired, two male guards roused Alex again. They led her down another yellowing corridor and into an office. They shoved her into a chair in front of a man who wore the insignia of the Havana police.

He sat behind a desk with a Cuban flag to his right. In the center of the wall behind him was a picture of three heroes of the revolution: Fidel Castro, Che Guevara, and Frank Pais, an early rebel leader who'd died in an assault on one of Batista's army barracks in 1957. The poses were neo-Stalinist heroic, three handsome, macho young men in jungle fatigues, outlined against sky and mountains, presumably in the Sierra Maestra.

The officer gave her a moment to settle in. She looked at him and recognized him. He waited until the two guards had departed and closed the door.

"Hello," he said in extremely good English. "Welcome to the Democratic Socialist Republic of Cuba. What a pleasure. We meet for the third and final time. I am Major Ivar Mejias of the Cuban National Militia."

She processed his name and face immediately. He was the commander who had headed the reception committee on the beach and the officer who had examined her passport in the lobby of the Ambos Mundos.

She tried Spanish. *"Mi llama Anna Marie Tavares y soy ciudana mexicana,"* she said. She then took it a step further and requested a lawyer.

With no smile whatsoever, he shook his head.

"No, no," he said, remaining in English. "No lawyers. Not necessary. A trial is not even necessary. You're an American criminal and counterrevolutionary," he said. "And you've had the misfortune to be captured. Ten years in prison? Twenty?" He shook his head. "I wouldn't want to be you. Your luck has run out. Unless you cooperate with us, your freedom is gone forever."

SIXTY

Alex was sweating profusely. The white dust from the prison had formed in patches on her skin. It itched and was beginning to cause a rash. Now her heart was jumping too. She knew the man in front of her not only had been on her trail since the moment she arrived, but he was a professional interrogator.

Several seconds passed. They looked eye to eye. Nothing from Alex.

"I have a theory," Major Mejias continued in Spanish. "It's my own theory but I'm proud of it. It goes this way: each one of us has only a certain limited amount of deception in us. We can waste it incrementally on the small things, or we can blow the whole bundle on one big life-size lie. Either way, it runs out eventually, our supply, and what we're left with then is the truth." He paused. "What do you think?"

She blinked, stared at him, and said nothing.

"All right. Let me put another question to you," he said. "You would seem to be an educated woman. Cultured. Not what we normally process here. Are you familiar with a film director named Luis Buñuel? He was a Mexican citizen, though born in Spain. Went to university with Dalí and Lorca, the painter and the poet. It was said they were all Communists together in the 1930s." He lapsed into Spanish. "Buñuel. The director. You know of him?"

She made a decision. She would try to follow his conversation, to see at least where he was leading. "Yes, I know who Buñuel was," she answered in Spanish.

"Good. What was he known for?"

"Films," she said.

"What sort of films?"

"Enigmatic ones," she said. "Buñuel's films were famous for their vibrant and distorted imagery."

"Very good," the major answered. "There were scenes where noble young men who aspired to sainthood were tempted by prostitutes. There were women with beards, bears in living rooms, and chickens populating nightmares. He was also well-known for his atheism. Buñuel once made a film in Mexico about a village too poor to support a church and a priest. Yet the place was happy because no one suffered from guilt. 'It's guilt we must escape from, not God,' Buñuel once said. He also once said, 'Thank God, I'm an atheist.' Now. Talk to me, *mi amiga*. What do you think of all that?"

"I don't think anything about it because I haven't thought much about it," Alex answered.

They had worn her down physically. Alex now knew they were starting the mind-twisting games. Mejias wasn't even taking notes. She assumed that, somewhere, others were listening and that a recording was being made. She held by her cover story, that she was a Mexican citizen and had come into the country legally on the twenty-fourth of May. At this point, she was praying they were plain stupid, or inefficient.

"I'm going to ask you several more questions," Major Mejias continued in English. "You would be wise to cooperate. If you answer all of our questions, we can afford to be extraordinarily generous. We might even send you back home after a short time. Home is America, isn't it? Now, why don't you begin by telling me your real name?"

"Anna Tavares," Alex said again. The major steepled his fingers.

"Very well," Mejias said, adding in English, "let's try another. *En realidad*, let's try this again from the beginning. Why are you in Cuba, and why did you enter the country illegally?"

"Hablo español," Alex said.

"Yes. Of course you do," Major Mejias said. "But you also speak English," he said, switching back to Spanish. "We all know this. How is *my* English, by the way? I think I speak it reasonably well. I spent two years at the University of Toronto. Have you been there? It's quite a beautiful institution. Beautiful city also. But they only have two seasons — winter and July."

"Hablo español," Alex said again.

"I'd like to see your hands," Major Mejias said.

Alex didn't make a move. Her hands were already on the table out in front of her.

"Sus manos," he said.

He reached to Alex's hands and turned them palms up. She did not resist. A condemned feeling started to creep up on Alex, one that went with her sense of panic. It wasn't just the situation, the filth, the danger; it was also the unrelenting isolation. The heat continued to assail her as well. She could even hear the occasional tick of her own sweat hitting the floor. And there was a stench in this office, even worse than the stench of backed-up plumbing in the jail. At least the bugs were gone, for now.

Major Mejias examined the interior of Alex's hands, paying special attention to the palms and fingers.

"Interesting," he said in English. "It is amazing how much one can tell about a woman by her hands. You have very nice hands. The hands of a wealthy woman perhaps. No scars, no nicks, no calluses. You work for a living as something professional, such as a lawyer or an accountant or a businesswoman. Or you don't work at all, which means you're married to a man who is highly affluent."

He pulled his own hands away and gave Alex's back to her.

"I'm told that you insist that you are Mexican," he said. "But a Mexican lady of your social status would speak passable English. At least that's my experience. Yet you refuse to speak to me in English or acknowledge my efforts. That tells me you're hiding something." He paused. "You already owe me one enormous favor," Mejias continued. "You were in line for some of the more brutish inquisitors, people who have trained against the drug traffickers and who use unspeakable physical means to obtain answers. In some rare cases, yours being one, I am allowed to intercede when we have a more sophisticated prisoner. So I have limited time with you. How limited, even *I* do not know. I will need to leave today with *something*, or the more thuggish in my trade will take over. Do you understand what I'm saying?"

"Hablo español, no hablo inglés," Alex said.

"Let's cut the charade, shall we? How are you feeling?" he asked in Spanish. "Have you been treated well?"

"No," she said.

"Good," he answered. "This is a prison. That's the way prisons should be. Prisons are the sewers of civilization. Do you wish to spend the rest of your life in a sewer, maybe die there, too?"

He again took her hands, gently, not roughly, but as a physician might.

"Look at this white powder, for example. It's from the jail cell, isn't it? I'm told that there is a microscopic bacteria in it that infects the flesh. A small parasite perhaps. Hydrocortisone cream soothes it. Perhaps you'd like to see a doctor after you start to speak with me."

He released her arm, and she pulled it away.

He sighed. "Very well," he said. "I've attempted to be cordial. I've known some criminals who took a long time before they finally decided to speak. Months, years sometimes. Eventually all of them wished they had spoken sooner. We will hold you as an enemy of the Revolution for as long as you need before you decide to talk to me. And yet," he mused, "the travesty of all this is that it would be unnecessary in your case. We are disposed to send you back to where you came from or at the very least trade you for something we want. What is the point of spending time with common prostitutes, burglars, and drug pushers in prison when you could be free in a matter of days? On the other hand, I can walk out of here and you cannot. Until categorized otherwise, you are an enemy of the Cuban Revolution. Do you know what the women's prisons are like in this country? You would be sent to a very rough one where there are ten to twelve women per cell.

A very pretty white-skinned woman like yourself, well, the results can be unspeakable."

"I will speak to you only in Spanish," Alex said in Spanish.

"Muy bien," he said. *"Hablamos español."*

"I wish to see someone from the Mexican Embassy," Alex again said in Spanish.

"That is not going to happen."

"Why not? Have I no rights?"

"To start with, you are American. You see, here is the problem. You gave us a name and told us that you came into Cuba on a Mexican airliner on May 24. That is in the police report and it is what you told me. But you are lying. We looked at the flight manifests for that day. There was no one by that name on the plane. Nor was your passport stamped. We could take the time to review the immigration video surveillance for that day, but that would only further prove to us the lie that you are telling to us. So let us begin again. What is your real name?"

Alex fell silent. Her cover was blown, and they both knew it. The prospect of spending ten years in a Cuban prison hit her like a kick to the stomach.

"You see, we can be very patient in Cuba. Those in the first revolutionary generation outlasted Batista, and then our enemies felt that they could outlast Castro. Yet half a century has passed and *la Revolución* still controls Cuba." He paused. "Do you support the Cuban revolution or not? My guess is you do not."

She remained quiet.

"Last month they sent two American women to Cuban prisons, one for twelve years, the other for fifteen. One was a black-market currency dealer. The other was someone who was arranging foreign passports and exit conduits. You know, I tried to help them also. They resisted me. Twelve years. Fifteen years. That's a terrible price to pay, isn't it?" He paused. "I would think you might be sentenced to twenty. Is that what you wish to do with the middle years of your life?"

He lit a small cigar.

"They will work on you in the crudest of ways. No sleep, a lot of physical pain, disorientation, no days or nights, either a hood over your head or the white light of the cells nonstop for weeks. It will be a slow contest between you going insane and breaking physically. And then of course," Mejias continued, "there are other things. Female prisoners are sometimes subjected to injections of drugs to make them physically dependent. They become the forcible mistresses of certain guards. Officially, this does not go on in the socialist paradise, but I have seen it myself. You are a very pretty woman. I can only shudder at what could happen to you in the penal system."

"I don't know what you want from me," Alex said.

"An admission of guilt," he said. "You've been under surveillance since you arrived in Havana," he said. "From Havana to Cojimar. Do you think we cannot track from the air? Do you think we are backward here?" He paused. "Where did you go after Cojimar?" he asked. "Back to Havana or some other place of interest?" She squeezed her eyes shut. He paused again. "Who is the man whose residence you were leaving when we arrested you?" he asked.

"I don't know."

"But you spent the night with him."

"We met at a hotel. We had some drinks. That's all."

"You're a liar."

A thought was upon her, a desperate one. She had one card to play and almost resisted playing it, for if it failed she had nothing left.

"Figaro," she said.

"What?" he answered rudely.

"You mentioned Spain before. There is an opera. *The Barber of Seville.*"

"I *hate* opera," he snapped. He was suddenly angry. "Pomp and extravagance, the indulgence of the capitalist ruling classes. My wife listens to opera. Drives me out of the house with it! Maybe I should lock her up too. Why do you even mention it, opera?"

"I don't know," she said softly. "It was just a thing to say."

"Why do you fail to understand the gravity of your situation?" he pressed. "No one outside of Cuba knows where you are. I am your only chance, and you are babbling, giving me nothing. I need a confession from you," he said. "Who are you, who came to Cuba with you, and what is your purpose?"

She stayed silent.

"All right," he said. "Have it the way you wish. He reached to a side drawer of his desk and pulled out a box, the type used to hold evidence. He opened it. He pulled from it her credit cards and her Mexican passport and laid them on the center of the desk. Then he pulled out her Walther and set it on the table with a loud flourish. The magazine had been removed.

"These are the tools of a saboteur." He pushed them around disdainfully. "Why don't you at least identify the agency that sent you to Cuba? CIA? A nod will suffice and get you a better cell, a private one."

Nothing from Alex.

"You will tell me nothing, but I will tell you this," Mejias said. "The airplane that came to take you back to America left the country without you this morning. The aging defector, the man you came to get, Roland Violette, was on it. He is mentally ill and no use to anyone. He also murdered an old adversary in love the other night in Havana. A Frenchman. So of course Violette wished to flee. Also on the plane was the man who came into Cuba with you. His name is Paul Guarneri. He sends his regards, I would suppose, as he left you behind to face the wrath of Cuban law. How do you like that?"

She refused to answer, much less believe what she was hearing.

"Where were you six nights ago?" he asked.

"I don't remember," she said with a shrug.

"You don't remember!" His voice rose sharply in anger. "*You don't remember?* Six nights ago a patriotic Cuban named Julio Garcia was shot to death as he peaceably ate his dinner at a restaurant in Habana Vieja. A single assassin walked in, a man connected with American gangsters, and shot him in the face with a Browning .38 special. You are telling me that you have no knowledge of this? Do you insist you were nowhere near the scene of the murder?"

"Yes, I do!" she said. "I had nothing to do with anything like that!"

"The murder was done by your gangster friend to settle an old family grudge. So you are linked to that also, as well as the man who committed the murder of a patriotic Cuban! That is what we have on you. Illegal entry into Cuba. Sabotage. Espionage. *Gangsterismo.* Links to two homicides. What do you say? You and you alone have been left behind to face the wrath of the law."

She looked up.

"I have nothing to say. Speak to my embassy."

"If you think you will be spared a firing squad because you're a woman," he said, "think again!"

"I have nothing to say," she said softly.

"We will speak again," he said. "You are my prisoner. Indefinitely."

In a fury, he stood. He gathered his evidence and went to the door.

He shouted profanely to his guards who were a short distance down the hall. Then two new ones appeared. They each took Alex by an arm and roughly ripped her from her chair. They marched her down several unfamiliar corridors and opened an iron door that led to a small cell. They pushed her in. The door slammed behind her.

There was a sink against one wall, a mattress and a hole in the cement floor. There was one window, way up high, maybe twelve feet off the ground. There was no way she could get to it, nor would she have been able to get through it.

She was in isolation but had no idea for how long. She sat on the stone floor, let her face sink into her hands and prayed as she hadn't prayed in months. Then she broke down completely and cried.

SIXTY-ONE

For the next two days, Alex remained in isolation. A brutal overhead light burned all the time. Breakfast was served at 5:00 a.m., a piece of bread, a banana, and a dirty plastic bottle filled with water. The water contained particles of something and had a strange tint to it.

Strangely, there was no more questioning. Alex feared that her captors, in their incompetent but Third-World way, were trying to find out more about who she was. Maybe Paul hadn't really fled. Maybe they were searching for him. All she knew was that her head was turning mushy. Thoughts of suicide returned to her, like an old, unwelcome adversary, an evil black spirit, that she had already defeated once in the dark days after Kiev.

Against these dark impulses, she tried to weigh everything that her Christian faith had brought to her: having been on the threshold of suicide before, she was later grateful for not having pulled a trigger. But where was God now?

The old phrase came back: a permanent solution to a temporary problem. But how temporary was this problem? Thirty years' worth of temporary? Would her government really get her back? Had Paul Guarneri set her up? Had he really killed a man in Havana perhaps to avenge an old family grievance? Could she believe a single word that Major Mejias had said? Or would she have been wise to believe every word of it?

In her tiny cell, as her mind tilted and rambled, she looked for ways to kill herself—theoretically, at least. She saw none, other than a hunger strike. But then, if she died in custody, wouldn't that just be a victory for those who'd imprisoned her? A stubborn streak started to kick against her suicidal impulses. Her spirits seesawed by the hour.

On the third day she was taken out of her cell with four other women.

They were marched to a shower and told to disrobe. A male guard came by, amused, and sprayed them for lice. Then they were led to the next chamber, which was a shower. They were given a crude piece of industrial soap and told they had five minutes to wash as two fat matrons stood at the portal to the showers and watched.

The five-minute limit was the first mention of time since she had arrived. Time: she wondered if her existence over the last few days presaged the coming years.

She was led back to her cell. That night, for the first time, she felt herself start to freefall mentally. She turned toward the wall, prayed, thought of home, the long road that had led her here, and she cried for hours. She prayed that some force — human, God, Jesus, anyone who could save her now — would somehow intercede and get her out of here. She thought of her fiancé, Robert, whom she had lost on the bloody streets of Kiev, and she thought of growing up in California and her grandmother's funeral in Mexico where they prayed and sent paper lanterns down the river. She knew she was getting delirious, but it didn't matter because the delirium was a mechanism that would take her out of this hell on earth. If she couldn't leave physically, at least she could leave mentally.

Then she wondered if that was what had happened to Roland Violette. Had his sanity been a sane reaction against the insanity of the life he had led? She didn't know and had too much time to think about it.

Then came another night in solitary.

Alex must have been sleeping, she realized with a start, sleeping in a sitting-up position on her mattress, because the rattle of keys awakened her. There was the grating, creaking, banging noise, of the door being opened. Then she was looking at three guards who were staring at her without saying anything. She had never seen them before, and they looked unpleasantly official.

The first two were female, one a thick woman with grayish hair pulled back and a thick middle. The younger one was slimmer and looked as if she might be part Russian. Behind them was a man. He carried an automatic weapon across his chest. The weapon was chained to his belt so that no one could grab it from him and run.

"*¡Levantse!*" the older woman demanded. Alex tried to blink the fatigue out of her eyes. "You're moving."

One of them threw a pair of rubber thongs on the floor.

Alex stood. She was hardly in a position to resist. Emotionally, she was flying blind. She hoped that somehow the police had contacted the Mexican government and some steps were being taken to get her released. But she had no reason to believe anything of the sort.

She stood and slid the thongs onto her feet. She held out her hands for cuffs. The older woman curtly said that the manacles wouldn't be necessary. They indicated she should walk. The matrons went first, followed by Alex, and finally the guard with the automatic rifle followed.

They went through two checkpoints. Alex tried to remain alert and observe as much as possible. She caught her first view of a courtyard. It was night and the yard was empty. Her eyes went to the walls. They were old, maybe fifty feet high, and patrolled with guards who commanded heavy searchlights. There was a flock of gulls far beyond, circling, and from the tone of the sky she guessed that she was somewhere near the water.

After the checkpoints, they walked her along a corridor. The path was long and dim. There was a ceiling fan that didn't work. The paint was peeling off the concrete walls, which were yellowish, discolored, and wet with humidity. She stole a glance at a wristwatch on one of her guards. It was 2:00 a.m. It occurred to her that it was around this time of morning that she had been on her way into this island, twelve days earlier, she calculated, unless it was thirteen.

They took her through another gate. This one was metal and

more modern. It led to another building: modern, glass, and steel. A walk down another corridor, this one with linoleum, and her keepers led her into a small room. They ordered her to remain standing.

"Now you wait," the male guard said in Spanish. Quietly, she stood and waited. In her mind, a prayer was never far way.

They left her alone and closed the door. The room was stuffy and humid, even at night. There were windows with lateral bars. The building had an imprint of Russian architecture from the 1970s. There was a dreadful condemned feel to it and it leached quickly onto her.

Her tunic was scratchy. At this point, it occurred to her, she would have given a year of her life for some soap, deodorant, and clean clothes. She tried to distance herself from the thought because she knew that she didn't want to start measuring things in years of life.

There was an animated conversation on the other side of the door, so brisk and profane in Spanish that she could barely understand it. Then the door flew open, and a very angry man rushed in. She recognized Major Mejias immediately. He was in a military uniform now. He wore a sidearm that could have brought down a charging elephant. He was dangerously agitated.

His eyes fixed quickly upon her.

"You!" he said to her in Spanish. "I curse the day I first saw you!"

"I can say the same for you," she said.

"Shut up! Hold out your hands!" he said.

She obeyed. The guards didn't think she needed cuffs, but Mejias did. He cuffed her hands. Beyond the doorway, two of her guards stood, watched, and smirked.

"They pull me out of bed in the middle of the night," Mejias raged. "You're my prisoner so *I* have to transport you. More trouble than you're worth in my opinion! We should shoot you and be done with this. But this is Cuba."

"Transport?" she asked.

"Maximum security. Middle of the island," he said loudly and with a snarl. With a sharp yank, he tested the cuffs to make sure they were secure. They were tight. He was so rough that the sockets of her shoulders ached.

He took a blindfold out of his pocket. He wrapped it around her eyes.

"Army base in Santa Clara," he said. "They're going to bury you alive so deeply that no one will ever find you."

"Is the blindfold really necessary?" she asked.

"Standard," he said. "Ugly place you're going to. You'll see when you get there."

He yanked at her arm to get her moving. She cursed back at him and he yanked harder. Then they were moving quickly down a corridor. She felt extra hands upon her, and the next thing she knew they were helping her down a short flight of steps.

"A transport van's waiting," he said. "Get in and keep quiet."

They led her to a vehicle whose engine was running. There was a female with the vehicle, a guard or a soldier, Alex guessed. She could hear her voice. The driver probably. Then Alex heard a door open and she was pushed into the backseat. Someone put a manacle on her right ankle and cuffed her to the interior of the car. The doors slammed, and she heard two people jump in.

One of them, she knew by his voice, was Mejias. The other was the female. The vehicle started to move. It stopped and started. Alex guessed it was going through prison checkpoints. Then it was out onto an open road. She could tell it was accelerating, moving onto a highway, probably the one that led to Santa Clara.

Mejias and his female associate talked in hushed voices that she couldn't hear. There was an occasional crackle of a longwave radio on the dashboard and a GPS that operated in Spanish. Every few minutes, Mejias took a call to confirm his location. The vehicle bounced as it moved along the highway. Alex managed to brush her blindfold against her shoulder so that she could develop a narrow sight line. But that gave her very little. It was an official vehicle of some sort, with boxes and crates next to her. The woman in the front seat was wearing a military uniform. That was all she could see of her: just dark hair and a shoulder with an epaulet. In front of the vehicle, all she could see was the night and the headlights along a winding highway that cut through the center of the island. Maybe it was best that she couldn't see more, she told herself. Mejias was driving like a wild man. The vehicle hurtled forward at a mad speed. What his urgency was, Alex could only guess.

Guess, hope, and pray.

Another incoming message crackled across the two-way. Mejias answered it and signed off. Then Alex heard him speak to the woman.

"*¿Ahora?*" he asked. Now?

"*¡Ahora mismo!*" she said. Right now!

Something had changed. Or plans were being jerked around. All Alex knew was that the vehicle came to an abrupt halt. She heard a window come down. She peeked through her sliver of sight and saw both of Mejias's hands on the two-way GPS.

She saw him pull it from the dashboard. She heard a clatter and guessed that he had jettisoned it. Then the car was in motion again. He ripped a vicious U-turn and from the feel of the tires, it seemed they were cutting across dirt or sand for several minutes. Then they accessed another highway or the same one in the other direction, Alex couldn't tell which. And they were underway again.

First gear, second, third, and fourth, as fast as he could shift. It was like they weren't driving now, more like flying low. Alex spoke out of instinct. "What are we doing?"

Cryptically, *"No es lo que parece,"* he answered. It's not what it seems.

But Alex didn't even know what it seemed like. She could only tell that the car had accelerated. The conversation between the driver and his accomplice was terse and hushed. Above the rage of the vehicle's motor, Alex couldn't hear anything.

The drive lasted many minutes. Eventually, Alex pushed the blindfold farther away from her eyes, so she could at least get a sense of where she was being taken. Outside, the sky was lighter. Dawn was in the offing. She wondered if it would be her last. Distantly, she recalled being warned about the military installations in Santa Clara and Camagüey. But she no longer knew where she was going. Someplace better? Someplace worse? Someplace to be incarcerated for years or hours? Or someplace to die?

The vehicle eventually turned onto what felt like a bumpy off-ramp. The boxes in the backseat slid toward her. Alex steadied herself. Next, they seemed to be on a back road, judging by the speed, then on a very bumpy narrow road, then finally what seemed like a pot-hole-ridden dirt driveway. Then the car rolled to a halt.

Both driver and shotgun rider leaped out. Alex struggled with her blindfold again, and this time she managed to push it half off. It barely mattered. The door flew open, and the woman in uniform reached in and pulled it off.

"Hurry," the woman said in Spanish.

The other door opened, and Major Mejias reached in with both arms. He too was operating as quickly as possible. He removed the three crates from the seat next to Alex. One by one, he stacked them in a small red wagon that waited nearby. The woman pulled Alex out of the vehicle and moved her a few feet away.

"Where are we?" Alex asked, blinking against the sudden exposure to light. It was dawn and the sky was red.

"You'll know shortly," the woman said. Major Mejias was too busy to answer.

They were in a courtyard surrounded by walls. But Alex could hear surf. Like so much of Cuba, they were near the water. She took a reading of the light in the sky and determined where east was. There were two gates. The one behind her, behind the car, faced north. The other faced the other way, and the driveway sloped down toward it. She guessed that it led to the water and that they were, therefore, on the south shore of the island. Mejias went to the outside gate so that no one could follow them into the driveway.

"The Venezuelans took an immediate interest in you," the woman said in Spanish. "You're wanted by the government in Caracas. So—"

"Juanita!" Major Mejias shouted.

The woman fell silent.

"Take her inside," he said, motioning.

Juanita, the woman in the uniform, pulled Alex by the arm. They reached a door to a small ramshackle building.

"Come along!" Juanita demanded. "You have Caracas to thank. This is better than Santa Clara!"

They reached the door and the woman pushed it open. She stepped into the building. In the dim light, two figures rose and stood to meet her.

Alex gasped as if she were receiving a visit from the dead.

Down the beach in his sniper's lair, Perez, after days and days of waiting, finally got the high sign. He sat ready, his rifle across his lap. His cell phone rang. He answered. Perez and the caller spoke in Spanish.

"Alex is here," the man announced. "She just entered the building. Everything is complete."

"How many minutes?" Perez asked.

"Less than ten," the caller said. "Watch the horizon. You'll see a bird."

"I'm watching it now," said Perez. He spotted a small dot far off, maybe six miles from shore.

"Don't miss," the caller said. "You miss, we leave you in Cuba. You hit, and you're on a plane to Mexico in two hours."

"I never miss," Perez said.

"We'll see," the caller said.

SIXTY-TWO

There are moments made up of too much stuff to be remembered correctly or to be assessed fully at the time they occur. For Alex, this was one. As it was, the morning had had its own peculiar madness. Events happened too quickly to fasten on any of them too firmly.

She recognized Roland Violette first. Then her eyes shifted to the other man.

"Alex! Thank God!" came the male voice. Paul rushed to her and embraced her. Juanita in the uniform was close behind with a key to the handcuffs.

"What—?" Alex began.

"We're going home," Guarneri said. "Back to the U.S. That's if our plane gets here. If the Cuban army or air force stops them we're all shafted."

Violette said nothing. He only twitched and stared.

Juanita worked on the handcuffs and undid them. Behind Alex, the door opened and closed again. It was Major Mejias. He had taken his cargo down to the end of the pier where it waited. Alex had to fight back her emotions. The loneliness in solitary. The suicidal thoughts. The fear. The torment. She turned toward the major.

"Sorry," he said, placing a hand on her shoulder. "I had to be rough. We had listeners. All the way. In prison."

"Seville," she said.

"Figaro," he said with a nod and an awkward tip of his cap. "This is my wife," he said, turning to Juanita, who now smiled. "Those boxes out there are for your employers. Everything I could copy for five years, plus a lot that I didn't have time to copy. There are papers, discs, flash drives. Defense records, police, militia security. A few personal items as well."

"Poison. Poison," Violette said, making no more sense than ever. He moved over to the window and peered out.

"The CIA is bringing us to Miami," said Major Mejias. "My wife is coming with me."

"A seaplane's coming in," Guarneri said. "Should be here any moment."

"I was told you'd already gone," Alex said. "Along with Violette."

"Without you?" Guarneri asked. "Don't believe everything you hear. You should know that."

"I should have known that, yes," she said.

"Airplane," said Violette. "Airplane, airplane, airplane."

They all went to the window.

"That's our exit," said Guarneri.

Alex watched the Cessna drop low on its approach. The plane hit the water, kicked up a wake, and began to taxi toward the pier. It was an old craft, propeller driven, but had its own beauty.

"If the plane doesn't lift off, none of us are going," Alex said.

"I'm going. I'm going. I'm going," Violette said. "Back to the U.S. of A."

She looked at him and then looked at Major Mejias. There was no question which of them was the bigger prize. And things started to come into focus.

"Let's get to the pier," Guarneri said. Then they all froze. From somewhere there was the sound of a loud bang. Then several more. Someone was trying to crash through the outside gates.

"Army!" said Major Mejias. "Or police!"

"We need to move," Paul said.

Perez waited. He perched his rifle in the second-story window. He had a clear line of sight to the small house with the Brazilian flag. He could see the commotion at the other side of the wall too, army trucks unloading soldiers, probably from Cienfuegos. But they weren't his concern. He was used to shooting under pressure.

He lowered his eye to rifle's sight. The rear door of the building opened, and a limping man with a hickory cane emerged. Then a woman in a police uniform came out. He waited. Then the woman emerged whom he had missed in New York. He grinned. That tiny miss a few weeks back had created all these complications. The woman, Alex LaDuca, was followed by a man. They were moving quickly, all of them, everyone except the crazy-looking old guy with the cane. Alex and the younger man were holding hands. Well, so be it. Let the lovebirds have their moment.

Perez moved his rifle onto his intended target. The right side of the victim's head was beneath the red dot of his laser. This was such an easy shot that he almost felt bad. Just as the first of the escapees reached the pier, and he prepared to pull the trigger, an explosion erupted at the gate. The army had blown the door inward. A wave of smoke rolled across the courtyard. Still, it wasn't enough to distract Perez. His future with his family was at stake, and these CIA guys he had been dealing with would have to make good on their promise to get him and Nicoleta and the girls back together.

He swung the rifle around, put the red beam on the head of his victim, and pulled the trigger. There was nasty recoil to the rifle but a tremendous satisfaction. He knew a single-shot kill when he saw one, a human head blowing apart, a crimson mist of blood and brains exploding from the bullet's impact. And that's what he saw.

Alex never heard the rifle shot. But she heard the crack of the bullet on Roland Violette's skull. She heard a strange guttural sound escape his lungs and mouth, and almost instantaneously, she heard his body hit the ground. His attaché case landed nearby.

She pulled her hand free of Paul's, turned, and stared. And at the same time, she could hear soldiers pushing through the wreckage of the iron gate.

For too long a moment, she stopped and stared at the fallen man. His last wish had been to return to the country he had disdained and be buried on American soil. But old grudges died hard. It was never meant to happen.

The noise of advancing soldiers grew louder.

"Alex! Alex!" Paul was back at her side, barking at her. "Come on! Now or never! We have to get out of here!"

He tried to pull her toward the aircraft, but she balked. She grabbed the attaché case from the ground. There was a splattering of blood on it. Then she turned and ran toward the pier.

Major Mejias and his wife were already in the airplane. The propellers started up again, and the door was open. Alex and Paul reached the end of the pier, and the soldiers opened fire. Paul turned and brazenly drew a pistol. He fired wildly at the oncoming soldiers, but, as on the day of their arrival, his volleys only caused them to scatter.

Alex reached the aircraft and darted onto it, crouching into a far seat in the second row. The aircraft started to move from the pier, the door still open and Paul outside. Alex realized that without help, as the plane accelerated, he was in danger of being left behind. Alex bolted to the door and extended a hand as Paul turned toward the plane. A bullet punched the body of the plane and then a second. A third shot hit a few inches above her head. Paul jumped forward and Alex pulled. His foot slipped but he grabbed part of the door frame. She pulled him on board. The aircraft turned rapidly in the water and the passenger door closed. Then a bullet blew out a side window.

The pilot threw the throttle forward, and the plane fishtailed on the water. Facing away from the shore, it was a harder target to hit. But shots ripped past it and into the water. All four passengers kept their heads down. The navigator sat low in his seat, as did the pilot. The plane gained momentum as the first rays of sun started to streak across the sea.

They lifted off, and the Cessna rose above the water. The aircraft was a thousand meters from shore, then twelve hundred. A final shot pinged against its fuselage but didn't penetrate. Then they were in the sky, getting as far from the island as possible before the pilot banked and turned to the southeast.

A palpable sense of relief flooded the passengers, tempered by the parting sight of Roland Violette lying dead on a Cuban beach. For several minutes no one spoke, aside from the pilot who checked in with air traffic controllers in the Cayman Islands. Alex muttered a silent prayer of thanks.

Finally, Paul broke the silence. He turned to Alex. "Communists," he said. "Can't do anything right. Can't run a captive country and can't even shoot straight."

SIXTY-THREE

For the next week, Alex lived in limbo.

In New York, her employers insisted that she go for a physical at New York Hospital, where they had all the proper doctors lined up. Since she knew this was both protocol and a wise health decision anyway, she didn't protest. So she spent her first three days back in the U.S. in a private hospital.

It could have been worse. She managed to sleep a good deal. Friends came by to see her, including Ben, with whom she made up. She entrusted him with the two letters given to her by the young boy Guillermo and asked him to mail them for her. He said he would.

When she got out of the hospital, on her fourth day back, she took a taxi to her home on West 61st Street. The living room window was still boarded up. The place reminded her of pictures she has seen of Berlin during World War II. The building manager told her that repairs could be made just as soon as they received signed permission.

She signed the form and packed up a few things, called her old mentor, Joseph Collins, and arranged to stay at his son's unused apartment on East 21st Street.

Then there was her first trip back to Fin Cen. She did this in the evening when most of the personnel were out. It would have been too much to see everyone at once, and there were parts of her trip that she simply didn't feel like discussing. She spent ninety minutes with her boss, Andrew De Salvo, over Chinese takeout and cold beer. She was put back in charge of Operation Párajo and learned the two most salient details of where Operation Párajo stood:

Numero uno: the gunman who had shot at her had been taken

into custody by the CIA and "turned into an asset," whatever that meant these days. He was, in short, "neutralized." Then again, other enemies would always be out there.

Numero dos: The Dosis were still out there somewhere, having slipped thought the holes in the worldwide dragnet. Alex's indictments and the arrests she had ordered had brought much of the Dosi worldwide enterprise to its knees and just about ruined it financially. But the snake still had its head.

"So where are we now?" Alex asked. "Back at the beginning?"

"No, we're entering an endgame," Andrew De Salvo said. "These things take years, not months. And that's if we're lucky. You did a whale of a job once again. That's what they tell me from D.C. Came back with an interesting haul from the Pearl of the Antilles. They want to see you in Washington, by the way. Things are under control here. You can take another ten days for R&R if you want."

"I want."

"Washington actually means Langley," he added.

"Doesn't it usually?"

Two afternoons later, Alex found herself in the familiar office in the west wing of the CIA headquarters, sitting in front of Maurice Fajardie, who was unraveling samples from the mishmash of notes, charts, and printouts that had traveled north with her on the Cessna. The Cubans hadn't quite entered the twenty-first century of intelligence compiling, so much of the information had a retro look — plenty of colors. Agency analysts were now trying to determine what red and green and orange pages meant. But the preliminary feedback from the intelligence analysts was highly positive regarding the material from both Major Mejias and the late Roland Violette.

"So it was worth my visit?" she asked.

"Very much so," Fajardie said. "A-list intelligence on a B-list enemy. Not akin to a top intelligence coup against our Muzzie adversaries, for example, but certainly when a hostile regime is ninety miles from our doorstep, an up-to-date snapshot is of great value. Most of Violette's material was dated and harks back to the sixties, seventies, and eighties. Think bell-bottoms to big hair. But it puts some old cases in order, lets us know who's still living in Cuba, and fleshes out some other cases. As for the stuff from Major Mejias, we've only had a week to look at that, but it's excellent stuff. Here, let me show you. Look at some of the initial conclusions."

Fajardie handed Alex a series of documents. Alex riffled through. She read a few of the conclusions that American intelligence analysts had come to:

> ... Cuba remains in the midst of its worst economic and social crisis since the fall of the Soviet Union ...
>
> ... The Cuban people, frustrated with massive unemployment and food shortages, could revolt at any time ...
>
> ... Raúl Castro drinks very heavily since the death of his wife. He is more in touch with the people than his brother was, but he would not hesitate to use the military to repress threats to the Communist regime ... On the other hand, the overtures of reconciliation to the United States that he has made through the Spanish ambassador to Washington are sincere ...
>
> ... More than 90 percent of all Cuban diplomats assigned to New York and Washington are engaged in espionage ...

She looked up. "What about Violette?" Alex asked. "I assume he genuinely wanted to return. Am I correct?"

"You are," he said. "But old antagonisms die hard around this agency. We had agents butchered in Angola, Colombia, Spain,

Cuba, and Venezuela due to this man. Do you think that anyone here was ready to see him return and receive free health care at a federal prison hospital? Do you think anyone had any real affection for seeing that vacuous, deranged, sneering face returning in pseudo-triumph?"

"I doubted it all along," Alex said. "I posed that question to him myself, but he was too far gone to comprehend."

"When the possibility of reeling in 'Figaro' arose, the possibility of a trade-off took shape. So if someone such as yourself was going to be kind enough to go to the island, scoop up Violette's final bag of goodies, and return with an even greater additional haul — well then! Stuff began to arrange itself behind the scenes. The Agency beat the FBI to Manuel Perez and made its own deal. Pretty good one, don't you think? We turned him back to our side and had him take care of some business in Cuba for us."

"Hitting Violette, you mean?"

"That was part of it."

"What was the other part?"

"Have you heard the name Julio Garcia recently?"

"Too many times, yes. I believe I should talk to Paul Guarneri about that."

"I believe you should," Fajardie said. "Have a nice chat."

"I have one other stop first," she said. "Some final points of interest. I'm going to take my queries directly to the source."

"Be my guest," said Fajardie.

That afternoon, Alex drove back across the Key Bridge into Washington, where she located a Cuban restaurant called Los Matamoros on a tiny side street in Georgetown. She spotted ex-Major Mejias and Juanita, his wife, at a rear booth.

The émigré couple faced front. Their backs were to the rear wall. They looked as if they were settling into their new life but knew they still had enemies. Mejias's eyes worked the room as he rose to greet her. A slap of a new cologne assaulted Alex during a token embrace. They sat. In the background, someone had fed the jukebox. Shakira was rocking the place. Nice and loud, great for talking off the record.

For the next ninety minutes, over plates of spicy Montuna chicken and glasses of cold drinks, Señora Mejias kept quiet as her husband told his own story to Alex, who slipped easily into Spanish for the encounter.

Mejias had been five years old when Fidel Castro marched into Havana in 1959, he said. In his youth, he became fervently pro-Castro.

"I believed socialism would eradicate the problems of the Cuban people," he said. "But after the fall of communism in Eastern Europe and the crash of the Soviet Union in 1991, I had my doubts about socialism. Because of my profession, and my position in state security, I was able to travel. I could see that the socialist system had not functioned in my country or any country that I had seen."

He paused.

"As years went by, I learned that my parents had come to Cuba from Spain as political refugees, fleeing the fascist Franco. I had the rights to a Spanish passport. You know this, I think. I wanted to return to my parent's homeland now that sanity had been restored. Juanita wished to leave with me. But the Cuban government routinely blocked passport applications from any of us in sensitive positions. And they took away security clearances and financial allowances for anyone who applied. So I held back because I wished to bring my wife with me. I never applied. That was six years ago. I've been preparing my exit since then."

"I understand," she said. "Are you applying now? You should."

"I already have," he said. "We may stay in America, or more likely we may emigrate to Spain. We will decide. I cherish the freedom to make that decision."

"I'm sure you do," Alex said.

Señora Mejias kept nervously watching the door. Alex had a hunch the little lady was packing a pistol just in case. But Alex didn't ask.

Juanes followed Shakira on the restaurant's play list, then the sounds went retro with the Buena Vista Social Club. Mejias seemed happier with the latter.

"Cuba remains in the grip of an economic calamity," Mejias said, shaking his head. "Tourism is shrinking with the global recession. There are crises in the pricing of nickel mining and in the sugar industry. The government is closing half of the sugar mills. No one has anything. People pretend to work; the government pretends to pay them. Human rights are nonexistent and the European Union plays along with Castro to protect their trade agreements. It is disgusting. The situation becomes worse by the year. The people are frustrated," he said. "Even Castro admits, after a half century of misery, that the Cuban model has failed." He sighed and looked deeply troubled. "How long must Cuba wait?"

"It took the Soviet Union almost seventy years to collapse," Alex said. Her words were meant to console and they failed.

Then, perhaps feeling that he was coming across as too dour, Mejias lightened. "There aren't even any Marxists left in Cuba," he said, with a wink. "They've all emigrated and found teaching positions at American universities!"

Alex smiled politely. Señora Mejias, who had probably heard the same joke a thousand times before, never looked up from her chicken.

Mejias laughed strangely, and so did Alex. The ex-major went back to business. Alex let him talk. One never knew what he might reveal, though she also sensed that Mejias was singing the tunes that he believed everyone wanted to hear. It wouldn't have been the first time the CIA had bought such a catalogue. Yet Fajardie and his analysts seemed pleased with their acquisition so far and, who knew? They might even be correct in their assessments. It happened from time to time.

Alex then moved to the only question that remained of which

the answers might interest her. "What about the Venezuelans?" she asked.

"What about them?"

"Were they really interested in taking me into custody?"

"Very much so," he answered. "And a deal was in the works and very near completion. Since you were never officially in Cuba, your government couldn't very easily track you. You would have been of great value to Hugo Chavez, and you might never have returned. That was why we left so expeditiously. I know solitary confinement was unpleasant, but it kept you alive. And as long as you were my prisoner, it was more difficult for the government to find you and move you. I'm deeply sorry to have frightened you and to have held you there."

"Forgiveness is nothing new to me," she said. "So, *muchas gracias*."

"De nada."

Then he leaned forward slightly. "You see," he said, "the fix was in from the very beginning. My squad was to take you into custody on the beach. Señor Guarneri would be allowed to have his moment with Julio Garcia and make his romp in the graveyard. We would connect you to Roland Violette, and the CIA would be allowed to settle their long-standing grievance with him. All the events came together at once and allowed me the perfect moment to leave Cuba, a moment that hadn't existed previously and would not have lasted indefinitely. Too bad the hotheads on the boat started shooting at us. They would have been home to Miami in a few days if they'd only surrendered."

"So when I arrived on the beach, you knew I was the one who was there to bring you to America," she said.

"That is correct. I wished to take you into custody. I was constantly being watched by secret police. So I wished to do my job and keep you under my personal supervision. Then we could both leave. Along with Juanita, of course."

"The CIA people told me they didn't know who you were. They only knew a code name. That was true?"

"Absolutely," he said. "There are traitors everywhere. If Cuban intelligence knew there was a major in the militia who wished to defect, I would be dead now. That's why they needed to send somebody and let me find him. Or her."

"Then why didn't you arrest me in the bar of the Ambos Mundos?" Alex asked. "We were *codo con codo* in there. Cheek by jowl. You could have arrested me then."

"Impossible."

"Why?"

"There were two men at the bar. Undercover police. Not very good and not very undercover. But they report to the federal authorities. They would have taken you away right then. Better to make a night-time arrest, fill the files with paperwork, and move you around at my whim until we were ready to leave."

Alex nodded. *"Muchas gracias otra vez,"* she said.

"De nada."

Alex switched to English. "And after I was in custody and the original escape dates were blown?" she asked. "Who arranged a new date for the CIA to make the pickup?" She smiled. "I'm guessing it was the only person who really knew when the prisoner, me, would be ready to escape," she said.

Mejias smiled. Juanita retained her silence. If Señora Mejias spoke English, she didn't let on.

"Of course," he said.

"You," Alex said.

Mejias nodded.

SIXTY-FOUR

Alex took the train back to New York that evening, but she was in no mood to face her office anytime soon. She made an appointment with Christophe Chatton of the Swiss Bank and went to visit her money. She wanted to see what would happen, how she would be received, and in truth, if it was all still there.

It was. She rearranged some of the accounts so she could accrue better interest. In fantasy, she played with the idea of buying a condo in Maui or a race horse, then decided against both. But for the first time, she fully understood that she was a wealthy woman, although she knew in her heart that wealth was never measured by a bank balance.

On that same afternoon, to put to rest some final perplexities about Cuba, she phoned Paul Guarneri. They arranged to meet in Brooklyn and take a walk together on the promenade across the bay from Manhattan. Alex worked on him for a while, allowed him to take her hand for the stroll, and got him talking.

Long ago, he said, when he had been just old enough to begin to understand such things and had repaired his relationship with his father, the old man had imparted some wisdom.

"If anyone ever comes after me," his father had said, "it won't be from America. It will be from Cuba." It was the 1970s after all, Paul explained, and people were looking into the dirty secrets from the 1960s. Castro and Kennedy. Hookers and hotel rooms, cash and casinos, Jimmy Fratianno. Santo Trafficante. Judith Exner and Jimmy Roselli.

"The whole venal backbiting worthless load of them," Guarneri called them.

As Paul and Alex walked along the promenade, he opened up to her as never before. It was a bright summer day with low humidity, perfect for a game at one of the new ballparks or an afternoon at Aqueduct, had the old man been around. It was equally perfect for skaters, strollers, and joggers.

Joseph Guarneri had made his peace with the American mob and was allowed a quiet retirement, his son explained. Even more quietly, however, shortly before his premature death, he was talking to investigators from the U.S. Congress about the Cuban connection with the assassination of John F. Kennedy.

"My father had theories and personal stories," Paul said. "They weren't backed by any evidence, but if true they filled in some dirty little pieces of history. You can only invade an island, poison cigars, hire homicidal mistresses, and plant contagious scuba gear for so long before the opposition hits you back."

"True enough," Alex said.

"Castro hated my father personally," Paul said. "Maybe no more than any other North American gangster, but I had the idea it may have been over a woman. Maybe even my mother. Who knows now? Everyone's dead. My father once told me, 'Castro's got a man named Julio Garcia who's been assigned to kill me.' "

Paul paused, admired the skyline, took in some air, and then continued. "We lived under the shadow of that for a long time. Garcia lived in Dallas and New Orleans in the 1960s. He took care of a lot of Castro's dirty work in the U.S. He knew Lee Harvey Oswald personally. Also knew Che and E. Howard Hunt. That's what my father used to tell me. What do you make of that?"

"Intriguing," she said.

"Later on, after my father was murdered, there was some underworld scuttlebutt. Garcia had gone back to Cuba. Castro gave him some sort of medal. Top stuff, was what I heard. Hero of the revolution and all that."

"But what direction does that go in?" Alex asked. "Does that mean that you went to Cuba to capture Garcia? Or kill him, like Major Mejias says?"

"I went there to kill him," Guarneri said. "Honest to God. I wanted to kill the man who took my father from me, even so late in life. Whether I could have looked him in the eye and done it was another question. So, when we were set to travel, your friends in Langley approached me. They said they had a man they were 'turning.' A sniper who had worked for them in the past. They were bringing him to Cuba, and he was going to take care of one assignment, so why not have him take care of another?"

"Then what was your part?" Alex asked.

"I just had to be the spotter," Paul said. "My team of diggers, the fellows you met in the cemetery, knew Garcia and led me to him the second night. I fingered him for Perez. Perez went in and finished the job and I paid my diggers handsomely."

"Thirty-eight years after the fact," she said.

"Better late than never," he said. Then he looked troubled. "You know, I've been thinking about it long and hard since then, and I still can't decide whether I'm glad I didn't pull the trigger or sorry that I didn't." He pondered. "Instead of my hands being dirty, I suppose they're only slightly soiled."

Paul slouched slightly, but strolled with a carefree air, as if some great burden had been lifted. He was remarkably calm and at ease.

"Oh, I think your hands are a little dirtier than that," she said. "You eliminated an old enemy, maybe your last enemy on the island. I can't tell whether it was a gangland hit or a political payback or something with elements of both."

"The world is gray like that, isn't it?" he asked.

"You also laid a solid groundwork for your own future in Cuba. After the thaw. In those inevitable first years when democracy creeps back in and corruption and criminal organizations come with it. You've already got your own boys on the street, don't you?"

"If and when," he said. "If and when. But of course, it would be ninety miles offshore. So why should you care? It's not your jurisdiction."

Alex processed all this. But Paul wasn't finished. "A good businessman needs to be prepared," he said. "Fidel Castro will be dead before the American presidential election of 2016, maybe before the one of 2012, if we're lucky. That's what everyone on the island was telling me. How's that for a 'feel good' moment, Alex?"

"I need to be getting over to Manhattan, Paul," she said. "I've got to be back at my desk tomorrow."

"So soon?"

"Yes. It's overdue actually," she said. "Señora Dosi is still out there somewhere, and I owe her some attention. So I need to find a taxi."

"The subway's on Clark Street; it takes you straight to Wall Street. If you live in New York now, you should know that."

"What else should I know?" she asked.

"You should know about a Tuscan restaurant in Greenwich Village called Vincente's," he said. "It's on Greenwich Avenue near Tenth. I know the owner. He's a connected guy like most of my friends. How about Saturday night? I can pick you up at seven. Car and driver. Then maybe some dancing afterward at some unlicensed dive in the Bowery with techno stuff, type of place where you can't hear yourself think."

"Are you insane?"

"No. I'm goofing around. Dinner's the real invitation, but I know some jazz clubs in SoHo you might like. What do you think?"

"Paul? May I share a secret with you?" she asked.

"Sure."

"After our trip to Cuba, and after the many, various, ingenious, and imaginative ways you lied to me, including the fact that a murder was on your agenda ..."

"Yeah ...?" he laughed.

"I wouldn't touch you socially with a ten-foot pole."

Guarneri scoffed. "Garcia was a bad man. He got what he deserved."

"Everyone does eventually. And you will too. Good-bye, Paul," she said.

Alex took a step to move away. His hand found her wrist. He held her firmly and stopped her.

"Good-bye?" he asked. "Don't be too sure."

She pulled her arm free and walked away. She ignored two taxis and went to the subway instead.

On the veranda of her beachfront property in North Africa, Señora Dosi steepled her fingers and stared at the Mediterranean. She had taken stock. She had assessed her legal problems in various countries and taken inventory of the vast wealth that she had stashed in various banks around the world, in Argentina, the Cayman Islands, Costa Rica, and the Dominican Republic—not to mention Panama and Israel, where she had citizenship.

There was a newspaper next to her, the *International Herald Tribune*. She picked it up and worked on the English-language crossword puzzle for several minutes. It was the Friday one, more difficult than most. She finished it quickly.

A pleasant breeze swept the porch. Her husband came to the sitting area and slid into a seat next to her.

Señora Dosi set the newspaper aside but kept the pen in her hand. It was a silver pen from a well-known jeweler in New York. She looked at Alex's name engraved on it and smiled.

ACKNOWLEDGMENTS

The author is grateful to many sources for background and research. Among them, *The New York Times*, *The Washington Post*, the United States Department of Justice, *Wikipedia*, *The Columbia Encyclopedia*, and *The Encyclopedia Britannica*. And as usual, I'm grateful to my good friend Thomas Ochiltree for his endless insights on international politics and diplomacy.

At Zondervan, at various times Andy Meisenheimer, Dave Lambert, and Bob Hudson saved me from my own words. Thank you, gentlemen. More than ever, I'm also grateful to my wife, Patricia, for her help, advice, and support in more ways than I can ever calculate.

The author welcomes comments and correspondence from readers either through the Zondervan website or at NH1212f@yahoo.com.

The Russian Trilogy

Conspiracy in Kiev

Noel Hynd

A shrewd investigator and an expert marksman, Special Agent Alexandra LaDuca can handle any case the FBI gives her. Or can she?

While on loan from the Treasury Department, Alex is tapped to accompany a Secret Service team during a presidential visit to Ukraine. Her assignment: to keep personal watch over Yuri Federov, the most charming and most notorious gangster in the region.

But there are more parts to this dangerous mission than anyone suspects, and connecting the dots takes Alex across three continents and through some life-altering discoveries about herself, her work, her faith, and her future.

Conspiracy in Kiev—from the first double-cross to the stunning final pages—is the kind of solid, fast-paced espionage thriller only Noel Hynd can write. For those who have never read Noel Hynd, this first book in The Russian Trilogy is the perfect place to start.

Available in stores and online!

The Russian Trilogy

Midnight in Madrid

Noel Hynd

When a mysterious relic is stolen from a Madrid museum, people are dying to discover its secrets. Literally.

U.S. Treasury agent Alexandra LaDuca returns from *Conspiracy in Kiev* to track down the stolen artwork, a small carving called *The Pietà of Malta*. It seems a simple assignment, but nothing about this job is simple, as the mysteries and legends surrounding the relic become increasingly complex with claims of supernatural power.

As aggressive, relentless, and stubborn as ever, Alex crisscrosses Europe through a web of intrigue, danger, and betrayal, joined by a polished, mysterious new partner. With echoes of classic detective and suspense fiction from *The Maltese Falcon* to *The Da Vinci Code*, *Midnight in Madrid* takes the reader on a nonstop spellbinding chase through a modern world of terrorists, art thieves, and cold-blooded killers.

Available in stores and online!

The Russian Trilogy

Countdown in Cairo

Noel Hynd

Why won't the dead stay dead?

Federal agent Alexandra LaDuca travels to Egypt to investigate the sighting of a former mentor, a CIA agent everyone thought was dead. She is thrown into the deadliest game of double cross of her career as the events that began in Kiev and continued in Madrid find their culmination in the volatile Middle East.

Her assignment is to locate a man she once knew. But to find the answers, Alex needs to move quickly into the underworld of the Egyptian capital, a nether society of crooks, killers, spies, and Islamic fundamentalists. And she must work alone, surviving by her wits, her training, and a compact new Beretta.

If you've been waiting for Alex LaDuca's next adventure, this fast-paced thriller is it. If you've never met Alex, *Countdown in Cairo* offers a first-rate introduction. You will be holding your breath from its explosive beginning to the very last twist.

Available in stores and online!

Share Your Thoughts

With the Author: Your comments will be forwarded to the author when you send them to *zauthor@zondervan.com*.

With Zondervan: Submit your review of this book by writing to *zreview@zondervan.com*.

Free Online Resources at

www.zondervan.com

Zondervan AuthorTracker: Be notified whenever your favorite authors publish new books, go on tour, or post an update about what's happening in their lives at www.zondervan.com/authortracker.

Daily Bible Verses and Devotions: Enrich your life with daily Bible verses or devotions that help you start every morning focused on God. Visit www.zondervan.com/newsletters.

Free Email Publications: Sign up for newsletters on Christian living, academic resources, church ministry, fiction, children's resources, and more. Visit www.zondervan.com/newsletters.

Zondervan Bible Search: Find and compare Bible passages in a variety of translations at www.zondervanbiblesearch.com.

Other Benefits: Register to receive online benefits like coupons and special offers, or to participate in research.